108

DAYS

LISA LINDELL

March

5

Publishing

ISBN: 978-0-9767673-3-6

Cover Design: Thomas Howard
Book Design: Kelly Fochs
Copy Editor: Marci Bethel
Cover Photos: Lisa Lindell

March 5 Publishing,
Texas
United States of America

This book is dedicated to the power of the human spirit.

She would accept nothing less
Than quality care at its best

She suffers nothing but fools
On her quest to enforce the rules

For 108 days she devoted her life
To save this patient and his wife

Words will never have the power
To hail the savior of our darkest hour

With eternal gratitude to my sister, Dawn Bloomer, BSN, MS, RN

Contents

Preface

This is a true story. It is based on my experiences during my husband's 108-day hospitalization following a burn injury

Writing and publishing this book would have never happened without my mother's steadfast encouragement and support. That was the fuel that created this book.

Thank you to all the employees of Top Roofers*. They rode this nightmare out with us for years.

Tom Basinski, who patiently provided advice and guidance to this rookie, first-time author.

Thomas Howard, a talented artist who created the cover art for the book.

Marci Bethel, whose tireless devotion to perfection helped me make my book the best that it can be.

Fictitious names are marked with an asterisk (*) the first time they appear.

Day 1: Wednesday, March 5, 2003

One of my coworkers, Willy*, is having brain surgery today. He is an older gentleman, and there is great concern in the office for him. Other than that, it is an unremarkable day. So far.

Five minutes after I return from my lunch break, I receive a phone call from Lucy* with Unified Tubing*. It doesn't immediately register that this is my husband's employer, as I get calls all day long from ladies in offices. I am typing away at my computer after she identifies herself and I offer my usual greeting, "Hi, how can I help you?" She replies, "Curtis* was burned and went to the hospital."

I shift out of customer-service mode and realize she is talking about my husband. I ask her, "What happened?" She explains, "He was burned on the tip of his nose and a little on his hands. He is at Ben Taub Hospital in the Med Center*."

We live in the suburbs of Houston, Texas. This large city contains a world-renowned complex of hospitals and universities known as The Texas Medical Center. Of course, I have heard of the Med Center, but having my dream home two minutes away from my wonderful job, and anything I could ever want within one square mile of my house, I haven't the foggiest notion of where this famous complex is. I ask Lucy where Ben Taub Hospital is. She doesn't know. I ask her, "Who drove him?" I am thinking that a coworker took him. She responds, "An ambulance." *Wow! This is more serious than I thought.*

I thank her and hang up. I go to the internet, search for Ben Taub in the Med Center, and print out a map. Easy enough. I grab my purse and shut down my computer. I stop at the office of the Human Resource Director, Ginger, and tell her I am on my way to pick up Curtis because he got hurt at work and is in the hospital.

My husband works for a metal fabricating company as their Stationary Engineer. The company is relocating to the freeway frontage road. Driving down the freeway, I pass the facility and see a fire truck in the parking lot with its lights on. *Oh my God, the building is on fire!* This immediately strikes terror in my heart. I didn't get much of an explanation, so in my mind I'm thinking something spilled on him and he had to get bandaged up. I am pretty panicked after seeing the fire truck, but I remember that Lucy said "the tip of his nose and a little on his hands" and try not to jump to conclusions.

I drive to Ben Taub, but I have no idea where to park in the ocean of parking complexes. I locate a spot as close to the emergency room as I can get. It still turns out to be quite a long walk. While I am waiting at the information counter, I scan the waiting room, thinking I'll see Curtis sitting there with some bandages on his arm waiting for me to pick him up. It has taken me at least forty minutes to get here. It sure is crowded, but there's no Curtis. Finally, it is my turn. No, they don't have a patient by the name of Curtis Wright*.

"Any burn victims brought in by ambulance?"

"Two. Let me check. Nope, neither one of them is Curtis Wright. Check Memorial Hermann*.

" "Where is that?"

"Right next door." She calls Memorial Hermann and confirms that Curtis is right next door.

As you can imagine, in a massive hospital complex—one of several in a large downtown area dedicated to health care—"right next door" is a sizeable walk. It's like walking from one strip casino to the next in Las Vegas. It takes a while to walk to the emergency room at Memorial Hermann. Again, I scan the waiting area, thinking he'll surely be waiting for me by now. It has been over an hour since he got hurt! Nope. No bandaged Curtis in the waiting room. I get in a long line.

"No, we have not admitted anyone with the name Curtis Wright. No, we don't have any burn victims."

"Do you have a phone? Phonebook?"

I call Curtis' employer to find out who actually knows where my husband is. A voice on the other end of the phone informs me that Curtis is at Ben Taub Hospital.

There is no way that I have beaten the ambulance to the hospital and he hasn't arrived yet. They don't know where he is, maybe Memorial Hermann. "Nope, I'm standing here in the waiting room. He's not here." Well, they don't know, but Curtis' boss and his wife are on their way to Memorial Hermann. *I'm glad to know the whereabouts of the boss and his wife.* I ask this person who knows nothing, "Which ambulance drove him?" Knows Nothing has to consult with others, and I am finally informed that the city provided transportation. I look up the number to the city ambulance service and call them, trying to find out where my husband is. They have no record of picking up Curtis Wright.

I'm asked the address where the victim was picked up. I guessed it to be around the 10000 block of the Gulf Freeway. Aha! They had picked up a Roger Lindale* at that address and dispatched him to the emergency room at Memorial Hermann.

Who is Roger? Maybe Curtis isn't hurt after all! I turn to my new friend who let me use the phone. She doesn't find a Roger

Lindale, but she does locate a Curtis Hart. "Is he burned?" "Yes, the doctors are with him now." "Well, that must be him." I am finally granted the invitation to take a seat and wait.

This is becoming a surreal day. It is now after three o'clock. It's been over two hours since the accident occurred, I just found out where Curtis is. Surely we'll be on our way soon, but there is no way, even if we leave right now, that we'll make it home in time for the kids to get home from school. I go to the pay phone and try to track down my brother. No luck. Try to find my sister. No luck. I call my dad at work and explain what little I know and that we'll probably be headed home soon enough, but who knows with these hospitals. Can he please go to my house and stay with the kids? Yes, he will.

I call Ginger to let her know what little I know and that it is very unlikely I'll make it back to the office today. She says, "I know, Roger called and talked to Mike," referring to Mike Mann*, my boss. I ask, "Roger who?" She says, "Roger Hart." "Who the heck is Roger Hart?" I ask. Ginger says, "Roger was a paramedic on the ambulance." Why would a paramedic call the employer of the spouse of a patient on an ambulance? *I am in the Twilight Zone.*

It seems Roger, in addition to being a paramedic, does some work for our company, Top Roofers*, repairing siding or gutters or something. When Curtis told him where his wife works, he knew who to call. In any event, Ginger goes on to say that she and Mike are on their way to Memorial Hermann, and I am aghast. "Oh heavens no, that is so unnecessary, please don't do that." She says, "He's going to be OK, Lisa, but prepare yourself. It's bad. It's real bad, but he's going to be OK."

I don't know what to say. I think Curtis will come out any time with his arm in a sling and we'll be on our way. I have spent the afternoon asking people in hospitals where my husband is. Who knew ny to find out everything ... hard-won seat and wait.

...le arrive and are direct... ...d's boss, Gary*, and his ...ce themselves, and I feel the need to chatter and make small talk. They have come all the way down here on our behalf. I feel like I need to be a hostess.

Priscilla tells me not to worry about a thing. "Workers' comp will kick in right away. All the medical bills will be taken care of." It occurs to me again, "Wow, this must be serious," but I don't dwell on it. I mean, c'mon, this is Curtis—a healthy, vital, happy, strong, male, macho man. Unless he is dropped from an airplane at ten thousand feet, y'know, he'll be fine. He'll be home in a couple of days. I have no idea the details of the accident, but I think either these are super-nice people or something serious has happened and they're worried about liability.

Priscilla goes on to say that she held Curtis' hand and prayed with him while they waited for the ambulance. This is when I decide that these are really-nice people.

For the almost three years that I have worked at Top Roofers, and especially for the past year since we bought our house, my days are very much a routine. I get up, take the kids to school, go to work, and go home at five o'clock. Every day is exactly the same, with the exception of the daily roofing drama. My routine is very much disrupted today. I've been ripped away from my desk in the middle of the day; I'm downtown at the Med Center, where I certainly don't belong; and Curtis has been in some type of accident*. I think I might be in shock. It just isn't sinking in.

I chatter away and entertain my guests while waiting for news. Sometime later, a man and woman in white coats come out and I am singled out once again and summoned over. I will never remember word for word, but it goes something like this:

The male doctor, Dr. Richard Head*, says, "Your husband was electrocuted and is very badly burned. We have him stabilized and have taken X-rays to look for internal damage, heart damage, or broken bones from the electrocution. They haven't found any internal damage, but it doesn't always manifest itself immediately. He's breathing on his own. There's no smoke inhalation. He's awake and conscious, but very badly burned. He has second- and third-degree burns over thirty-five percent of his body; seventeen percent are second degree. He will need skin grafts to help the burns heal and resist infection. The number one reason burn patients don't leave the hospital is infection, and your husband has a very bad burn. The length of the hospital stay is about one day per percent burned, so you're looking at about thirty-five days in the hospital. Do you have any questions?"

He goes on a bit about the electrical shock, but I'm not worried about that nonsense anyway. *Pfft! Please. Curtis will be fine.*

Nice Blond Lady Doctor* nodded and smiled comfortingly while he talked.

My big, well-thought-out question: "Can I see him?"

"Yes, but just for a few minutes because he has to be moved upstairs to the burn unit."

Burn unit sounds so neat and professional and medical and businesslike, but I'll soon find out that it's just a pseudonym for its real name—barbaric pit of Hell.

I am escorted to a room, and the first thing I see looks like burned pieces of paper in a pile and scattered about the floor. It doesn't register until I'm on my way home later that the pile of charred paper is Curtis' burned skin all over the floor. The next thing I see is a heaping pile of blankets on a gurney, shaking like a big mound of jelly. I keep walking alongside this shivering mass and find a head. I can tell it is Curtis, but it sure doesn't look like him. His face is all white and blistered, loose pieces of burned skin are hanging all over, there are no eyelashes or eyebrows, and there's a very distinct line on his forehead. The top of his head looks the same, and I can tell he'd been wearing a hat, so I instantly put my hand on his head and say something like, "Oh, Curtis, you poor thing, everything will be just fine." My heart is broken. He is clearly suffering. It is horrible and so unfair.

Curtis says, in a weak, shivering, struggling-to-talk, teeth-chattering voice, "I'm so sorry." I say, "No, no, I am so sorry to see you hurt like this. You have nothing to be sorry for." He says, "I am so thirsty!" Some medical person walks in, and I ask if he can have a drink. She says, "No. They are taking him upstairs to the burn unit. You can see him then." She hands me a plastic bag, which contains his charred boots, his wallet, his burned cell phone, and a specimen jar with his charred wedding ring in it. They had to cut the ring off his finger.

After all these hours, I'm able to spend three minutes with Curtis. I am horrified and heartbroken. Curtis is the nicest person I have ever met. He's always so peaceful and easy-going, and this is so unfair. I decide this minute that I am going to dedicate myself to making him as comfortable and comforted as I can while he's in this hospital, and to get him home as quickly as is humanly possible.

A crew of medical folks arrives to wheel him away. They tell me to go to the waiting room on the seventh-floor burn unit, like I'm supposed to know exactly where that is. I must look lost, because Nice Blond Lady Doctor comes out of nowhere and tells me and Gary and Priscilla to follow her. We get a personal escort to the seventh floor. We travel up some stairs and down corridors, then ride in an elevator and turn right and turn left and go through some more doorways with more stairs. I don't know how I'll ever find my way back out of that maze she just took us through, or ever find my way back in. We are invited to take a new seat in this new waiting room.

So we sit. I chatter away. I don't know these people at all. I'm sure they have better things to do, and I'm thinking how nice are they to sit here and keep me company. After a while, I'm sorry that I told Ginger not to come. I appreciate the company. We are in the waiting room for a very long time. Hours. It seems like days. Gary leaves at some point and comes back with a parking pass for the parking garage and coupons for food from the cafeteria. Conversation turns to business, and I realize that Curtis' truck is still at work and I don't have the keys. There are no keys in the hospital bag. Gary calls some guys at work and tells them to look around on the ground for a set of keys. Apparently, Curtis' clothes were burned off his body. There is no clothing left, just ashes. No pocket for keys.

They don't find any keys on the ground; they say they'll keep looking. Priscilla asks about the kids. I mention that Curtis is supposed to be home with them next week because they are off school for Spring Break, but I will have to take the week off. Priscilla says that Curtis is in the right place, the burn unit is A-number-one. She recently had a family member in the same hospital, so that's why she knows all about the parking pass, but her loved one wasn't burned.

Dr. Plastic Surgeon comes into the waiting room looking for me.

Curtis is burned badly on both legs, abdomen, groin, face, hands, and a few other spots here and there. He will need at least three skin graft surgeries, possibly four. He wants to do the hands first, as quickly as possible, as third-degree burns heal with debilitating scarring. Hands are a vital area, and to retain as much function as possible, they need to be grafted as soon as possible. I ask a question about the electrical shock, and Dr. Plastic Surgeon says Curtis wasn't electrocuted.

Well, that absolutely contradicts what Dr. Richard Head told me in the emergency room, but really, it doesn't matter. A few volts won't hurt Curtis anyway. Dr. Plastic Surgeon is brusque and to the point, but I have immediate confidence in him. I feel like we're in good hands. I ask about the use of Curtis' hands and possible nerve damage and he says there is no way to tell that yet. But he wants to graft those hands next Monday or Tuesday. Wow. Finally, we can go see Curtis.

Nice Blond Lady Doctor shows us the gown room. We have to wash our hands and put on a hat and gown before we can enter the burn unit. As we enter the burn unit, I take note of a sign. "No overnight guests. Visiting hours 11 AM–6:30 PM and 7:30 PM–10 PM. No children under 12. Only two visitors at a time." I think that stinks, no overnights, but rules are rules and he's in the finest facility. They know what they're doing. We get into our gowns and hats and exit the gown room. The door slams behind us, making me jump almost out of my skin. We are escorted to Curtis' room.

I see a body wrapped in bandages all over; even his head and face are bandaged. All of the bandages are covered in white netting. I can still see areas of his white, burned face, but now it is cleaned up and treated and he's already looking better. And that awful shaking has stopped. Priscilla says she wants to pray for Curtis, so we all hold hands, she says a nice prayer, and they leave. I thank them for coming and thank them for the stuff they have given me, although I don't realize at the time how valuable that parking pass will be. I always want to remember my manners, and I feel like we are imposing on them.

Curtis is out of it. I tell him again how sorry I am and that he shouldn't worry about a thing, just focus on resting and getting home. I mention to him that visiting hours don't start until eleven o'clock and that I will see him tomorrow. Curtis doesn't have much to say. He is tired, probably drugged. *Geez! This poor guy had a heckuva day and just needs to sleep.*

I tell him I'll call his family when I get home, and this is the only time he speaks. "Please don't tell my mother." "OK." He says again, "Lisa, please, don't call my mother." "OK. I won't. I'll call your brother Andy* and Andy can call whoever he needs to call." He repeats, "Please don't tell my mother." "Curtis, I won't, I will go home and call Andy, and I will only call Andy." He is finally satisfied.

That makes sense. He doesn't want to worry his mother with this. Curtis is forty-four and the youngest of seven children. His parents are elderly, and they have their own health problems to deal with. I barely know his family, really, as they live almost four hundred miles away. I do know his brother Andy fairly well, though. He'll know better than I do who to tell and how to tell them.

I haven't spent a lot of time with Curtis today—probably all of fifteen minutes. The rest of the day I just sat in waiting rooms. But he needs to rest, so I go home. I cry all the way home; it is heartbreaking to see such a gentle, peaceful person suffer such a painful injury. I know what my mission is: to get him healed and home as quickly as possible.

I get home expecting to see my dad, but my sister is on the couch.

I flash her a "not in front of the kids" look. My kids are eight and nine. She asks me, "What percent?" "Mostly third, some second." She says, "No, total percent." I answer, "Thirty-five percent." Dawn's eyes get as big as saucers.

Dawn is a registered nurse. She spent years as a floor nurse specializing in pediatric infectious disease, then as a visiting nurse taking care of terminally ill children in their homes. She went to Saudi Arabia when my youngest was an infant to work in a hospital there. After a few years at the hospital, she went on to live in a palace as a nanny for a Saudi Royal princess. She came back stateside to work as a nanny for a wealthy family, but soon decided that she missed working in the medical field and found another opportunity in Dubai in the United Arab Emirates. She had worked as a nurse only briefly when she was offered an opportunity to work as a liaison between the nursing staff and a software manufacturer who was developing nursing software. Shortly after September 11, 2001, she got out of the Middle East and came back for good. Just in time. We missed her during her seven years or so overseas. She's now pursuing her Master's degree in Health Infomatics, the computer age of medicine, at a prestigious university that's located in the world-famous Med Center.

Dawn is much more familiar with the medical world than I could ever be. But ever since she got her nursing diploma, well, she tends to over-dramatize things. I won't go so far as to say she uses scare tactics, but... I don't let those eyes as big as saucers scare me. When it comes to sickness and injury, my sister's glass always seems to be half empty.

After I put the kids to bed, she asks me again about this percentage. "They told me thirty-five percent second- and third-degree burns, I think they said seventeen percent are second degree." She asks, "Is thirty-five percent the total body surface area, or thirty-five percent plus seventeen percent?" I don't know. She thinks I should call and find out. She tells me, "Anything over thirty percent could be mortal; this is very, very serious."

I'm shocked. Up to now, nobody has given me any indication that Curtis could be mortally wounded. If I even had an inkling I was leaving Curtis in that hospital to die in his sleep, I would not have come home. I figure it's just Dawn's half empty glass, but I am a little freaked out. I've spent less than forty-eight hours in hospitals my entire life, and that was to give birth. Dawn knows what she's talking about. To humor us both, I call the nurses' station and clarify the percentage. "Thirty-five percent total." Dawn thinks this is very serious and grim. I am so sad for Curtis and his suffering, and she depresses me even further and also scares me. I have half a mind to race back to the hospital, but then I come to my senses: no overnight visitors, and Curtis isn't going to die, for crying out loud, that is ridiculous. Dawn lets me know that Curtis is in the best place he can be. The burn unit at Memorial Hermann is the best burn unit west of the Mississippi. The gravity of the situation is starting to sink in.

I start repeating the events of the afternoon. When I get to the part about me calling Top Roofers and finding out how badly Curtis was hurt from Roger the paramedic, she makes the comment that next month that will be a HIPAA violation. She is taking a class on HIPAA, the Health Insurance Portability and Accountability Act, which contains new rules for patient privacy that go into effect on April 14, 2003. She gives me a brief rundown. After April 14, 2003, doctors can't discuss patients in elevators, patients' names can't be on the doors to their rooms, paramedics can't call the employer of a patient's spouse from an ambulance and give them the lowdown on the condition of the patient. Stuff like that. Well, that's all very interesting, but if HIPAA were in effect, I'd still be looking for Curtis. The hospitals didn't know anything, I had to find out from Top Roofers.

This is the first time I've heard the term HIPAA, but it won't be the last—oh, no, certainly not the last.

I cut my conversation with Dawn short because I have to call Andy. Nobody in Curtis' family has any idea what happened. A lot of them were just here two weeks ago as a surprise birthday visit for Curtis. I call Andy and tell him about Curtis' accident and what little I know. He asks, "What happened?' I answer, "He got burned pretty badly." I tell him to do what he needs to do, but Curtis asked me not to call his mother, so I am going to respect his wishes and not call her, but for him to do what he needs to do. He said, "I'll be out as soon as I can." I said, "That isn't necessary, but to do what you need to do and let me know when you're coming."

I don't want to burden anyone else or cause anyone unnecessary expense. Of course, his family will want to see him and help him (at the time, I probably thought us) in our time of need, but there's no need to drop everything and come running. I assume folks will want to stay here at our house. Y'know, the normal things that families do when crisis strikes. Whatever normal is.

About four minutes after I speak to Andy, the phone rings. It is Curtis' sister Betty*, and she wants to know what happened. I repeat, "Curtis got burned pretty badly, but he'll be fine." I repeat Curtis' wishes that his mother not be told. I assume Andy called Betty. She said, "Mother called me." Apparently, Andy hung up with me and called his mother and opened the pipeline. That didn't take long, but I kept my word to Curtis, and that is all that matters.

After Dawn leaves, I head for bed, but I don't sleep a wink. My heart is broken, just broken. My mind is racing with all that I can do for Curtis and all that I will need to organize —I still have a job, kids, a house, and a life to manage. The phone rings all night. All the Wrights call. "What happened?" "Curtis got burned." "What happened?" "Curtis got burned." "What happened?" "Curtis got burned." I don't even know how he got burned, and it doesn't matter. I don't know who all I talk to—a lot of Irma's, a lot of people with the same names. "We'll come out as soon as we can." "OK, just let me know." Over and over again.

I talk to my mother. She has just returned home after spending an extended period out of state taking care of her elderly parents.

She can't come to help. I don't expect her to or need her to; it doesn't even occur to me to ask her. Everything will be fine. A bump in the road is all. My dad, brother, and sister live sixty miles away on the west side of downtown. My mother lives nine hundred miles away. There is no need for her to come here. My mother says she's so sorry she can't come out. Of course, I'm going to need some help, but it never occurs to me to bother my mother with it. I know her plate has been full with her parents.

My first priority is to get through this with as little disruption to others as possible. I just need to organize and keep chaos to a minimum while I'm on my "bring Curtis home" mission. I know my mom feels bad that she can't come, but I don't. All will be fine.

Curtis is scheduled to be off work next week, as the kids are off school for Spring Break. This is now problem number one. I can't go to work next week, and that is that.

I get no sleep at all.

I grab Curtis' Bible and some pictures the kids have drawn for him. I take the kids to school and explain to them that Curtis has been hurt and will be in the hospital for a while, but he will be fine. I get to work and Mr. Mann tells me, "Take all the time you need." I take this opportunity to let him know I will be out all next week as the kids are going to be off school for Spring Break.

I keep mentioning this like it is an issue. I know all we do is install roofs, but I have a lot of responsibility in the office, and there really isn't a lot of cross training. A lot of coworkers and the company depend on me to be there and take care of my responsibilities, so this business of just taking the week off is, in fact, a huge issue for me. The only time I ever take a week off at once is around Christmas, when it's slow, and I've planned for it ahead of time to keep the disruption to a minimum. I'm not saying that I'm not as expendable as the next person, but it just isn't that simple to say, "I can't come in next week." Whatever is not getting done while I'm gone, which is a lot, is just going to pile up on me and make this whole ordeal that much harder. Mr. Mann doesn't have a problem with it at all, of course, but it is a huge burden for me. There are simply things I have to get done. The only good thing is that it is a good time of the month, as far as deadlines go, for this to happen.

Ginger tells me Willy's brain surgery was successful. He is in the same hospital as Curtis. Small world.

All of my coworkers want to know what happened. "Curtis got burned." I can't understand why it matters how it happened. That is in the past. I repeat all day, "He got burned." They all tell me to let them know if there's anything they can do. All of them. "We're praying for you." I appreciate it all, I really do, but I have to "hup-to double-time" if this is going to work out. I have work to do.

Priscilla calls and says they found Curtis' keys. One of the many coworkers who wants me to let him know what he can do for me is Gary*. I make arrangements with him to bring Curtis' truck home on Friday.

I take off at ten-thirty like I'm on fire to get to the hospital for eleven o'clock visiting hours. I can't get there fast enough. That poor man has been on my mind nonstop. Off I go finally! I find the right parking garage and this is when I realize what a thoughtful gift the parking pass is. Nine dollars a day to park. If they didn't buy me a pass, I would not be able to afford to see Curtis every day. By the time our ordeal is over, parking will go up to ten dollars a day.

Another advantage to this cool pass—I don't have to stand at the aggravating machines with long lines of people waiting to put their money in and get a ticket. Usually, the machines eat their money and give them no ticket, so they have to call for assistance and wait interminably for a human being to fix the machine so they can get their exit pass out of the parking garage. Hence, it's always a long line.

I park, ride the elevator up to the fourth floor, walk forever and a day to another bank of elevators, then ride up to the seventh floor. Stop in the gown room to wash, hat, and gown, then walk down the hall. Finally, there is Curtis. He is asleep and clearly loopy on drugs. That's OK. I speak softly and let him know I brought him his Bible. I realize immediately that he can't pick it up, and I feel like an idiot. At least he knows it's nearby. I start to read one of the kids' cards to him when in walks this lady I've never seen before in my life.

She says her name is Bertha* and she is Curtis' cousin. She sits down next to Curtis and mutters a few things I don't hear. I tell her I am his wife, Lisa, and thank her for coming to see him. It really is a struggle to get parked and get to Curtis' room. It is not for the faint of heart.

Bertha eyeballs Curtis and asks me if the color on his neck is his normal skin color. I say, "Yes, that wasn't burned." She says, "Hmm... He's lighter than I remember." This is not a close relative—I've never seen her before and never heard Curtis mention her name, and she is asking about his skin color. A few minutes pass and she says she wants to pray for Curtis. I say, "OK, thank you," thinking she can pray whenever she wants, she doesn't have to ask permission. I realized later she wasn't asking permission, she was letting me know the show was about to start. I guess I was supposed to participate.

There is a dramatic difference between the way that Gary and Priscilla pray and the way that Bertha prays. She is putting her hands all over Curtis, and she is feelin' the spirit. I tell you, she is **ordering** Jesus to **heal** this man! If I were Jesus, I would be scared to do anything less. She goes on and on for at least thirty minutes, speaking in tongues and all sorts of things. I've never seen or heard anything like it. I know Curtis loves Jesus. She is his relative, so this is no doubt a great comfort to him. Whatever brings Curtis help or comfort is welcome. I just sit there in wonder.

Bertha needs to breathe, so she finishes praying. Then she picks up a cell phone and says, "Yep, it's Curtis. Yep, he's burned. Yep, I prayed for him. Hold on." Then she put the phone in my stunned face. I'm half expecting Curtis to jump out of bed a healed man after that show. I say, "Hello." It's Curtis' mother. She says "Don't you worry about a thing, darlin'. Alfred* [Curtis' dad] and I *will* be there tomorrow!" I reply, "Oh, you don't need to make that trip right now. He's still heavily medicated...." She says, "I will be there tomorrow!" I ask, "OK, what time?" She says for me not to worry about it. I ask her if she needs directions to the hospital or if she is coming to the house first. She says, "Don't you worry about a thing. I can take care of myself!" I say, "OK," and give the phone back to Bertha. Fine. Do whatever you want. This poor woman is seventy-five years old, she clearly doesn't want my help, and she says I don't need to worry about it, so fine.

A lady named Karen Vidor* comes by and introduces herself as the medical case manager for the insurance company. She asks if I'm all right and, "Is there anything I can do for you?" "No, not at this time, thank you." She lets me know Curtis is in the best of hands.

A nurse comes in to fiddle with Curtis' equipment and Bertha asks her if they have housing for families. The nurse tells her there are area hotels, and Bertha gets more specific. "Does the hospital provide free housing for out-of-town relatives?" The nurse says no. I tell Bertha we have a large enough house for people to stay there. People are welcome if she'll just let me know who's coming and when. It occurs to me, but apparently to nobody else, that I could use some extra hands and company at home. She says she doesn't know about anybody's travel plans.

Bertha finally leaves at about three o'clock. Curtis is long since worn out, and he is out cold. No whispering, no muttering, out cold.

I don't get to talk to him. Nothing. It's time for me to head back south before the traffic gets bad so I can be close to home when the kids get home from school. I tape the kids' cards to the wall and leave, not really feeling any better than I did yesterday. I have things I want to say to my husband, but I didn't get a chance.

I go back to work. It is easy to go to work in the morning, but it is emotionally and mentally draining to go back to work directly from the burn unit. Who cares about shingles? Who cares what the date on that invoice is? Is this really important? It is hard. I go through the motions, but my heart isn't in it and my concentration is elsewhere.

I call my dad's house and ask my dad, sister, and brother to go to the hospital this evening. I can't leave the kids, and I really do not want Curtis there alone. They are happy to go visit Curtis. I sort of expect to hear something from Curtis' family, but nobody calls.

A lady named Heidi* calls from the insurance company and says that they waived the waiting period so Curtis' benefits will kick in immediately. This is as much time as I spend thinking about benefits or money or paying bills or insurance.

Later in the evening, my dad calls. I had asked him to call me from the room so I could get updates from my sister and maybe talk to Curtis. I am irritated because I know they've been there for hours, and the phone is right on the wall. I ask how it's been going and my dad says they just got into the room. "Where have you been?" He says they've been in the waiting room. They couldn't get in to see Curtis because so many of his family are here! "What? Who's there?" He tells me, "A big praying woman named Bertha, a brother Richard* and Richard's wife Lucy*, and other people whose names I don't know." I say, "Let me talk to Richard."

Curtis' brother Richard was at our house for the weekend two weeks ago with his girlfriend, Imelda*, so either this can't be the same Richard, or my dad is confused about Imelda's name. He puts Richard on the phone and, yep, it is Richard and he is there with his wife Lucy. I didn't know he had a wife. They came with another sister, Irma*.

These people all live hundreds of miles away, I had no idea they were coming. If I had known, I sure wouldn't have sent my family there to keep the waiting room chairs warm. I ask Richard, "Does anyone need to stay at the house?" He says, "No, my wife and I are getting a hotel, and Irma is staying on the north side of town with some other in-laws." I ask him who else is coming to town. He says his mother is coming (I know that), and Andy is coming this weekend. I ask him to let me know if anybody needs to stay at the house.

My dad calls again later from his house and tells me a little more about the hospital scene. Bertha says she is not leaving Curtis' bedside until he is well enough to go home. How brazen. She's definitely not a close relative, and Curtis has a wife, thank-you-very-much. I talk to my sister about coordinating our schedules for the weekend. She can meet me halfway between my house and hers at 7 AM Saturday to pick up the kids and take them to my dads house for the weekend. I don't know if I'm going to have Wrights at the house; they haven't said a word to me about it. It's Thursday night, I have to arrange care for my kids.

Another long, tear-filled sleepless night. My mind is racing. I'm frustrated that I can't have five minutes alone with my husband. It rips at my heart to think of him getting burned like that, so I try not to think about it. He was on fire. He was engulfed in flames. His clothes turned to ash. His skin turned to ash. His tissue turned to ash. It will torment me if I think about it, so instead I think about getting his tool chests home from work.

In the morning, I take the kids to school and go to work. Jill* had everybody chip in and buy me a ham, and Jill made soup. I leave work at ten-thirty and race through the drill again. I can get to the hospital parking lot in thirty minutes with no traffic. It takes another fifteen to twenty minutes to get to Curtis' room. Then wash hands, put on hat and gown. Finally, I get to the room and find Curtis sitting in a chair, wide awake!

I am pleasantly surprised, and he is so happy to see me. He is still covered in bandages, and clearly in pain, but he's alert. This is really the first time I've seen him in two days. I tell him how proud I am of him making progress so quickly. Shirley*, his nurse, tells me that cocoa butter will be good for his skin after the wounds heal. Curtis is thirsty, and Shirley brings him some juice. She shows me where the kitchen is and tells me I can bring him almost anything he wants and keep it here for him. Say no more. She also says they will be moving him across the hall later today. Still an ICU room, but not as small and it has a TV, more of a long-term room. I ask her if I can bring a DVD player, and she says yes. I want it to be as much like home as possible. We like lying in bed watching a movie on a Friday or Saturday night. I'm trying to make Curtis as comfortable and as comforted as possible.

I lift my digital camera up to my face to click a picture of Curtis. I plan to do this every day for him, so he'll have a visual diary. Shirley sees the camera and tells me, "No! You can't photo-graph him!" I ask Curtis if he minds if I take his picture. He says no, he doesn't mind. Shirley says I can't take photographs; the only photographs the doctor will testify to are the ones the doctor takes. Who said anything about testifying? This is my first exchange like this, but won't be my last. This hospital is full of people who are trained to respond from a position of liability. They don't know how to be human. They all went to the same seminar. After she leaves, I take three pictures of Curtis just because she said I couldn't. I can take my husband's picture. Last time I checked, one of the items on my country's resume was "Land of the Free."

Curtis was photographed his first day here, while I was bab-bling away in the waiting room. All his burns, in all their glory. I never saw his raw burns; I only saw him bandaged. His chart states that he was photographed, and Curtis told me they photographed him before he was bathed. The hospital "lost" those photographs. Those photographs turn out to be very important over a year later. We never got copies

The adventure to the kitchen and the exchange over the camera all take place in the first fifteen minutes after my arrival. I start to tell Curtis that I will be bringing his truck home later today, when in walks another guest. Somebody I've never seen or heard of before. It's another sister-in-law, another person named Irma*. So, here we go with the praying and carrying on again. No doubt a great comfort to Curtis. I'll have plenty of time to talk to him, no worries. This new visitor tells Curtis that his mother will be here this evening, and Curtis shoots me a dirty look. I said, "I didn't call your mother, Andy must have." It's not that Curtis doesn't want to see his moth-er. He doesn't want her to put herself through that arduous trip and expense. He worries about her, and I don't blame him.

We don't get any more time alone before I have to head back south again in the afternoon. I know he won't be alone this evening. I am satisfied enough to see him sitting in a chair and alert. What a treat. On my way to the gown room, I can hear the screams of pain from another victim. I am starting to dislike this place.

Curtis has a large tool chest full of tools at work. I know this has to get home, I idly figure that his brothers can get that whenever they're here. I go back to work for the afternoon, then Gary and I get Curtis' truck and bring it home. I swiftly start some laundry while I have the opportunity, do a little tidying up, pack the kids' suitcases (they're spending the weekend with my dad), pack a suitcase for Curtis, disconnect the DVD player from our room, stuff like that.

Taking the kids to school and going to work have become the best part of my days. I would rather be at work than anywhere near that hospital. It is easy to go to work in the morning. But after only two days, what is killing me is leaving the hospital and returning immediately to work. It is extremely difficult to leave that environment of indescribable suffering to go back to office work and be able concentrate, or even care, y'know? It's emotionally draining. It sucked the life right out of me after only two days. I am exhausted.

My daughter Amy* and I head to the grocery store to load up with things for Curtis. I buy all manner of individually packaged food. Anything at all that can be eaten from its container or easily prepared in a microwave and lots of it.

We're unloading the car at home when my son Ben* says that Curtis' mother called and wanted to know when I was picking her up. What? She didn't say anything about that when I talked to her. I put the clothes in the dryer, start another load, and go back to unload the last of the groceries. I debate calling the phone in Curtis' room. The phone is on the wall, and he can't get up to answer it. How aggravating is that, to be stuck helpless in bed with a phone ringing? I don't want to do that to him. But I also don't want his poor mother sitting there all night thinking I am coming to get her. Because I'm not. I can't. I don't know what else to do, so I call the room. Richard answers. I ask him what is going on, and he says he is heading back home. "What about your mother?" He says she is staying on the north side of the city with another Irma. "Oh, OK." I ask how Curtis is doing and if he knows of anyone else's travel plans. He does not. "OK, 'bye." Now it is after nine o'clock.

Amy starts unwrapping all the packaged items so we can write Curtis' name on each individual package. I bought him Popsicles and ice cream bars and other cold or frozen foodstuffs. I put the cooler in the trunk so it will be ready to load in the morning. The plan is to meet my sister at seven o'clock in the morning to exchange the children. That's too early for me to go the hospital, but it's the only time she can meet me. I am trying to hurry and get everything done so we can get to bed at a decent hour. I help Amy finish writing Curtis' name on everything. Bags and wrappings are all over the place. The house is trashed. I keep the laundry going. Finally, at almost eleven, we are starting to put the food into the freezer and refrigerator when the phone rings again.

It's another person named Irma. She wants to know what time I am picking up Curtis' mother. I ask, "Where am I supposed to pick her up and when?" She says she has been waiting for me to pick her up at Memorial Hermann. They left a message with Ben. I say, "I called the hospital and talked to Richard. He said his mother is staying with Irma's sister-in- law. That was hours ago." Irma says no, she wants to stay with you. "I have no plans to go to the hospital tonight. I can't leave my kids home alone to drive all the way down-town, and there is no room in the car for everybody as I already have it loaded for Curtis because I have to leave early in the morning."

Well, I don't know what to do. "There is just no way I can go to the hospital tonight, I'm sorry. I wish she had let me know what she had in mind when I asked her yesterday, but I was told not to worry about it and I can't help you now. I'm sorry. I am finishing up laundry and leaving at six-thirty in the morning to meet my sister. Nobody will be here all weekend. Sorry, but I can't help you now, sorry."

I feel really, really bad about this. If I had known she was coming, she would have had a clean bed and a five- star breakfast. Anybody who knows me—but especially Curtis—knows this. I am mildly aggravated. It is awfully presumptuous of somebody to assume I am just waiting to accommodate out- of-town visitors on a moment's notice. I asked everyone I've talked to, "Who's coming? When are they coming? Do they need to stay at the house? Just let me know." Nobody has said "boo" to me. I have to make my own plans for my kids and Curtis, but they want to call me at 11 PM and ask me to taxi people around. I feel badly for his mother but I'm also annoyed. Ten minutes later, Bertha calls and asks for directions to my house. I give her directions and ask her what is going on. She says Curtis' mother is staying at my house and that is the end of that. *Fine, whatever.*

Immediately after I hang up, I realize I have to leave at the crack of dawn to meet my sister, I have no room in my little car for another body, Curtis' mother is elderly and can't get up the stairs to the guest room so she will have to take my bed, and my room is a mess and I'm too tired to start picking up my dirty underwear on top of everything else I have to do. In my exhausted state. I suddenly feel very put-upon. Why, on top of everything else I need to do, do I have to start cleaning my house and making last-minute arrangements to accommodate a guest? It is simply out of the question. I know this will surely put me in the doghouse for life, but I am in no position to worry about taking care of anybody else except my husband and children.

I call Andy and tell him there is no way, at this late hour, that I can accommodate his mother. I am very sorry. If I had any notice or communication about anybody's plans, I could have planned accordingly. I asked her yesterday what her plans were and whether she needed to come to the house, and she told me not to worry about it. I'm sorry, but I can't help her tonight. He says, "No problem, I'll take care of it."

Well, I don't dwell on it. Much later, I will find out that I was already in the doghouse with his mother since day one, for life, because I didn't call Her Highness myself the day Curtis was burned.

Day 4: Saturday, March 8, 2003

We get up at six, I load the cooler, and off we go to meet Dawn. I am very, very tired, "in my bones" tired. I drop the kids with Dawn and head to Memorial Hermann. I park and, carrying as much as I can, make the long trek to the burn unit. I am there well before visiting hours start, but the nurses let me put Curtis' stuff away in the kitchen. I unpack the first load and make the long trek back to the car to get more. By the time I make the last trip with the DVD player, it is eleven o'clock and I can see Curtis. I have more family photographs and drawings from the kids to hang in his room. I stop in the gown room to wash, hat, and gown. While I am standing at the sink washing my hands, I feel like I am swaying, but I am standing still. My stomach is queasy. It occurs to me this might be motion sickness, as this is the first time I have stood still in a very long time. I start to wonder when I ate something last. It was Wednesday, at the Black-eyed Pea. Two-and-a-half days ago. I'm not hungry.

Finally, I see Curtis in his new room! I am so happy to see him. I beam and chatter away about all the stuff the kids and I brought for him. I chatter about everything that is in the kitchen, while I try to hook up the DVD player. Curtis directs me. Well, it turns out I'm missing a cable. The nurse comes in and tells us it is time for his bath. He asks the nurse to let me come with him. "Please, I need my wife with me." She says no, they have their hands full just taking care of him. It breaks my heart, but rules are rules. This is a world-class burn unit, and he is in the best of hands. The more we cooperate, the sooner he will be healed and coming home. Yes, ma'am, no wife in the bath.

I try to comfort Curtis and pretty much tell him my thoughts. "They know what they're doing, and we'll both be better off in the long run if we do everything they say. It's all to get you well and home quickly. It isn't going to be easy for you. Stay focused on the goal, going home." He asks if I can walk with him to the bath, that he wants to try and walk, and she says yes. I keep the IV and hoses out of his way, and he makes the attempt to walk down the hall. It takes a good long while for him to just get outside his doorway, and that is it for walking today. The nurse puts him on a gurney and wheels him the rest of the way to the bath. When we pass the hallway I enter from, he sees the exit sign and says he wants to walk to the exit sign. He becomes committed to walking to that exit sign. We constantly hear about it, and I constantly encourage him to do it. But he always has to bypass the exit sign hallway and go straight to the tank room. It is pathetic. The man just wants to walk to the exit sign, but he never can.

We get to the room that I'm not allowed to go into, and I see a large stainless tub. I think, "Man, that's gotta hurt, having water on that poor burned skin. Ouch!" I really feel badly for him. And that is an understatement. I am excused, and leave him to his suffering. I leave and drive around until I find a Radio Shack. I get the cable I need and head back to Curtis.

I have been gone less than an hour. When I get back, Curtis is in his room, sitting in a chair, shivering uncontrollably. Oh, poor baby! His teeth are chattering and he tells me how cold he is. Why wasn't I here when he got back? He is so cold. I put as many blankets as I can find on him and rub his feet; they aren't burned. He shivers and I rub and try to get him to think warm thoughts. This goes on for a good long while. Oh, he is so miserable. I just want to warm him up and stop that shaking and shivering. I tell him I got his truck home and that he doesn't have to worry about not having a paycheck. As it turns out, he has been quite concerned about what the kids and I will do without his income, and how on earth we will pay these medical bills. t's been three days and we haven't had an opportunity to talk about anything privately, thanks to all the traffic.

I let him know the medical bills won't cost us a thing. I let him know about how nice Gary and Priscilla are. I tell him he can just relax and focus on getting well, as it will be just him and me all weekend. The kids are at my dad's, no worries. "You don't need to concentrate on anything except getting well." I opt not to tell him about the incident with his mother Friday night. There is no place for that nonsense in his room. I've decided that nothing negative is allowed in his room. He asks what he looks like. I tell him, "Not too bad at all," and get him a mirror. He doesn't seem too happy with what he sees, but it all looks like second-degree burns to me, which will heal right up, and some people pay big money to get facials like that! He tells me about his "bath." They have to scrub the burned skin away. Oh, I still wince at the thought. Twice a day he has to go through that torture. That's why we were waiting for so long the first night. He was being tortured. He says it hurts, and I have no doubt it does. I can still hear the screams of other victims having their torture. I say all the right things about what a painful recovery it is going to be, but to stay focused on the goal. Before we know it, a month will be up and he will be home. This suffering and torture will not go on forever.

So, we have almost an hour alone together, and then our weekend of quiet healing is over. Another Wright invasion. All weekend long, there is a constant stream of Curtis' family. Only two people are allowed in the room at a time. The first visitor is his cousin Calvin*. They visit while I fiddle with the DVD player and get stuff put away. Calvin says he will bring Curtis a radio and some CDs; he doesn't stay long. Curtis is just starting to doze off when in comes Bertha with his mother. That's three people, so I excuse myself. I figure I'll let his family visit with him, as I'll have plenty of time with him after they lose interest. I go downstairs to the rehab floor and finally check on my coworker Willy. His daughters are in his room and I introduce myself. I give Willy some of the treats I brought for Curtis and some of Jill's soup. One of his daughters and I go outside to have a smoke. After that, I mill around for about an hour and head back to the room.

I will become a frequent guest in Willy's room. He is on the rehab floor, so there is no limit on how many people can be in the room. His daughters are good company, and I have somewhere to go when I am frequently kicked out of Curtis' room, for treatments or other guests or who-knows-what.

Neither Bertha nor Curtis' mother show any signs of getting ready to leave. After about twenty minutes, I leave again because only two people are allowed at a time. I go to the waiting room, since I am "waiting" for his family to leave. Another family is in the waiting room: a little girl about four, a woman about my age (her mother), and an older woman (her grandmother).

Peter* had been in Mexico. The car he was driving went off a cliff. The car exploded and he was burned, among other things. The wife says she had to cut through a mountain of red tape and shell out a lot of money to have him flown to this facility. She has done her homework, and this is the best place for him to be. They are not native to Mexico. I gather he was there on business or something. In any event, Peter (who I nicknamed "Mexico") has been here a couple of weeks. He is in the room one door down and across the hall from Curtis. I think the mother and daughter live in this area, and the grandmother has been staying in a local hotel. Today they are overjoyed that Mexico opened his eyes briefly. He is on his way home; they are convinced of nothing less. Wow. Such a big event, his eyes opened. Wow.

You think you've got it bad, and then you meet someone who's got it worse. They are as tickled as lottery winners that their loved one opened his eyes, briefly, for the first time in two weeks. This breaks my heart. Once again, I am reminded that people travel from all over the country to be treated in this fine facility. Boy, are we lucky. We don't have to pay for a hotel. I can keep my job. Curtis is miles ahead of Mexico. I am humbled and so grateful. I wish them luck and head back to Curtis' room.

Bertha and Mamma are still here. Curtis looks so sleepy. Mamma asks me for something to drink. Curtis asks me to bring her a banana, too. So I do. I also get myself something to drink and a frozen Frappuccino bar. Bertha finally leaves, which means I can stay because now we're back down to two.

Curtis seems agitated, and I ask him what is wrong. He asks why I keep leaving. I tell him about the "two visitors at a time" rule and that I am trying to accommodate his family and let them visit with him. I tell him about that poor man from Mexico. I ask him if he wants to get back in the bed and take a nap because he looks so tired and uncomfortable. He says no, he has company. I ask him if he wants me to put in a movie. He says no, his mother won't like any of these movies. Well, his mother is in the only guest chair. There is no place for me to sit, and I am very tired. I lay on the bed crossways so my legs or feet aren't on it, only my gown. I shut my eyes and start dozing.

Just then, more visitors arrive. Three or four of them. I very loudly tell Curtis, "Only two people at a time are allowed in the room, so I'll step out and let you visit." I hope others will take the hint, as there are still more than two and he is so tired. Nobody else leaves. At least four visitors remain in the room after I leave.

This is how it goes all weekend. Curtis will not eat, really, as he has "company." The physical therapist has shown me different exercises to do to with his legs and hands, but I never get the chance because he has "company." He gets scrubbed again, and we do the feet rubbing thing again. It is obvious to me that he is in a lot of pain. This poor man. Why won't these people leave and let him rest? All weekend long, "I'll step out and let you visit with your family." I grit my teeth and figure I can endure it for one weekend. They will lose interest and go back to their lives. They can't stay forever.

At one point Saturday evening, I am outside smoking with one of Curtis' sisters. She asks how I am, and we chat a little. I ask her if she knows anything about anybody else's plans. She says no. I ask her to spread the word to everybody to please let me know what their plans are. We have a big house where folks are welcome to stay, and I can use some help, especially next week. I am nice about it and everything, it just seems to me to be common sense. I am desperately trying to get this point across to her so she can get it across to everybody else. Wrights are pouring in by the truckload.

Day 5: Sunday, March 9, 2003

Today starts like Saturday ended. By now, I have had the privilege of hearing the screams of pain from other victims having their torture many times over. I am starting to hate being in this place. I remember coming to see Curtis on Friday and seeing him sitting in a chair. Such progress! That's what I expect, leaps and bounds, or baby steps each day, whatever it takes, as long as we keep going in the right direction.

I arrive Sunday and Curtis looks worse. Just miserable. I know the cause is all this traffic. I am angry that he seems to have taken a step backwards. *No, no, no. We want progress, and it is never going to happen with a constant parade of Wrights. The poor man just needs a nap.* They take him for torture again this morning. I don't go to the waiting room. I wait in the hallway because I know he will need me when he gets back.

After about an hour of constantly peeking through the window, I see Curtis walking very slowly. I go back in to wash, hat, and gown, then help him walk back to his room. It takes a very long time. He sees the exit sign down the hall, and he says he wants to walk to that exit sign. He talks about it all weekend. He wants to walk to the exit sign. Good goal.

Of course, before we even get to the room, the invasion is back. I have to "excuse me," "oops, sorry, pardon me," just to get to him and try to warm him up. They all just stand around talking or praying. I guess not a one of them can pick up a blanket. They can't tell that the netting on his face is stretched too tight across his nose. Snip that tight thread! His gown is twisted uncomfortably around his neck. His foot has popped out from under the blanket. He needs another pillow under his arm. They are all useless and in the way. This man needs all the help he can get. Why can't they see it?

I am standing next to Curtis with my hand on top of his head, as it is the only place I can touch him. He whispers to me that he doesn't want me to leave anymore. I say I won't. And I don't, for most of the day.

Later in the afternoon the nurse comes in, admonishing us for having five visitors in the room. Finally, after four days, a real hospital employee comes in and says something about the two-person limit. Nobody moves. She gets a little firmer about it, so I say, "I'll leave." I am too angry to wait around and see if anybody else does. I check on Willy and fetch my smoking buddy, and we go outside and chain smoke. Willy is starting to get ornery, moaning about going home. I don't want them to leave. I have nowhere to go, nobody to talk to. But his "piss and vinegar" tells me that he is back to his old self and he isn't going to be around much longer.

After a while, I go back up. Bertha is the only one here. I am suddenly starving. I ask Bertha if she wants something. She says no. I go to the kitchen and fix Curtis and I a sandwich and some of Jill's soup. I make an extra sandwich for Bertha. I bring it back and sit next to Curtis and fix him all up and try to get him to feed himself. He says, "I'll eat later, I have company." I invite Bertha to eat with us, but she says, "No, thank you." I eat. I am starving. Thirty minutes later, Bertha finally leaves. The second the door closes behind her, I have a talk with Curtis. I know I might only have five seconds to have a conversation with him, so I don't waste any time.

I remind him that the only reason he is in this place is to get well. I understand how much comfort he gets from having his family around him, and I know how hard and painful his recovery is going to be. I tell him it is his job to rest, eat, do his exercises, and make healing a priority—he shouldn't be playing host. I tell him he looks terrible. I know he is in pain, and he needs rest. "If you're tired, close your eyes. End of story." I tell him if he loses sight of his priorities, I will clear these people out of here so fast his head will spin. I tell him I don't want to be the bad guy and shoo the family away, and to please not make me do it, but not to think for one second that I won't. I know he feels it is an honor that so many people have come so far and gone to such trouble and expense to see him, but he isn't in this barbaric pit suffering so he can be the center of attention and entertain the travelers. "Get well and go home. That's your only job." I'm sure I sound harsh, but I need to get my point across before the next invasion.

Curtis apologizes and says I am right, they are wearing him out. I tell him he needs only to worry about himself and do what he wants as long as he is here. So he eats. I help him get into the bed he has been aching for. I settle him in and settle myself in the chair. We are both ready to take a nap—when in comes the next round.

Individually, none of them sees themselves as causing any trouble. They can't see that, collectively, they are all an overbearing problem.

And so it goes, through the rest of the day, past the afternoon torture, past shift change, and into the night. But Curtis does do his exercises, and he does close his eyes. The important travelers ignore the drooping or closed eyes, but that isn't Curtis' fault. He is now taking recovery seriously, and that's all I can ask for.

In the "wash-hat-gown" room, on my way back from another chain-smoking marathon, I see two of Curtis' nephews there, crying. I ask them if they saw their uncle and they nod and sniffle.

I tell them everything will be fine. Curtis is hurt badly, but he is getting better. Everybody is here to support Curtis and help him get well. It's OK to be sad and to cry, but not in front of Curtis. "If you can't stand at his bedside and talk to him like he's your uncle without falling apart, then you don't need to be in his room at all. Curtis is very worried about his appearance. How do you think it makes him feel to have his nephew stand next to him and start blubbering? Like some sort of freak, that's what. Don't do that to him!" I let them know that only positive vibes are allowed in that room and that they need to save their tears for the trip home. They thank me and say I am right and they're sorry. "There's nothing to be sorry about, just go back in there and hang out with your uncle, talk to him about what's going on in your life and just be normal, no worries." They agree.

I find out later that they went back in and started the crying again. As far as I'm concerned, that's just selfish. If you can't put Curtis first, then stay away from him. All my compassion and sympathy is with Curtis. I have none left for anybody else.

I have to meet my sister and pick up my kids at nine o'clock. We are meeting at a gas station by the side of the road, halfway between my dad's house and my house, and south of the hospital. That means I have to leave no later than eight-fifteen. Shift change is at six-thirty, and no visitors are allowed back in until seven-thirty. After the shift change, the Wrights are gone. I don't know if they'll be back, when they'll be back, how many of them will be back.

Finally, it is quiet and peaceful in Curtis' room. I turn the lights down and get him situated. He says his stomach hurts. I ask him if he wants to go to the bathroom before somebody else comes back in. He thinks about it. I can tell he really doesn't want to get out of bed, but the thought of having to go when "guests" are about is even less appealing. He says no, but his stomach is really hurting. I call the nurse, and he brings Curtis a bedpan. I tidy up the room and round up my stuff. Curtis is aching and moaning about his tummy. Nothing is coming out. The nurse leaves to get permission to give him something for his upset stomach, and gives it to him eventually. This all takes a while, and poor Curtis' tummy is really bothering him. I don't know if it's because he had to go all weekend and never got the chance, or perhaps all the traffic is stressful to him, or maybe it's something else entirely.

Curtis is not a weak man. He is a strong, macho, very nice man. It is very new and distressing to me to see him in such a weakened, helpless state. I'm not really worried about a tummy ache. It is just so sad that a tummy ache, on top of everything else, is bothering him so much. He has been in pain all weekend, I can't even imagine how much, but I can only say comforting things. Of course, this is going to be painful, but I'm sure the medical experts know what they are doing. Poor thing. This just sucks.

I get him settled and as comfortable as I can get him in the bed. "It's ten after eight," I tell him. "I am so sorry, but I have to say goodnight now." I am just so sad. He has deteriorated over the weekend, I hardly got to spend any time with him, the whole experience is stressful and heartbreaking, and to say I feel bad about having to leave him is an understatement. He says, "No, spend the night." "I can't. Overnight visitors are not allowed, and Dawn is meeting me at a gas station on the side of the road with the kids. I have to go, but I am off all week. I'll figure out what to do with the kids, and I'll be here at eleven o'clock on the nose tomorrow. Try to relax and focus on getting well and coming home. Please try to get some good rest." I kiss him on the forehead, say goodnight, and turn to leave—and there is Andy in the doorway!

Right behind him is his ten-year-old daughter, all gowned up like she is going to come in. They start to walk in and I put my hand up and say, "No, no. She can't come in here; no children." Andy says, "The nurse said it is OK." I am so stunned I don't know what to say. I ask him where they are staying; he says he doesn't know. I tell him I have to go, but they can follow me to the house. "I am just leaving. I have to meet my sister and pick up my kids." Andy says, "OK. I just want to pray for him." "OK, I'll meet you by the elevators."

Out at the elevators is Mrs. Andy. I say hello and tell her I am on my way out as I have to meet my sister, and they can follow me to the house. Five minutes pass; no Andy. Five more minutes. Now it's eight twenty-five, and I envision my sister sitting in her car at night alone with my children and I don't like it. How can I expect her to babysit for me again if I just leave her cooling her heels? I go back in and tell Andy, "I **really** have to go," and go back to the elevators. Finally, at eight-thirty he shows up and we're off and running to the parking garage. His car is on the seventh floor and mine is on the eighth. "I'll drive down, and you follow me as I pass you." Out we go. I exit with my pass and pull ahead. I'm waiting and waiting and waiting for him to come through the gate. It occurs to me that he probably didn't go to the money-eating machine. He didn't.

I pull back in and he backs up. I wait while he goes back into the hospital to get his parking ticket. He comes back out. I loop around to come back through the exit gate and he passes me, going the opposite direction back up into the parking garage! It's the Three Stooges trying to exit the parking garage.

Now it's eight-forty! I am starting to get annoyed with the idiot who came up with the brilliant parking plan for this facility. People are used to paying for parking when they exit the garage, not before they exit the building. I really don't like this hospital's practice of charging for parking to begin with, and the fee is exorbitant. This is supposed to be a place of healing and caring. Sixty-three dollars a week seems greedy, and it leaves a bad taste in my mouth.

Finally, we get out and I race to meet my sister, fifteen minutes late. I load up the kids and their stuff and tell Andy to follow me. When we get home, the kids and I situate the guest bed and the guests. Then I unload the dishwasher, and Ben takes the trashcans to the curb. It is well after eleven before we get to bed, I am exhausted. I'm shaky and nervous from being so tired. Physically, emotionally, and mentally, I am worn out. My mind is racing. I can go to work in the morning before visiting hours, as now there are adults in the house with the kids. (See, why can't they let me know?) I write a note stating I will be home at ten-thirty and we will leave for the hospital. I promised Curtis I'd be there at eleven. I set my alarm for six o'clock, planning to go to work for a couple of hours in the morning. I don't get any sleep all night.

Our dog Brownie, a Boxer, always sleeps in our room. She is not allowed upstairs. She can open our bedroom door, so there is no way to confine her, but there is never a reason to. She sleeps in our room and has no interest in being upstairs. But tonight, she keeps going upstairs to the guestroom. She stands by Andy's side of the bed and whines and cries.

"Lisa, I need you. Lisa, why aren't you here? Lisa, I had a terrible night, please come and see me. Lisa..." I wake up to Curtis' weak and pleading voice on the answering machine. My alarm is going off. It is ten-fifteen! My alarm has been going off for over four hours, and I am out cold. Curtis' voice is as weak as a kitten's and shaking.

I jump out of bed and leap into the kitchen to grab the phone. Tangled in the blankets, I go splat! on the tile floor. *Mental note: Get a phone and plug it in near the bed.* I grab the phone and tell Curtis, "We are on our way. Visiting hours don't start until eleven. I am so sorry, but they won't let me in until then. We're getting ready to leave right now. I'm coming."

"I had a terrible night, I never want that nurse near me again!" I tell him, "Calm down. Everything will be OK. We are on our way out the door right now."

I run upstairs shouting, "Get up! Get up! Time to go right now!" I shout this into every bedroom. Everybody is still sound asleep. Amy and Curtis' niece had stayed up until all hours having a sleepover, so Amy is just as ornery as she can be and I am not much better. Amy will not get up. "I don't want to go, I'm too tired." "Get up **right now** or I will throw you in the car barefoot and in your jammies. We're late! I promised Curtis we will be there at eleven. We have to go right now!"

By the time I get downstairs, Ben is already eating a bowl of cereal. I throw on the same clothes I wore yesterday. "Let's go! Let's go!" I shout up the stairway. Her highness comes down scowling and whining about being hungry. I hiss at her, "Go get in the car right now!" Andy, his wife, and his daughter are already standing by their car.

My sister told me I should put a photograph of Curtis on his door so the nurses and doctors will know what he is supposed to look like. My boss' son Elmer* volunteered to print one that I had on my digital camera for me. I'm supposed to pick it up this morning. My office is only six blocks from my house and on the way to the hospital. We all get into our cars, run by the office and grab the photograph, then off we go.

When we assemble in the parking garage elevator, it is 10:55 AM. I tell Andy, "Curtis had a bad night and called almost in tears. I promised him I'd be here at eleven, so when we get off this elevator I am going to run. I'll meet you upstairs." The doors open and I start running. I run down the long corridor and turn right turn left, run down this long hallway to the next bank of elevators. Ride up to the seventh floor. Run to the gown room. When I come out, it is 11:01 AM and Curtis is walking down the hall for his torture. I almost missed him.

He is so happy to see me. I take the IV pole and help him down the hall. I get a hug. He says again, "I had a terrible night! I never want to see that nurse again, she hurt me, and she's mean. I'm afraid of her. I want to walk to the exit sign! I don't want to go in that room, Lisa, it **hurts**."

"I know, I know. Curtis you're doing so well. You're getting closer to home every day. I will take care of the mean nurse. Try to bear it, Baby, try to find somewhere else in your mind to go to. All of this will bring you home, I'm so proud of you." I am stressed and tired and frazzled, but I'm as cool as a cucumber around Curtis. I don't know how I do it. I'm excused at the torture room and walk back down the hall, just as Andy is coming in. "You just missed him. They took him to torture, and that will take at least an hour."

Now is as good a time as any to use those cafeteria coupons. With three kids underfoot, it takes a long time for everybody to get what they want. I grab a bagel and a Pepsi. This is my second grand meal in five days. At the time, though, I don't realize how seldom I'm eating. When we finally sit down, Andy's wife says, "You need to slow down, Lisa. You really need to just slow down." *If I hadn't run from that elevator, I would have missed Curtis. I'm so glad I ran.* "I can't."

Andy tells me he thinks Richard is coming tomorrow with Andy Junior*. *Mental note: Call Richard*

By now, it has been at least forty-five minutes since Curtis started his torture. The kids are behaving, and Andy and his wife are still eating. I ask Andy if he minds if I leave the kids with them and meet them upstairs. He says, "No problem, but I want to see Curtis, and we have to leave at one o'clock." I say, "OK, I'll see you upstairs."

When I get back, Curtis isn't done being tortured yet. Karen Vidor is there and once again asks, "Anything I can do for you?" I tell her, "Actually, I do have a concern. Curtis has two stepchildren, ages eight and nine, who are not allowed in his room. Last night, the nurse allowed his ten-year-old niece into the room, and I think somebody should know about that. Who should I talk to?"

She calls Mitzi*, the unit manager, and hands me the phone. I introduce myself to Mitzi and tell her about the night shift allowing a ten year old in the room. She says she'll send Kid Counselors* to talk to my children, and if they think my children can handle it, then they can see Curtis. That's not what I expected to hear. I thought kids weren't allowed, plain and simple. "Oh, that will be nice, but that isn't my point. I just thought somebody should know that the night shift allowed a ten-year-old child to see him." She again says she'll send the mind-benders up to talk to my kids. OK, whatever. Since she is the unit manager, I figure I'll start here with problem number two. "Look, I don't know if you're familiar with my husband, but he was admitted last Wednesday." Just then Andy comes up to the nurses' desk. I tell him that Curtis isn't back yet and that I have some business to take care of and I'll see them in the waiting room when I get off the phone. I continue with Mitzi, "He was admitted last Wednesday, and he is badly injured. I am well aware he is in for a painful recovery. I haven't had a chance to talk to him much today, but he's had no complaints about anyone until now. He is normally a very easygoing, peaceful, cooperative person, but whoever his nurse was last night he really doesn't like at all. I'm sure, whoever she is, she is a great nurse and nobody is saying she's not doing her job or anything like that, I don't know all the details, but I gather from Curtis that he feels as though she was a little rough on him, in his opinion. I'm not trying to make trouble for anyone, but maybe, just to give him some comfort and peace of mind, is it possible to throw him a bone and not let this nurse take care of him?" Mitzi says, "Absolutely, I will find out who she is and I'll make sure she is not assigned to Curtis again."

OK, so, this isn't so bad. I thank her and I thank Karen, who has been standing right next to me during the entire conversation. I tell Karen that the Kid Counselors are coming to bend my children's minds and that Mitzi is going to make sure Mean Nurse is not assigned to Curtis again. Karen lets me know Curtis is in the best of hands. I've heard this so many times, I naïvely believe it. I have blind faith in this hospital. It is the best! I am operating in the mindset of a woman whose husband is being cared for by one of the finest hospitals in America. I am humbled by their greatness. I have been brainwashed.

I start toward the waiting room, and see Curtis coming down the hall. I go to help him back to his room. I get him situated in his chair and rub his feet and try and stop that God-awful shivering and shaking. "Oh, Lisa, I'm so cold, and it hurts so bad. I hate those baths. They scrub me Lisa; they scrub all these burns. It hurts so bad, and I'm so cold. That nurse hurt me last night, my stomach hurt so bad and I had to use a bedpan and missed and she wouldn't help me. It took forever, and she kept leaving the light on and the door open. I am so cold, Lisa. And she kept grabbing my legs where I'm burned and, Lisa, it **hurts**. She's too rough. I'm afraid of her. Last night was terrible."

I tell him I already talked to the unit manager and he will never have that nurse again. "It's going to be a painful, tough road, but you've already made it through almost a whole week! A fourth of this is over! Every day, you're closer to home. I'm so proud of you. You're walking up and down the hall. You've come leaps and bounds already. It's going to get better every day, and today is already half over!" It makes me feel good to be able to tell him Mean Nurse will never be his nurse again. I actually did something for him, gave him some peace of mind. It made him feel better, too. But I don't want to baby him and suddenly find that he has a problem with every nurse. I can't go complaining all the time to these world-class medical folks who are saving his life.

The violent shivering and teeth-chattering lessen. I tell him that some counselors will evaluate Amy and Ben and maybe they can come to see him, but only if he is up for it. He smiles and says he can't wait.I tell him Andy and his wife are in the waiting room with the kids. "Do you want me to send them in?" "No, please, no, please don't leave, keep rubbing my feet. I'm so cold."

By now, it's almost one o'clock. Andy said they have to leave at one, and I know they have a long drive ahead. I also know this is not Curtis' problem. But I am all too aware that I need to get them in to see Curtis. For fifteen minutes, I rub and speak warm thoughts and decide to try again. I delicately tell Curtis that Andy and his wife are in the waiting room and that they drove out last night but I had to rush them out of here to pick up the kids. "They needed to leave for home twenty minutes ago, Curtis, and I know they really want to see you. Would you like me to get them for you?" He replies, "No, please, no, I'm not up for it right now." OK. Fifteen more minutes go by. Curtis is starting to doze off and isn't shivering as much. "I can call them in here, Curtis. I don't have to leave. I'll stay with you, but Andy really wants to get home." This time, he firmly says, "No!"

About two o'clock, some woman (now known as Twila*) pokes her head in the room and says to me, "There are out-of-town visitors in the waiting room who have to get home. You'll have to leave so they can come in. Only two people at a time!" Curtis isn't asked whether he wants to see them. I am simply ordered to leave. I look at Curtis and say, "I'll be back later."

In the gown room, Andy and Mrs. Andy are donning their hats and gowns. They look angry. "I told him you were waiting and need to get home. I kept asking him if he wanted me to get you, but it takes him a while to recover from those baths. He just isn't up for it." They finish suiting up and leave without speaking to me.

I go out to the waiting room to sit with the kids. I tell Amy and Ben that they can visit Curtis if they want to. "Yeah, yeah. Can we go right now?" I tell them, "His brother is visiting him right now, and some people want to talk to you first, but maybe later today." "Yay! Yay!" A few minutes later, two ladies in white jackets come in and call for the kids and me. Curtis' niece Irma* is with us. I figure if Andy already let her see Curtis, then he won't mind if she gets counseled. There is really no other choice because I can't leave her in the waiting room by herself. Off we all go to a conference room. The white jacket ladies have a doll that's wrapped with gauze and has IV tubes in its arms and stuff. They talk to the kids about what a burn patient looks like and all the potentially traumatic things they might see. Irma is already the expert. So, jolly day, Amy and Ben pass the mind bending. Andy and Mrs. Andy come into the conference room looking a little worried. I guess they were wondering where their daughter was. They collect Irma and leave without a word. Amy, Ben, the White Jacket Duo, and I go to Curtis' room.

Curtis is still sitting in his chair, and is very happy to see all of us, but especially the children. Amy is a little uncomfortable, but she is a natural nurturer. Curtis is cold, as usual. I tell Amy that I rub his feet to warm him up. She doesn't have to if she doesn't want to, but Curtis will like it. She starts rubbing and chattering. Ben is very uncomfortable; he can't even look at Curtis. I show him one of the coolest things about a hospital room, balloon gloves. That's all it takes. They can see all their artwork displayed on the walls of Curtis' room, so Ben sets to work on a new masterpiece. The White Jacket Duo leave, never to be heard from again.

Priscilla comes by. She makes frequent short visits. She is a very considerate woman who obviously has lots of experience with loved ones in the hospital. She is always thoughtful and considerate. She never stays long or shows up empty handed, although she certainly could. In addition to a weeklong parking pass, she hands me an envelope. All of Curtis' coworkers pitched in to help me with the children. This envelope has four hundred dollars in it! I am very appreciative and touched, but I have another reaction: now we are some of "those people" who have tragedies happen and people donate money to them because they feel really bad and don't know what else to do. I have done the same thing. Being on the other side of it is an entirely different matter. I envision Curtis' face on a pickle jar at the convenience store. I try to shake it off. It is a very kind thing to do, but it leaves a very strange sensation.

When I get home, I call Richard to confirm his arrival for tomorrow. Curtis is having his hands grafted tomorrow. I ask if they can come by the house first and if maybe Andy Jr. can stay with Amy and Ben while we go to the hospital. Curtis' surgery could be a couple of hours, or it could be all day. He says sure, they'll come to the house first.

Before the accident, we signed up for a satellite dish service. They're scheduled to install it this morning. I could cancel it, but I would have to pay a two-hundred-dollar cancellation fee. Visiting hours don't start until eleven anyway, so I plan to wait for the dish people and Richard to show up. The weekend came and went with no opportunity for Curtis' brothers to bring his tools home, so I arranged for Gary and Joe*, my coworkers, to pick up his tool chests from his work, which is very gracious of them. His tool chest is in three pieces, as tall as a person, and very heavy. The dish guy comes and installs the service.

I call the nurses' station and confirm that Curtis has already gone to the OR. The skin grafts to his hands were scheduled for eleven, and he left on schedule. I take a shower and wait for Richard, as he should be along any time. He calls shortly after noon, and says they are still four hours away. I am disappointed, but there's nothing I can do about it. "OK, I'm just waiting for y'all."

He says his wife Lucy is with him, and that Andy Jr. wants to see Curtis. I suggest that Lucy stay with the kids. He says, "Oh, no, her dad is sick." and something else really boneheaded. I wonder why he even brought her. Then he says, "We're going straight to the hospital because we need to check on Curtis. We're not coming to the house."

Everyone who has come to the hospital has given me his or her phone number. When I took Curtis his Bible the first day, I also put his address book in my backpack. Whenever anyone gives me his or her number, I dutifully put it in his address book, as he would have done. What's funny—though I didn't even realize it at the time—is that his friends' and relatives' numbers went right into that book without fail. But when my family, friends, and coworkers gave me phone numbers, I wrote them on scraps of paper or the backs of envelopes, whatever was handy. My backpack is full of scraps of paper with phone numbers on them and I have no idea which ones are whose. But all of Curtis' numbers went right in that book.

Bertha told me a couple of days ago to call her if I need help with the kids. Well, the kids don't know her, but my back is against the wall, so I find her number in Curtis' book and call her. She says she'll watch them and gives me directions to her house. The kids don't want to go and they promise to be on their best behavior, so I call Bertha back to tell her thanks, but the kids want to go with me. The kids pack some snacks and activities in their backpacks, and off we go.

We get into the parking garage elevator and who's already in there but Richard, Lucy, and Andy Jr. Four hours away, my foot! I don't speak to them. Amy and Ben recognize them—they were at our house just a couple weeks before—and chatter away. I get the kids situated in the waiting room and go to the nurses' desk. Curtis isn't back yet.

We sit in the waiting room for a while. Hours, and hours, and hours. The kids can only keep themselves entertained for so long. They are getting bored and starting to bicker. I can hear other Wright voices in the waiting room. What possible reason is there for fifteen people to be sitting in this waiting room? I can't understand why one of them can't be in the comfort of our house, watching TV and letting Amy and Ben play at home. No, we all have to be in this uncomfortable waiting room for who knows how long, listening to these kids bickering and whining and me getting after them. I think they just feed on drama, and there's no drama like a burned man having skin graft surgery. Curtis himself would have asked one of them to stay at our house with the kids, but they wouldn't have listened to him, either. They aren't here for him, they are here for themselves.

Priscilla stops by with another weeklong parking pass. I update her on Curtis. She tells me, again, that she's happy to do anything she can do to help. She and Gary have discussed it. She is more than happy to drive Curtis' mother to and from the hospital but, she is so sorry, they won't be able to pay for her hotel. "You must have misunderstood somebody because neither Curtis or I would ever dream of asking you for money." It seems that Curtis' sister called her and asked her to put Curtis' mother up in a hotel. I apologize to her on behalf of Curtis and myself and suggest that she not take any more calls from Curtis' family.

Curtis gets back from surgery about six o'clock. The nurse says I can go in, but only for a few minutes. He is out cold and snoring soundly. The nurse, Shirley, asks what that noise is. "He is probably just snoring. This is probably the first time in six days he's gotten any rest." She says, "That isn't snoring, it's something else." She wants me to wake him up. "Oh I don't have the heart, why can't we let him rest?" She asks me if he's ever made that noise before. "No, he hasn't, but he's probably never been this exhausted before." Again she says, "Wake him up, Lisa." I wake him up. Poor thing. I tell him he is done with surgery and I am so proud of him. Almost home. He is drifting off again, and my five minutes are up. Shirley makes me leave so she can fuss over him some more. It is almost time for shift change, anyway, and Curtis is loopy and out of it. I collect the children from the waiting room and head home.

The very first day, I vowed to leave all negativity outside his room. I never tell Curtis about all the trouble I am having, or the issues with his family. Nothing. I don't tell him that days pass before I realize I haven't eaten, that I really don't sleep at night, that I get motion sickness any time I stand still (which is rare), or that the pool is black and I don't know how to take care of it. Nothing but good things. Except last Sunday, when I told him that he'd better get serious about getting well or I'll stop the visitors. But that was for his own good.

I will not bother him with the family mess. He knew the plan was for Andy Jr. to stay with the kids. I will not tell him any differently. I will not say anything that may make him feel guilty or stressed about the weight of the world being on my shoulders. It doesn't matter what his family does. He can hear all about it after he gets home. I am always calm and smiling, and I say all the right things to him to keep him encouraged. I'm not saying I'm perfect, but I am starting to realize that somebody or something must have their hand on my chin and be putting all the right words in my mouth, because no mere mortal can do this all by herself.

So, Curtis has no idea how stressed and distraught I am. How many balls I'm juggling. How hard I'm working to keep everything together. Easy as pie, no worries, no problems. He will hear all about it when he gets home, that's for sure, but there is a time and a place for everything. I put all the nonsense right out of my mind when I am with him. It isn't important.

Curtis calls me at ten o'clock. I am so surprised to hear from him, after the way he looked a couple hours ago. I figured he'd be knocked out all night, finally getting some good rest. He is wide-awake and alert. Leaps and bounds, I tell you, leaps and bounds. I am so proud of him. I just can't believe I'm sitting here on the phone with him! "Did the nurse dial the phone for you?" I am giddy and really, really proud of him and I tell him so.

He is not sharing my enthusiasm. He seems distracted. I ask him what is on his mind. "Lisa, you know I love you very, very much. I miss you so much and wish you were here. You have helped me so much. I can't do this without you. There is something I have to ask you. It hurts me to even ask you this, it hurts me a lot, but...did you tell my mother she can't stay at our house?"

What!? I am so mad that someone would even mention this nonsense to him! It just figures that, as soon as I left, all those Wrights pounced on him and stirred up a mess. And now I have to defend myself! Curtis knows me better than that. Well, the gloves are off! I tell him no, that isn't true. I tell him exactly what happened that Friday night with his mother. I tell him word for word the conversation I had with her on Thursday. I let him know that I kept asking her when she was coming and where she was staying, and told her just to let me know if she needed to stay at the house. And she told me not to worry about anything, she can take care of herself. And the next thing I know, it's eleven at night and I'm suddenly ordered to the hospital to pick up mother, who wants to stay at the house. Not one of those people had said a word all week!

I tell him all about my week. I tell him that my coworkers brought his truck and his tools home. I had some vague notion that his brothers would help with that, but I never know what they're doing until they show up, and they're not interested in doing a thing other than being seen at his bedside. No, I never told his mother she can't stay here. I just said that I couldn't accommodate her that Friday night. I told Curtis that if I'd had any notice, I would have made it happen—and he knows that!—but it was just impossible at eleven o'clock at night.

He says, "OK, OK, calm down." Boy, I am pissed! I demand to know who told him that, and he says it was his brother Richard. OK, so now we have two troublemakers, sister Irma hitting up his employer for money and Richard starting this trouble! I tell him about Irma asking Priscilla to pay for his mother's hotel. I tell him everything.

He says he is going to put a stop to this right now. He says he doesn't want his mother out here anyway, and that he's told her to stay home. He says they are wearing him out. And I tell him, "Remember the plan? Richard and Andy Jr. are going to come to the house today and Andy Jr. is going to stay with the kids. Well, Richard called at about noon, said he had Lucy with him and Andy Jr. wanted to see you. I suggested that maybe Lucy could watch the kids, and he said her dad is sick and some other boneheaded thing. Curtis says exactly what I thought, "Why'd he even bring her?" They changed their minds and went straight to the hospital and left me hanging. I feel really bad to unload on him, but they started it and it wouldn't do to have him buying in to their drama and malarkey. They are pouring into the state in droves. Curtis says they are wearing him out, and a lot of people are asking if he has a lawyer and telling him that he should do this and he should do that—all up in his business, which is none of theirs. He is tired of it.

I tell him everything and unload both barrels. As soon as my guns are empty, I feel bad. I tell Curtis I know it's a comfort to have your family around, and I can endure it for as long as you need me to. You do whatever you want, don't worry about me or anybody else. He repeats that he wants his mother to stay home. He's worn out and he doesn't appreciate everybody offering his or her two cents on his legal situation, if he even has one.

Today is just more of the same. The kids are in the waiting room attempting to kill each other, and I am fighting my way through Wrights to visit with Curtis and help him recover. Oh, it is getting so old. His nurse, the same one who told me I could bring him whatever he wanted, now tells me that I have to take the food home before they get roaches.

I will never again mention any of the issues we discussed regarding his family. He can do whatever he wants. I'm not bringing any mess to his room, no matter what they do or say.

The nurse tells me they are going to move Curtis to a private room at the end of the hall tomorrow. He doesn't need to be in ICU anymore. Progress.

The family has cleared out, finally. The ones who don't come to the hospital call his room all day and night. Curtis can't pick up the phone because his hands are bandaged, so they call the nurses' station. The nurses answer the phones. Every time his family members call, they take nurses away from Curtis and other patients who need them. And the nurses can't give out information over the phone anyway. Any time I know anything, I call Andy, just like I said I would. That starts the phone chain.

Eventually the maintenance staff set up a phone for Curtis that answers as soon as it rings. So, if the phone rings, he can just start speaking to whoever is calling. It rings constantly and wakes him up. I don't call his room or the nurses' station if I can help it, as I know what a problem it causes.

We get Curtis all situated in his own room with its own bathroom. The nurse shows me how to help him out of bed to get to the bathroom. My sister comes to the hospital to visit with Curtis and take the kids for the weekend.

Curtis still has almost constant complaints about the pain, the terror of the scrubbings, the miserable shivering and shaking, the constant cold, and the staff who come into the room and leave the light on and the door open. He is helpless in bed. The room gets warmer when the door is open, and he starts to sweat under his bandages. It's such a small thing—close the door for this man. It causes him so much discomfort, but nobody can ever remember to turn off the light and close the door.

While my sister is here, she notes his level of pain and writes on the dry erase board, "Please manage my pain!" I naïvely assume that this is going to be very painful for Curtis, and that these experts in this world-class facility are doing all they can for him. They see this all the time. All I can do is encourage him to cooperate, to do his exercises, to stay focused on coming home, to try to endure it, and to keep his mind off the misery as much as possible.

My sister, with her medical background, sees things quite a bit differently. She thinks his suffering is inexcusable, and that it could and should be abated quite a bit. Next thing I know, he has a morphine pump. I express concern about taking a dope addict home, and my sister tells me that a person who's in that much pain is not going to become addicted. I can't believe it! And furthermore, she says, "I told them to fix that door to the gown room. It always slams!" Within days, it is fixed.

I thought these were world-class experts, yet my sister has to prompt them to give him pain medication. It's not that they aren't giving him any, it just isn't enough. I don't see that. I am so grateful to her, but not as grateful as Curtis is. After nine days of misery, he finally has some measure of relief. These are my first inklings that maybe I need to watch him a little closer.

We still have the constant battle with people leaving the door open. He is so sensitive to the temperature, and his thermostat doesn't work. It is a constant activity, trying to get the temperature just right and get folks to close the door behind them. I wish that were my biggest problem. Getting people to close the door is such an issue, and it makes Curtis so miserable when his room temperature is disrupted.

I brought Curtis his burned cell phone. Turns out, it still works. He asks me dial his mother's number. I am standing right there and hear everything he says. He tells her he loves her and he appreciates her coming to see him, but that he wants her to stay home now. There is nothing she can do for him here. She can come and take care of him after he is home. He'll be home in a couple weeks. I can tell she is arguing with him, but he is very firm and very clear with her. She should stay home and pray for him, then come and stay with him after he gets home.

This evening, two more visitors show up. Curtis is really pleased to see them. He introduces me to his cousin Ken* and friend Dudley*. They make some jokes about the gowns and hats they have to wear, and visit with Curtis. I hang a calendar on the wall and put a large number "1" on March fifth, the first day of the rest of his life. I put an "X" over every day that he has been here, so he can see how far he's come.

Dudley notices the calendar and asks, "Today is the twenty-first?" I say, "Yep. See, back here is the day he was hurt; the first day of the rest of his life. He just moved to this room today, and I put the calendar up." Dudley says he had a court date on the nineteenth, and he missed it. Boy, is he in trouble! Am I sure today is the twenty-first? Oh yes, Curtis has been here two weeks and two days. He's halfway home! Dudley doesn't seem to trust the date at all. I know that Curtis was burned on March fifth, and he has been here over two weeks already. It is correct.

A few minutes later, they say something on the news about a St. Patrick's Day Celebration on Monday the seventeenth. Dudley says, "See, it's not even St Patrick's Day yet! Today is only the fourteenth!" He is right. Curtis has only been here nine days. I can't believe it. It seems like forever. I am so confused. I erase all the Xs from the fifteenth on. That sucks. I stand there and look at the calendar stupidly for a few minutes. In the words of my dear, departed Grandmother, "What a revoltin' development." I am stunned! Maybe he wasn't burned on the fifth. I must have that wrong. It seems like we've been here at least a month already.

We invite them both to stay at our house and come back in the morning. I leave my car in the lot and use my pass to get Ken's truck out of the parking lot. Dudley goes right to bed when we get to the house. I think he's been drinking. I update Ken on the past harrowing nine days and all the family mess, then go to bed. I can't believe it has been only nine days. What in the heck...? Three weeks to go. Three more weeks, minimum.

That's not so bad. I'll recruit some babysitters next week and spend the evenings with Curtis. Dawn can take care of him during the day. Three weeks will be over before you know it.

Day 11: Saturday, March 15, 2003

I wake up and see Ken outside cutting the grass. I am so touched that I start crying. I call Curtis and tell him that Ken and Dudley are cutting the grass. Curtis says he asked Ken to do it. It is amazing how much it has grown in nine days. The pool is black, but I can't worry about that. This is the first time any member of his family has lifted a finger to help, and it really means a lot to me. I let Ken and Dudley know it, too. I notice some purple flowers on a tree in the backyard and recognize them as wisteria. I have never seen them before, but I don't mention it to Curtis because I don't want him to feel bad about missing it. It's only been nine days, and I'm weeping because somebody is cutting the grass. This is a graphic illustration of my battered emotional state and how trampled I've been by his family.

The rest of the weekend continues very much like the last. Curtis has a tummy ache and has to go to the bathroom a lot. One time his mother is sitting in his room. (She came back.) I help Curtis sit on the side of his bed, put my foot in front of his and my arm around his back to help him up, the same way the nurses taught us, the same way we've done it so many times. His mother is nervous and thinks we should call a nurse. She is full of suggestions about how I shouldn't be assisting Curtis, that the staff should do it. Curtis assures her we have done this many times.

The occupational therapist lady arrives with a metal cart like a hot-dog vendor would use. She heats some blue plastic, bends it, and works it over to fashion splints. His hands are heavily bandaged and these splints fit over the bandages and go up to his elbows. They have taken skin from his calves and grafted it on his hands and a large area on his left elbow. Curtis constantly complains about people leaving the door open and the lights on and about his pain, but he wants to get up and go home. He never stops talking about walking to that exit sign.

I have to return to work and the kids go back to school on the seventeenth. Curtis has his second skin graft scheduled for the nineteenth. This one is to graft his left thigh. During his first skin graft, the kids and I sat in the waiting room for hours on end to see him for five minutes. He was out of it and didn't remember seeing me, anyway.

My sister is taking classes in the Med Center and I have already started to coordinate my schedule with hers. She can see to Curtis during the day, and I can see to him in the evenings. I have a lot of volunteer babysitters—my neighbors and folks from work—but that's like gold, y'know. You have to use it sparingly.

My sister will see Curtis on Monday; I will be there Monday night. Tuesday, I'll go both day and night because Dawn can't. I don't ever want him left alone if it can be avoided. The Wrights never tell me when they are planning to appear but, by now, I figure they'll taper off, especially after Curtis told them to. Wednesday is his skin graft. Dawn is planning to go after class Wednesday evening. There is no reason for me to sit in the waiting room all day while he is in surgery when I need to be at work. My plan is to leave Curtis in Dawn's care Wednesday night and get some laundry and grocery shopping done. Since my son Ben is all but failing school, he really needs to be kept up with, so I figure I'll take advantage of the evening at home. Dawn is going Thursday during the day, and I am going Thursday night. Friday, the kids will go to my dad's again, so I can be there for the day and night shifts all weekend.

The rest of today is very much like every other. Wrights are everywhere and I'm constantly being evicted. By now, Willy has been discharged. On one of my many excursions to the waiting room, I encounter Mexico's family again. Mexico is now on a ventilator. They are hopeful that he will be off it next week. If they can't wean him from it, they will have to perform a tracheostomy. *Poor man. He'll be one of those people with a box in his neck.* Just when you think you've got it bad, you hear something like that. What a horrible reality. She talks about these horrid things—ventilator, tracheostomy—as if she's rattling off a grocery list. It makes my tummy queasy. Poor woman. Poor family. I wouldn't want those words in my vocabulary.

I take the kids to school and go to work. I work all day. I search the internet for pure cocoa butter. I finally find some and order a case. I ask Smitty*, another coworker who also has a pool, to come over sometime and teach me how to use my pool equipment. I just don't know when I'll find the time. I don't have a babysitter tonight.

Mr. Mann discreetly asks me if we've hired an attorney. I have not. Everybody always wants to know what happened. It doesn't matter what happened. All that matters is that this man is burned and suffering horribly. Mr. Mann gives me the number of an attorney. The attorney says he wants to come to the hospital as soon as possible and interview Curtis, so we set it up for this evening. I break my "no call" rule to let Curtis know.

I go to the hospital after work. By the time I get there, it is five-forty-five. That leaves only forty-five minutes until shift change, when I have to cool my heels until seven-thirty, and then get to spend only another ninety minutes with him. When I walk into the room, Curtis stands up from his chair all by himself and gives me a hug. Leaps and bounds I tell you. He stood up by himself! I am beaming like a lighthouse. Thirty-five days, my foot. We'll be done here in a week! I fix him a snack, then go and get the kids situated with their homework in the waiting room. When I get back to his room, the lawyers are there.

This is the first time I hear what everyone to wants to know: "What happened?"

A non-English speaking coworker pushed live wire instead of pulling it. This push caused the wire to arc and shot Curtis with 440 volts. He was instantly showered with sparks, which ignited his clothing. The coworker dropped the wire and ran. Curtis alternately tried to pat out the flames and to cover his face. So his face suffered only second-degree burns, as it was being burned only when his hands were busy patting out flames. Nobody came with a fire extinguisher. He was too panicked to remember to stop, drop, and roll. He started to take his hands off his face to pat again and saw nothing but flames everywhere, so he kept his face covered. I believe the building had caught fire, as well. His clothes burned completely off his body. He hit the ground at some point. He was lying on the ground, naked and smoldering, when Priscilla drove up and came running toward him while she was talking on a cell phone. She had been calling 911. She dropped down next to him and prayed with him and for him until the ambulance arrived.

His entire faced suffered second-degree burns, he was wearing a baseball cap, so it stopped at his hairline. The tip of his nose is burned very deeply. His eyelashes and eyebrows are gone. His left ear has a deep second-degree burn. His neck and extreme upper chest are unharmed. He has third-degree burns on a large portion of his left elbow area, which was grafted at the same time as his hands, as well as parts of the palms of his hands, and the backs of his hands from the fingertips to beyond the wrist. He has third-degree burns on 99 percent of both thighs, his groin (including the equipment), and his abdomen; spots of second- and third- degree on the calves; and a spot of second-degree on his back.

After Curtis finishes telling them the story, we sign some papers, and the lawyers leave. We never speak about it again.

I spend the rest of the evening with Curtis and the kids. Ben has to do his homework, the kids have to be fed, and Curtis needs help to the bathroom. It goes on and on. I'm not resting on my laurels, I can tell you. Curtis' hands, in addition to being heavily bandaged, are now in those plastic splints that go up to his elbows. They are very heavy and unwieldy. His entire body is covered in bandages and greasy cloths.

Day 14: Tuesday, March 18, 2003

I leave work at ten-thirty. I know it is going to brutalize me to come back to work after being at the hospital, but I try not to think about it. I get to Curtis' room and kiss him on the forehead as I always do. I spend a couple hours with him until I have to head back to work. After work, I go home and get the kids and we go back to the hospital. Once again, Ben has homework and the kids need to eat. To my surprise, Wrights strike again. There is nowhere for anyone to sit. I don't leave this time. As long as my husband is in this room, it is our home. I am sick and tired of being kicked out. I have the kids settled in with food and homework,

I just ignore the Wrights and try to work around them, although the room is very crowded.

Day 15: Wednesday, March 19, 2003

Skin graft day. I speak to Curtis several times this morning. He is scheduled for surgery at eleven. This is the last time I can talk to him before surgery. I offer him all the words of comfort and encouragement I can think of. "Dawn will be there when you wake up. Call me when you feel up to it. I'll be waiting to hear from you. I'm very proud of you, and I love you so much."

They are going to take skin off his back and put it on his left thigh. The entire left side of his body is more severely burned than the right. The skin graft to the right thigh is tentatively scheduled for next week; they are going to take the skin from his chest and parts of his calf. Dr. Plastic Surgeon also tentatively scheduled a fourth skin graft to his abdomen and manhood for the following week, but he is running out of donor skin sites.

I don't hear from Curtis. I think of him all afternoon and send him good thoughts. I get home after work, expecting an update from my sister at any time. Now remember, his first skin graft started on time and he was loopy and out of it and he was gone for hours. I'm trying to be efficient with minutes, minutes are all I have to work with.

Since I knew I would be at home this evening, I asked Gary to come over and look at something. I figure Curtis will still be somewhat bedridden after he gets home, and I want him to be as comfortable as possible. We have a TV in our room, but it just sits on top of a low dresser, and one of the posters of our four-poster bed slices right through the middle of the screen on Curtis' side of the bed. I want somebody to come by and look at it and let me know what kind of shelf I should buy to mount it on the wall. It is a fairly large, heavy TV. Gary comes by to have a look and is out in the garage cutting wood before I know it. He builds a shelf and we put the TV up there. Another item off the list.

No more than thirty minutes after I get home, my sister calls, "Lisa, why aren't you here?" She sounds frantic. I say, "What? I had no plans to go this evening, remember? How did the surgery go?" She says, "He hasn't even left for surgery yet!" She says he is miserable, in pain, has a tummy ache; he's just a mess! Oh, I feel like crapola. How could I let this happen? Last time I talked to him, he was fine and leaving for surgery any minute. It never occurred to me to call his room; I don't want to disrupt his rest. I am waiting for his call after surgery. I can't believe he hasn't even left and hasn't called me. I feel so bad. He's been there all day stressing about this surgery by himself. I have failed him miserably. Dawn puts Curtis on the phone, but he just doesn't feel well and doesn't want to talk. A totally different person from the one I spoke to earlier today. I don't know what to do. I tell my sister he is probably highly agitated after dreading this surgery all day alone. If I leave now, he might be gone by the time I get there. Dawn says for me to stay put and she'll call me later. I try to do laundry and get the things done that I planned on doing. Who knows when I'll get another chance. I can't really concentrate because I am so uptight.

Dawn calls an hour and a half later. She repeats the litany of complaints Curtis has: tummy ache, headache, pain, temperature. All the other things I chalk up to stress, but the fever perks my ears up. I ask her if she has told anyone. She says she's told every person that crossed her path in a white coat. She went down to pre-op with him and told everyone there, too. She's told everybody, but nobody seems concerned. I am very distressed, and so is Dawn. She says she is staying until he comes back from surgery, visiting hours or no visiting hours. She waits in his room. No Wrights tonight. She calls me well after midnight. He is back from surgery and is resting. He has a fever, but they think that is normal after surgery despite the fact that he had one **before** surgery. I don't get much sleep tonight.

I get to work in the morning very agitated. Visiting hours don't start until eleven, and I am desperate to check on Curtis. I give Ginger the update and tell her I have to leave at ten-thirty.

I could have taken time off work—a lot of time, I think it's three months—and still had a job to go back to. The Family Medical Leave Act secures your position of employment if your husband receives an electrical shock, is severely burned, and requires care. Well, here's the kicker. If I'm off work, I don't get a paycheck, so this is of no use to me. Furthermore, if you are in the upper levels of management and your absence will cause a direct detriment to the company, then you have no protection under the Family Medical Leave Act. If I were absent from my job for any length of time, there would be immediate and devastating financial consequences to my employer. My husband needs me, my employer needs me, and I need my paycheck. I never took advantage of my circumstances as an excuse to get out of work. I can't "get out of work" anyway. It just piles up. Except for the first week, I dutifully reported to work almost every morning. I missed a lot of hours and a lot of my co-workers, including Elmer, picked up what slack they could. I never had to ask them. I had a paycheck every week. There were some rough spots, but Mike Mann and his entire roofing company rode this out with us.

I race to the hospital very distressed about Curtis' deterioration. I won't let this happen. I thought we were on track. I'm trying to keep everything together and keep him cared for, but it seems like every time I have some semblance of a schedule, it falls apart. He is halfway home now; we can get through this.

I get to his room and kiss him on the forehead. He is in a bed that looks like a bathtub. It's a waterbed. They have removed the skin from his back and put it on his left leg. Almost all the skin from his back. He can't sleep in a regular bed until the donor site heals.

His leg is wrapped in red gauze, and under the sheet is a lamp that's pointed at his grafted leg. The nurse tells me every hour for twenty minutes, or something like that, they have to put the light on it to help the red dye dry out. He is all jacked up in this waterbed. There is a trapeze-like contraption hanging from the bed, so he can pull himself up and turn if he needs to. Please, he isn't pulling up or turning anywhere. His back is bandaged, and I'm sure it hurts with every move. His arms and hands are bandaged and in splints, his belly is covered in greasy cloths (the dressings for the other third-degree burn sites) his right thigh and leg are dressed in bandages and greasy cloths, and his left thigh is wrapped like a mummy in red bandages that look like they've been dipped in blood. He's hooked up to a morphine pump and other cocktails through an IV. But, all things considered, he is OK. He's a little warm, but given the circumstances, he is OK.

In walk his mother and sister! Curtis and I just look at each other. I ask his mother how long she is going to be here. She says, "A while." I ask if that means "a while" today, or "a while" the rest of the week, or "a while" several weeks. She says, "A while." I look at Curtis and he looks at me. I tell him I have to go back to work. He says no. "Only two people are allowed at a time. As long as you're not alone, that's all that matters. I need to be at work as often as I can, so I am going back to work." I leave almost as soon as I arrived. A wasted trip once again. Thank you, Wrights.

I go back to work, and they are all surprised to see me. I give Ginger the lowdown. I talk to her almost every day. It takes too long to catch somebody up from day one, so she and Dawn are the only people I speak to every day. I did talk to Willy and his family, but they checked out a week ago and left me all alone. I had secretly hoped that Willy would sprain his ankle or something so they'd keep him in the hospital. I was sad, almost despondent, after they left.

I work the rest of the day and call Curtis in the evening. Mother and sister are still present and he doesn't know how long they will be here. I take advantage of the bonus evening at home to get some chores done. Jill from work comes by to keep me company and help around the house. My cousin from Michigan calls and says she is thinking about coming down here, but she wants to know how I feel about it. Do I need some help? "Yes, please come as soon as you can. Please get on the next plane!" She can't get on the next plane, but she'll work on coming in the next couple of weeks.

My friend Penelope*, who used to work with me but moved three hours away, also offered to help. I tell her to please come any weekend she can. She is scheduled to come the weekend of April fifth. Bless these people. I desperately need some help, and I am not afraid to admit it. Whatever help I assumed Curtis' family would offer isn't coming and is never going to come.

My neighbors come by. They want to visit Curtis, but they want to check with me first. I tell them they have no idea how much I appreciate that. I tell them where he is and when visiting hours are. I tell them that they can go whenever they want to, but good luck getting in to see him because we are trampled by his family. The wife has experienced long hospitalizations with hip trouble, and they advise me to speak up. They tell me that people don't realize what they are doing, and I need to tell them. I tell them that I have spoken up, and Curtis and spoken up, but they're not listening.

I'm so frustrated and angry with his family. They've called Curtis' boss and asked for things. Karen Vidor tells me that she, too, is getting calls from Curtis' family asking for financial assistance or updates on Curtis. I have continued to call Andy with updates on Curtis as soon as I know them. That's been the plan since day one, at Curtis' request—I communicate with Andy and he spreads the word. I have little time to keep up with the doings of the Wrights. Curtis knows enough about what's going on, and he can deal with them as he sees fit. He's asked his parents to stay home, but they won't listen. He's asked his brother to keep his parents home, but he won't listen. Nobody helps him a bit. They all act as if I am trying to keep them away from Curtis and I am keeping information about his condition from them. It is just ludicrous! All we ever asked for was a little common sense. We never got it.

Curtis has told me that he has had numerous conversations with different family members about getting a lawyer. We discussed it briefly, we met with lawyers, and we haven't discussed it again. We have bigger issues at hand, but it sure as heck isn't anybody else's business. I don't think about them or their doings, but they are always popping up creating chaos. Curtis can handle them when he gets home. He will hear all about it. Until then, I am staying away from them and ignoring them. I miss my husband. I know he needs me, and I can't get to him.

I get to Curtis' room after work to find mother and sister still sitting there. I cannot believe how much he has deteriorated, and how quickly. I kiss his forehead and find that he is on fire. The whites of his eyes are as yellow as butter. I push the call button and ask his nurse to come to the room. Just then, Curtis says that he is going to puke. I grab one of those kidney-shaped plastic dishes and tell him to go ahead. It is hard to lift his head because his back has been skinned and he is in a bathtub bed. The barf is running down the side of his mouth, so I get a washcloth. Mother and sister just sit there. Shirley walks in and asks what is wrong. I tell her he just threw up and he is on fire.

I look right at her and say, "The whites of his eyes are butter yellow." She says, "I noticed that, but you're really the better judge of that than I." I tell her, "I haven't really seen much of him since Wednesday, but he is sick and this isn't right." She takes his temperature—101.2. That is a fever. She takes the blanket off him and goes to get some Tylenol or Motrin. Before she gets out the door, Curtis says his tummy hurts, and he throws up again. She says there probably isn't anything left to throw up, but if he is still nauseated, she can give him something for that. She presses on his tummy and asks him where it hurts. He says it hurts all over, and he throws up again. She leaves to get Tylenol and something for nausea. After Shirley leaves, his mother says to me, "It's a good thing you're here.

I wouldn't know what to do." *Then why are you here? If you don't know what to do, then you have no business here.*

I am wiping up barf when Curtis starts to freak out! "I can't breathe!" He starts grabbing at all the IV lines and equipment. He can't do much grabbing because he can't turn in the bathtub bed and his arms weigh about fifteen pounds each with all the bandages and splints. His eyes are huge and wild, and his voice is very ragged, "I can't breathe...give me oxygen...I can't breathe." This all happens very quickly. At his first outburst, I tell him, "Yes, you can breathe. Look at me, Curtis, and breathe with me. Slow, deep breath." At the same time, I push the call button. "Look at me, Curtis. Yes, you can breathe, and we're going to breathe together. Slow deep breath in..." I can't get his attention. He's frantic. I don't know how I manage to seem so calm. I am scared to death. I growl at his mother and sister, "Go get somebody!" The nurse is not responding to my call, and it is evident to me that **he can't breathe**! His mother leaves to get somebody. I keep telling Curtis, "Yes, you can breathe. Look at me, Curtis. Calm down. Breathe with me."

His color is changing, and I think he is going to die right in front of me. He is wild-eyed, frantic, and desperate for air. Nice Blond Lady Doctor and Shirley come in, and I get out of their way. Nice Blond Lady Doctor goes for the oxygen, and Shirley excuses us all from the room. This all happens within five minutes of my arrival. I can't help thinking that he was just waiting for me to get there before he fell apart. That's what happened. He literally fell apart before my very eyes.

I am so angry with myself. How, how could I have let this happen? It is all coming together: the tummy aches from as far back as March ninth; the strange breathing noises after the first skin graft; the fever and tummy ache and misery the night of the second skin graft; the "injury not always readily apparent," the seemingly endless pattern of two steps forward and three steps back. Something is very wrong with him, I should have seen it coming. I should have been watching him a lot closer and taking care of him. I shouldn't have concerned myself with accommodating all the out-of-town visitors. From this moment forward, game on! I am not getting out of anybody else's way, they are getting out of my way. They obviously are not here to take care of Curtis; they don't know how. I am angry with his family, but even more angry with myself. This is my fault. I am responsible.

I go straight to the waiting room to check on the kids. My adrenaline is pumping like crazy. I have no concentration for the kids. Ben has to go potty. I take him to the bathroom. The closest one is downstairs. They have to fight over whose turn it is to push the elevator button. Once we're inside the elevator, they have to fight and negotiate some more to determine whose turn it is to push the number button. I need a big, fat cigarette. Man, that child is in the bathroom forever. I am desperate to go back and see about Curtis. The kid must have been on that toilet for twenty minutes. Now they want something to drink. A little patience goes a long way with children, and it is bound to be a long night, so I take them for a soda. Finally, we head back to the waiting room. It's been at least forty minutes. The waiting room is full of Wrights, but none of them can take the kids for a soda or anything, because hey, they "have to check on Curtis." They're all useless.

Curtis is now in an ICU room right next to the nurses' station. Nice Blond Lady Doctor says they are coming to ultrasound his gut. Curtis is lying there moaning and groaning. He can't get comfortable because his tummy hurts so bad. Shirley tells me to just leave his things in his other room as they don't know how long he'll be in ICU, and if I have to move his things, I can deal with it tomorrow. He has a lot of stuff.

His mother returns and says something about indigestion. I am incredulous. *Indigestion?* My patience for these people is way past gone. I just ignore her and try to make Curtis comfortable, which is totally impossible as he is miserable.

The ultrasound tech arrives and lets me stay while he does his thing. Mother and sister also stay. He doesn't speak English very well. He keeps the wand on the left side of Curtis' abdomen. After he spends a good while looking over there, he acts like he is done. I tell him that Curtis indicated the pain is over here, and I point to the right side. He moves the wand around the right side, but doesn't spend as much time there; he seems to like looking at the left side. Of course, I have no idea what he is seeing. It all looks like a lava lamp to me. This all takes a while, and my kids are probably tearing the waiting room apart. I go check on them. They are playing well enough with Mexico's daughter.

I go back to Curtis' room and tend to him while waiting for news. He is just flippin' miserable, and there's nothing I can do about it. His temperature is up to 102, but he is cold. The door has to stay open and lights blazing. His tummy is causing him indescribable pain. It is hard to watch and it's so frustrating—the minutes tick by like hours.

Back and forth between the waiting room and Curtis' room. Eery time I make the transition, I have to take off the gown and hat, go to the waiting room and tend to the children, then go fight off motion sickness while I wash my hands, then put on a clean gown and hat, and go back to his room. Back and forth. Shift change comes, so I have an hour to go get the kids something to eat and let them run around outside while I smoke five cigarettes at a time.

I come back from shift change and go into Curtis' room only to find Mean Nurse checking his IV. I ask her if she is his nurse tonight, and she says yes. *What?!* Shirley is still here, so I tell her that Mean Nurse is not supposed to be Curtis' nurse ever again. Shirley says she does the scheduling, and Mean Nurse is his nurse, and there is nothing she can do about it. I'm talking to her away from Mean Nurse. I don't want to hurt her feelings, as I still have no reason to believe anything other than that Curtis just had a bad night and blamed her. I tell her that the unit manager told me she would never be assigned to Curtis again. He is afraid of her. Shirley says that nobody told her any such thing, and Mean Nurse is his nurse for the night shift.

I cannot describe how helpless and frustrated I feel. Curtis is in really bad shape and, on top of everything else, I have to leave him alone with this woman he fears. I am getting distraught. I promised him he would never see that nurse again. I feel an uncontrollable urge to wheel his bed into the elevator and take him home. To heck with this fine hospital! His family keeps parading in and out. I continue trying to get him to rest and relax and let his mind take him somewhere else. The Wrights keep coming in and stimulating him. He is so tired and in so much pain. Why won't they give him some peace? He tells me again that he wants his mother to go home. I don't know what to say, as I don't feel like it is my place, and I am already in the Wright doghouse. He is talking gibberish at times, getting confused and disoriented.

They lock the waiting room at ten o'clock, and there is nowhere for the children to go. At quarter to ten, Nice Blond Lady Doctor says that they think he has gallstones. The critical care team is coming to evaluate him, and they may take him to surgery tonight. She says these stones must have been there for some time and asks if he ever had tummy trouble before. No, not at all.

I am relieved. Yes, please, cut him open and fix him! I ask her to call me at home because they are locking the waiting room, and I have to take the kids home. As I turn to leave, Curtis' sister comes around the corner with a cart piled high with clear trash bags. It is all of our things from Curtis' room, including his hands-free phone that it took the maintenance people days to hook up. I see all our things and ask her, "What are you doing?" She says, "Moving his things, where do you want them?" I say, "Those are **our** things and I want them exactly where they were!" Those are his things, my things, and the children's things. They dumped it all in trash bags. I get my children and go home.

After I get the kids to bed, I call my sister to bring her up to date. I am hysterical—crying and cursing like a sailor. My sister tells me that somebody at the hospital can do something about Mean Nurse and the family. I tell her I talked to Shirley and what Shirley said. Dawn says, "You need to keep going over people's heads." I am worn out, but I have to do something. I tell my sister, "Nobody cares. This can't possibly be one of America's finest hospitals!" She says somebody cares and I should call the hospital and ask for the on-call administrator. She asks me if I mind if she calls. "No, I don't mind. Please do. I can't take anymore." I am distraught, at best.

Dawn calls me back and says a woman named Annie will call me. Annie calls and, of course, I have to fill her in on Curtis. That gets me going on everything with the family. By the time I get to Mean Nurse being his nurse again tonight, tears are streaming down my face, which frustrates me even more. I don't want to be a hysterical, crying woman. I want to get Curtis the help and care he needs.

She tells me she can't do anything about the nurse tonight, but that she knows Mean Nurse. She can only surmise that, given Curtis' condition, she is assigned to him because she is an excellent ICU nurse. I say fine, just don't let her bathe him. It is unlikely he will get bathed tonight, but I don't want her touching him. She agrees to make that happen and to discuss this issue with Mitzi. She is so nice. She tells me she will check on Curtis as she, too, used to be a nurse. She makes me feel so much better. She says, "What I'm hearing from you is that you're concerned about your husband's recovery. I'm not hearing that you have any personal issues with the family. We have counselors who can orchestrate a family meeting and help get everybody on a schedule and work together to benefit Curtis." She is no nice, and I believe she really cares. She isn't placating me, she is responding. I will never forget this woman. She turned me right around tonight. I call my sister back and thank her and tell her she was right. Finally, at long last, here is a shining glimmer that maybe this really is a world-class facility because this woman is world class. *This is how it's supposed to be.*

I go to bed, but don't get any sleep. I have calmed down quite a bit, but my breath still catches, as I am recovering and still have the sniffles. It is exhausting. *Mental note: Lisa, no matter what happens, don't ever let yourself fall apart like this again. This whole ordeal is exhausting mentally and physically, and a "good cry" doesn't help a bit. It just wastes energy and wears you out even more. Don't do this again.*

I wait for the hospital to call all night, still hearing Curtis' moans and yelps of pain. I can't get it out of my head; it is haunting me. Why aren't they calling and cutting him open? He desperately needs help! I break my cardinal rule and call the nurses' station. Nice Blond Lady Doctor says they decided not to operate, since they don't want to cut through burned skin. He has to stay in that bathtub bed. The gallstones are blocking his bile duct. They are going to perform a sphincterotomy, a procedure in which they make an incision in the bile duct to release the stones. OK, good deal. Do it quickly. I toss and turn all night.

Day 18: Saturday, March 22, 2003

I load empty suitcases into the car so I can bring home a lot of things that will not fit into the ICU room. My brother comes to stay at my house with the kids for the weekend.

I get to the burn unit and Sonny* is at the nurses' station. She says Curtis isn't here; he is getting his sphincterotomy. It is eleven the next morning! That means he spent the whole night suffering; for the past twelve hours, he's been in the same pain I left him in. I am horrified. She tells me where I can find him. I leave the suitcases in his room. Trash bags are heaped up on and around a cart. I am disgusted.

I set off for the other part of the hospital. Lydia*, another nurse, stops me in the hallway and tells me she told housekeeping not to clean his other room until I can go through it. I thank her. Another world- class glimmer. I see his parents near the lobby, but they don't see me. Obviously, they haven't left. I find the GI place and finally find Curtis. He asks me where I've been, why I haven't been here. Once again, I explain to him that visiting hours aren't until eleven. I thought they'd done this last night. He asks if his parents are here. "I saw them in the lobby. Do you want me to go get them?" He says, "No, I want them to go home!" I tell him I am working on that. He says, "I need my bed."

He is on a tiny little gurney, not in his bathtub bed, and he has no morphine pump. He is very agitated. The lady at the desk says she called the transport team, and they are on their way to take him back to his room on the burn unit. She seems nervous. Curtis asks for something to drink. It takes Desk Lady some time to track down Dr. Sphincterotomy to see if he is allowed to have a drink. He gets some orange juice. We wait a long time for the transport team. Curtis is getting increasingly unstable and miserable with each passing minute. Desk Lady is getting really nervous, which is making me nervous. He is nowhere near any ICU equipment should something happen. She calls to check on the transport team every five minutes. We must have been waiting forty minutes before they finally arrive. I can't ride in the same elevator, so I run back to the burn unit. I find Sonny and ask her who can help me clear the traffic out of his room. I tell her that he needs to rest and his family won't let him, and that he wants his parents to go home. I start crying. She says she'll call some counselors to talk to the family and me, but she cannot police visitors.

Nice Blond Lady Doctor and Dr. Richard Head are at the nurses' station. I see Wrights milling around. I ask the doctors what I can do about all this traffic. I repeat how stampeded he has been and how badly he needs rest. I tell them that he asked his parents to go home for the time being. Dr. Richard Head says he will clear them out without hesitation; he'll write an order. Sonny is walking by and says he doesn't need to write an order; she will take care of it. That doesn't make any sense. She just told me there's nothing she can do about visitors. I wish he would write an order.

Curtis comes back and I am kicked out again as they have to torture him and put him back in his waterbed and put some tubes in to pump out his stomach. I go to his old room to make sure nothing is left behind. There are a few items. I check the outlet behind the bed for the cell phone charger, but it is gone. They take quite a while with the bed and the tubes and the torture. I am in the hallway talking to somebody about something when I hear an indescribable, long, howling, scream of pain coming from Curtis' room. They can't take him to the "tank"; they have to torture him right there in the bed.

If I were in a dark alley, I would know that Curtis made that sound, although I'd never heard that kind of noise from him before. I have long since "gotten used to" his yelps and cries and moans of pain, but this is new. It is the sound of a human being getting tortured. Barbarically. It distracts me from my conversation. It goes right down to my toes and into my bones. That poor man. I can't breathe. The scream is shortly followed by a very ragged, loud whisper, like he can only whisper but is trying to yell and is catching his breath after every word "Don't --- you--- f---ing --- touch me --- again!"

That's followed shortly by a patronizing nurses' voice, "Don't curse us, Mr. Wright, we're just doing our job." I have to walk away. I have to walk away, or I'll go in there with an ice pick and stab that bitch's eyeballs out of her skull and see how she likes it. I go outside to chain smoke. I am itchy. I chain smoke, and scratch all over, and try to think of something else. I am not going to cry; that makes me too tired. What can I do about getting him some rest? He's been up for thirty-six hours in agony. Scratch, scratch, scratch. I need eight more hands to scratch all my itches and smoke all my cigarettes.

I go back up after a while. Curtis is flat on his back in his bathtub bed. He is sweating and looking very worn out. His breath is ragged. The splints are off his hands. His hands are open, and he has them elevated about six inches off his chest. They are trembling, like a very elderly person. He looks awful and isn't acting like himself. He is exhausted. I tell him to close his eyes, take slow deep breaths, and get some rest. He is muttering gibberish between ragged breaths. I keep trying to soothe him to sleep. His dad walks in with his big booming voice, and up go the trembling hands again and here comes more gibberish. Right then, we are kicked out again, as they have to put in a central line.

I've given this issue with the family a lot of thought, but I give it more good hard thought right about now. I need to step in for Curtis' sake. This is becoming a life or death matter, I kid you not. I am reluctant to overstep my bounds. I know how badly Curtis needs to rest and heal. I know how much comfort he gets from his family. I also know they are wearing him out. I know he has asked his mother repeatedly to go home. I hate to bother Curtis about this, but I have to be sure what his wishes are. I must have sensed I was losing him or would lose him if this continued for one more minute.

When I get back to the room again, he looks even worse. By now it's four or five in the afternoon. He's been up for over a day and a half, and for twenty-four of those hours he's been in excruciating pain. He needs to sleep. He needs to sleep for days. His hands are up, shaking violently. I kiss him on the forehead, and he is on fire. There is a large, clear, plastic canister on the wall. It is filled with about a quart of green stuff. It is connected to a hose. The hose disappears into Curtis' nose. There is another tube in the other nostril. Sonny tells me one is a feeding tube and the other is pumping his stomach. He isn't allowed to have anything by mouth. They gave him orange juice downstairs. Oh, no, no, no! He can't have orange juice! That nasty green bile has been backed up in his body, blocked, for an entire day.

He is so tired, it is an effort for him to take a breath. But I have to be sure. I tell him to concentrate on what I am saying. "Do you want your parents to go home?" He whispers, "Yes." I tell him he is sick and needs to rest, and that maybe we should keep the visitors down to me, my sister, Calvin, and Calvin's wife for the next week. Calvin's wife is also a nurse. I need caregivers, and no one can accuse me of "kicking out his family" if we allow two people from each side. He agrees. I ask him repeatedly to concentrate on what I am saying. I tell him I am going to send his parents home, and that I will involve administration if I have to. But I don't want to do any of this if it is not his wishes. "Are you sure you want your parents to go home?" He tries to say something but it is too much of an effort.

Throughout this conversation, I have to stop and get him refocused on taking slow, deep breaths. Taking a breath and relaxing requires extreme concentration for him. I get him paper and a pen so he can try to write what he is trying to tell me. He writes with his trembling, bandaged hand, "I told them not to come." That is it; the subject is closed. It took thirty minutes or so to get through this. Concentrate on what I'm saying, concentrate on breathing. I am trying to get him as clearheaded as he can get and to realize what I am saying to him. Although it is already clear, y'know?

I get kicked out again for X-rays of the central line. His mother is at the nurses' station. I ask her when she is leaving. She says she isn't leaving. I tell her that Curtis is exhausted and needs rest, that he asked her to stay home, that he is worried about her, and that he needs to focus on healing. It is time for her to go home. I slap my palm on the desk, "Go" (slap) "home!" (slap) and walk away.

I come back from my smoke and don't see any Wrights. I go back into Curtis' room. He is all worked up again. Oh, this is so tiring. I get him somewhat soothed and somewhat stable breathing. In walks Curtis' father with his booming voice, and this gets Curtis agitated again. I tell Curtis I am going to get my chair. I go scouting for a comfortable chair, and when I come back with it, Dr. Richard Head is in the room. I catch the tail end of the conversation. He tells them Curtis is very sick and needs rest, and he is not allowing any more visitors tonight. His mother says, "Oh, no, we need to be here in case he opens his eyes!" The doctor is quite firm and says no, not tonight, no more visitors, he forbids it. Curtis' parents leave. I feel bad for them, but this is unfortunately how they have to be treated. I am so relieved.

I set up my camp next to Curtis. He tries to throw the blankets off and whispers, "Let's go." I tell him we are going to take a nap. He keeps struggling to say something. His hands are shaking. I tell him that if he doesn't hush and take slow deep breaths, I will leave. The hands come down and the eyes close. A few minutes later, he says the doctor told him he can go home. Let's go home. On and on. I repeat if he doesn't hush and go to sleep, I will leave. The hands come down and the eyes close. It doesn't last. "Let's go home. Get the car." Finally, I tell him if he takes a good nap while I am off getting the car, I will ask the doctor if he can go home. I don't want to lie to him.

The bathtub bed is a heated waterbed. After a couple minutes of quiet, he mutter-whispers something unintelligible, but I hear something like "refrratr" and notice that his right hand is kind of near his right leg. You have to pay attention to the details. in his state, he can barely move. Although the gesture is weak, I know he is directing my attention to his right thigh, and it sounded like he was trying to say "refrigerator." I slide my hand under his thigh; it is ice cold. I am amazed at how well I can understand him. I calm him down and get him to focus on breathing again, then go to find Sonny. I open the door and Curtis' sister is about to walk in. I put my hand up and tell her that the doctor said no visitors. She says, "Get out of my way, Lisa. You will not keep me from my brother!"

They have been here for a week. I haven't kept her from her brother—what a drama queen! Her brother's doctor told them to leave him alone tonight, but they will not. I don't understand these people. They are killing him before my very eyes. I find Sonny and tell her about the bed. She says she'll call maintenance, but they won't come until Monday. *Great. I'd hate to see how slow mainte-nance is in a mere mediocre facility.*

I ask her, "Why doesn't his family care about him? The doctor said no more visitors tonight." I start crying. Sonny says she'll call administration. I tell her to call somebody! I go back into Curtis' room. His sister has him all agitated again. His hands are up, trembling like crazy, and he's taking erratic, short, struggling breaths. I leave again and ask another nurse why he can't breathe, why is he so confused? He is very childlike. She says, "Oh, that is very common in burn patients." Sister finally leaves.

Some guy comes in and puts a mask on Curtis' face. The mask is hooked up to an oxygen tank. I ask him what that is for, and he says sometimes burn victims inhale smoke and this is just to help him breathe. Curtis was burned seventeen days ago and didn't suffer smoke inhalation.

I get kicked out for shift change. I go into the gown room to take off the gown. A lady in a suit with a badge is putting a gown on. She looks official, so I ask her if she is here about the Wright family. She says she is. I tell her I am the patient's wife, and that the patient just needs some rest. "He has asked his parents to go home for the time being, and the doctor said no more visitors tonight, and they just keep coming back." She says I don't get to make those decisions and she doesn't need to speak to me. She is quite rude. I head for the waiting room, not at all worried about Rude Lady. She will go ask Curtis if he wants his parents to go home, he will say yes, it will be on record, and that will be that.

I get to the waiting room and Mexico's family is there. A doctor is talking to Mrs. Mexico. I glean that Mexico is now on dialysis. The doctor finishes telling her all these terrible things and Mrs. Mexico asks, "Is he still on track? We're at the halfway point. Is this where you expect him to be?" Man! I feel so sorry for this woman. I don't remember what the doctor said. I don't know what he could have said. "Oh, yes, kidney failure on day thirty. He's progressing right on schedule!" After Dr. Grim News leaves, I don't know what to say to her. I like her. She always seems smart and on the ball. We've always exchanged brief hellos and updates, but now she is a crazy woman. I find something to say, but I don't remember what. She tells me Mexico could not get off the ventilator, and they had to do a tracheostomy. Now he's on dialysis. His kidneys stopped working. I am once again horrified back into how lucky we are. These are such terrible things she is saying: ventilator, tracheostomy, dialysis. Holy cow! That poor man. I feel lucky all over again. They are really happy about his "progress" and are really positive people. What little I heard from Dr. Grim News did not sound good at all. I don't know anything, but my money is on "the writing is on the wall." These people are either deeply in denial or know something I don't. I feel really bad for them.

She asks, "What happened to you? You were in a private room!"

We are now back in ICU, right across the hall from Mexico. I say, "Oh, gallstones of all things!" I wave my hand dismissively. I feel so sad for her and this little girl who is going to grow up never knowing her father. A small roar erupts in the waiting room. It is full of other people in the midst of a burn survivor support meeting I hear, "Oh, yeah. Next thing to go is his gall bladder. It happens all the time to burn victims!"

All these doctors and nurses have said, "Oh, no, burns don't cause this." They have led me to believe this is wholly unrelated to the burns, even though I know he was as healthy as a horse before March 5, 2003. Now a room full of former burn patients are saying it is related. I believe the waiting room. They say the gallbladder is next.

I come back in after shift change and tell Curtis we are going to take a nap together. I remind him to take slow, deep breaths, close his eyes, and relax. The trembling hands come down onto his chest, and the eyes close. He tries to say something. I shush him.

The hands start shaking again. I tell him I am going to lie down next to him and we are both going to go to sleep. No more visitors. He can't mutter anymore, only whisper.

I continue my chanting, "slow deep breaths...breathe with me Curtis...close your eyes and focus your mind on taking slow deep breaths and getting some rest." Over and over. He wants to go home. He is delirious and childlike. I don't know how long he can go on in this sickly, exhausted state. I chalk most of the gibberish up to exhaustion and fever. The struggling to breathe is a deep concern to me. All the nurses I ask just placate me and pat my shoulder sympathetically. Nobody knows why he is having trouble breathing. Nobody seems concerned about it, other than the guy putting a mask on his face, and he doesn't know why he's doing it.

His cousin Calvin comes in and I say hello. Right behind Calvin is a guy with a more heavy-duty-looking portable tank-type thing, and he puts a serious mask over Curtis' face. I ask what this is for. He says it is his breathing treatment. I ask why, and he says he doesn't know. I have barely said hello to Calvin when in walks Mean Nurse again! I smile and ask if she is his nurse, and she says yes. After she checks all his cocktails and equipment, she leaves. I pick up the phone and call for the on-call administrator (OA for short). A lady answers and I say, "Hello, my name is Lisa Lindell. I'm the wife of a patient on the burn unit." She says she knows who I am and she's spoken to my husband. I tell her, "I'm calling about a situation with a nurse." I briefly explain that the unit manager, Mitzi, told me on March tenth that this woman would not be assigned to Curtis again. Last night, she was his nurse and I spoke to Annie, the OA, who said she couldn't do anything about it last night, but that she would make sure she wouldn't bathe him last night. Now, lo and behold, this woman is his nurse again. Who is it that I need to speak with to have this problem corrected?

She says she can't do anything about staffing, nobody can until Monday, and patients don't get to pick their nurses. "By the way, I asked your husband if he wanted to see his family, and he said of course." She says this in a really condescending way. I am taken aback by her attitude and I correct her. I tell her he just asked that they go home for the time being and that he is really confused and not clear-headed. She cuts me off and says she spoke with his doctors and they told her he is perfectly capable of making his own decisions.

That is it. I throw the phone on the floor and storm out of the room in hysterical tears. Her implication is clear. I am so frustrated. Calvin stops me and says, "Whoa, whoa, you can't leave like this." I can't do anything but cry. He follows me down the hallway and tells me to pull myself together and come back and say goodnight. I can't leave Curtis like this. I feel bad for Calvin, as he has been here all of three minutes, and I feel even worse that I have broken my most important rule and behaved this way in Curtis' room. I am pretty sure Curtis is oblivious to it, but atmosphere can have a great effect.

I get down to the smoking pit as fast as I can, crying uncontrollably. I am itching everywhere. I get outside and light up. I cannot stop crying and itching. I am thinking about everything and it occurs to me that some of these thoughts are coming out of my mouth as maniacal mutterings through my tears. I keep telling myself to get a grip before somebody puts me in a straightjacket. I cannot stop crying no matter how hard I try to calm myself down. Crying, smoking, itching. Scratch, scratch, scratch.

This goes on for thirty solid minutes. Scratching and crying, uncontrollably. I have never been a weepy person, and this has never happened to me before. I have never been accused of being vague, but for some reason, all the educated, experienced, skilled people in this fine establishment can't understand the English language. I just want to wheel Curtis' bed into the elevator and take him home.

I don't think it's at all unreasonable to ask that one nurse not be his nurse again, especially after the unit manager said she would not be. I also don't think it's at all unreasonable to stem the flow of traffic and let that poor man get some rest. All I'm trying to do is get him well. I can see so clearly what he needs, and everybody else is blind to it. Everybody. Oh, I am so upset. I am further frustrated that I cannot stop crying. I'm blubbering like a brokenhearted teenager, scratching like I have fleas, muttering like a maniac. I know I am going to a padded room if I don't stop, but I can't stop. I know this is going to wear me out. My batteries have so little juice. *Please, Lisa, please stop crying.*

I get back upstairs, and Curtis is resting. Calvin is at the foot of his bed and we go into a corner and start whispering. I tell him about the history of the nurse, I tell him about the trampling he is getting by his family, I tell him I told Rude Lady that Curtis said he wanted his parents to go home. I give him as brief and as thorough a rundown as I can through whispered tears. He leaves for a few minutes. When he comes back, he says he will fix the nurse situation and he is going to speak to the family. He says he's known Curtis since before he married me, and he knows how happily married Curtis is. He says he sees how I have taken care of him since he's been in the hospital and how Curtis responds to me. He says he understands, and he is going to speak to the family, and everything is going to be fine.

That makes me feel a whole lot better. Finally, I'm not so ganged up on.

Curtis wakes up, so I brush his teeth and get him sorted out. He is weak, confused, and hot. I take off his blankets and put my warm hand under his cold thigh for a while until he falls back to sleep. Visiting hours are over, and I have to leave. I make sure his call button is near his hand.

I cry all the way home. I get turned around somehow because I am not paying attention to where I am going. It takes me twice as long to get home. Everybody is asleep and I can't sleep. I will never be able to sleep again. It is too late to call my sister. I go to bed, but I don't sleep. I scratch all night. My eyes mist up a few times, but I refuse to cry.

I get to the hospital at eleven. Curtis is still the same, but weaker. He can't really talk at all now. He's working hard for every breath, so hard. In comes an even heavier-duty tank with an even more aggressive-looking mask. A guy hooks up some sort of dispensable liquid right into the tube going into the mask. Never one to give up, I ask this fellow what this is and what is it for. He doesn't know. I ask his nurse. "He's stable. Nothing to worry about." Another nurse comes in and I ask her, "Why can't he breathe? Why can't he talk? Why is he so confused?" She says burn patients get confused sometimes; he's OK. Then she puts the corner of his blanket over his face and pulls it away and says, "Peek-a-boo, Mr. Wright!"

Then she kicks me out because they are going to torture him. They stopped taking him to the torture room last Friday when he fell apart. They torture him right in bed. Just the thought of him having to go through that makes me want to puke. He can't. He can't do it. I am heartsick, and I feel so helpless. I see him slipping away in front of my eyes, and nobody knows what is broken. This is really frustrating. It is not a mystery. I know how badly Curtis wants to come home, and I know those burns are never going to stop him, but they won't fix him.

I no longer have a charger for the cell phone. Curtis' family lost the charger when they so carefully packed our belongings in garbage bags. I roam around, looking for a pay phone. I need my mommy.

My dad flew to my mother's two days ago for a week's visit. I don't care about her or my dad's plans or schedule. I don't care that she can't get any time off work. I need my mommy. Curtis is probably going to be dead before the sun sets, and there is nothing I can do to stop it because nobody is paying attention. It is so unfair.

I find a pay phone on the ground floor near the critical care waiting room, which is always crowded. I can't call long distance so I call my house, where my brother is. I am literally choking on the hysterical tears I know are coming, I don't want that to happen in front of all these people. My brother answers and I take a deep breath and choke out, "Please call mom and dad and ask them to come. I think Curtis is going to die." I can feel the tears coming. "Just call them and ask them to please come." And then I hang up.

I spend the rest of the day just trying to get him to rest and take slow, deep breaths. "Breathe with me, Curtis." I ask every person in a white coat why he is in this state. I get either shrugged shoulders or a pat on the shoulder "There, there, Mrs. Wright, we're taking the best care of him!" At one point in the afternoon, I come back and Nice Blond Lady Doctor and Dr. Richard Head are at his bedside speaking quietly to each other. I perk up.. I wait on pins and needles for them to finish their hushed consultation. They'll fix him! Nice Blond Lady Doctor tells me they can't take him out of the waterbed yet because his donor site hasn't healed. They don't want him flat on his back, so they are going to prop more pillows under his head to elevate his head and help him breathe. I'm told Curtis' pancreas has sprung a leak from the pressure of the blocked bile duct.

I'm no medical expert, and in these early days, I have no idea what all the numbers and beeps and hums and drips and monitors mean. I have no idea what any of it means, but I am a person of at least average intelligence and I can't figure out how a leaky pancreas can cause you to struggle to breathe. I don't feel much better. All this technology in this world-class facility and the best they can come up with is adding some pillows under his head. It is pretty disappointing. At least they are on to him now, and they acknowledge that he is working hard for air. Maybe they'll pay a little closer attention now.

I'm not a doctor, but I know my husband, and this isn't him. He needs help. He needs a huge dose of medication, or he needs to be cut open and fixed. He is getting worse with every passing hour, and after forty-eight hours of misery, the best they can come up with is to put some pillows under his head. If they will just fix him, he'll be back to his old self in no time. I know this as surely as I know my own name. Pillows aren't going to do it, but that is the only twenty-first-century medicine he is going to get today.

Later in the day, Curtis has a spurt of energy. He makes a gesture like he is tossing the blanket away and whisper-gibbers, "Let's go." I tell him to relax and take deep breaths and take a nap. He starts getting more distressed and lashes out at the IV tubes. "Wanna go home. Right now." He is getting more agitated. I don't know how I know or how he knows, but it's like we know things are about to go from bad to worse and we don't want to go there. That's why I finally called my mommy. That's why he's determined to go home. We both know the worst is yet to come, and we can't stop it. We are both fighting so hard to run in the other direction any way we can, but we can't escape our fate. He is waving those clubs of arms around the IV equipment. I go to get the nurse.

I get out of the room and another nurse says I have a phone call. It is Curtis' niece. She demands to know what is going on with her uncle. I tell her right now he's agitated and trying to escape. I have to get his nurse. I'll call you later. She says I don't know her phone number. I tell her I don't have anything to write with and I am in the middle of a crisis. I will call you tonight. I hang up and get his nurse.

I spend the rest of the afternoon and evening trying to get Curtis to take slow deep breaths and get some rest. It is exhausting.

When I get home, Mike tells me that our folks are on their way. I feel a twinge of guilt over being so selfish, but I need my mommy. I update my sister. She is asking me all the same questions I have been asking all weekend, and it is frustrating because I don't know the answers. She says she has a class in the morning, but she will meet me in the burn unit afterward and she *will* get some answers.

I make another hysterical call to Annie to see if she will watch Curtis again tonight so he won't take his last breath. She says she will. I don't ask like that, though. I am a desperate hysterical woman, and I am so frustrated because I don't want to be treated like a desperate hysterical woman and I don't want to act like one.

I track down the niece's phone number, call her back, and tell her what little I know. I tell her that I call her father every time I know something. I tell her that the case manager finds out everything she knows about Curtis from me. I tell her about the nurses having to answer the phones. I tell her how exhausted Curtis is and how desperately he needs rest. She is hostile. I tried.

I don't sleep much. Most of the night, I lay in bed telling Curtis to stay calm, take slow, deep breaths, and try to sleep. I figure if he sleeps, his body will breathe for him and he won't have to work so hard. I don't know what I am thinking but I am sending him ESP. It occurs to me that I might be going insane.

I forgot Amy has a field trip this morning and has to be at school early. It is a mad rush to get all of us out of the house. Quick, quick, quick! I am rattled that I forgot about her field trip. As I am pulling out of the driveway, my folks are pulling in. I pass them at the street and tell them I am late getting Amy to school. I run back and unlock the door to the messy house for them. I get Amy to school, get to work, and call my mom to thank her for coming. I update her on Curtis and tell her Dawn is meeting me at the hospital at eleven. I tell her what time the kids come home from school. My folks drove all night to get here, over nine hundred miles. My dad went home, and my mom is going to take a nap. I told her to pick the cleanest bed she can find. The house is trashed, especially the upstairs. She says she is going to have a housekeeper come out. That is nice, but really, I couldn't care less about a housekeeper.

At ten-thirty, I head for the hospital. I am in the parking garage going from floor to floor, looking for a spot near the elevators. It doesn't matter what floor. Curtis is always on my mind, of course, but I am in a look-for-a-parking-spot-frame of mind when, like a bolt of lightning, I am hit with a shot of pure panic. I know it is Curtis, and I start talking to him in my head, *"Stay calm, Curtis, take a slow, deep breath and relax. I'm coming. Slow, deep breath."* I have never been a believer in ESP, or the spirit world, or any of that nonsense. But I know that Curtis is terrified and he needs me, and I feel his terror as if I am the one who's suffocating. The "connection" passes, and I ponder my sanity.

When I walk into Curtis' room, he is flat on his back and his call button is on the floor out of his reach. The one little crumb they threw him, propping him up with pillows, and they can't even do that! Bastards. I am glad he lived through the night, and as hard as it is to believe that he could get any worse and still be alive, he is worse. I don't even go over to him or talk to him because he doesn't have the strength for stimulation of any kind. I stand against the wall, he doesn't know I am there. I stand there about ten minutes, watching him struggle and fume over the pillows and the nurse call button, until they come in to throw me out for his torture. I point out the call button and say something about the pillows.

When I walk down the hall to take off the gown and hat, I see my sister coming out of the gown room and tell her he is having his bath. He is not going to survive this dressing change; I just know it. No way. The only comfort I have is that medical personnel will be surrounding him as he is taking his last breath. If they are right there next to him, watching him die, surely then they will step in and do something about it.

My sister says she has to go to the school library, so why don't we walk over there while we wait? I still have no answers for her, and she assures me she is going to get some. I am very agitated and distracted. I'm trying to concentrate on Curtis and I don't want to talk. I tell her something bad is going to happen. He can't do this dressing change, he can't. Scratch, scratch, scratch.

We walk all the way around this sprawling hospital to her school bookstore. Dawn chatters away about this and that...she needs a lab coat...blah, blah, blah. I don't hear most of what she is saying. I am concentrating so hard on Curtis, trying to pick up his "signal." I am very tense. I want to go back. I am getting impatient. I'm not getting a signal, and I am very concerned that Curtis might be dead. I know he can't survive this dressing change. We've been gone about an hour; it's time to go back. We go back, get to the nurses' station and are told he isn't done yet. They tell us to go to the waiting room and they will call us.

We sit in the waiting room. Fox news is on, and Dawn is making a running commentary on everything that is on the news. War with Iraq. I don't realize I have gone into some type of trance. I don't realize I am staring out the window, turning my wedding ring around and around on my finger, telling Curtis, "*Everything is OK. There are people there and they are going to help you. Relax and stay calm, Curtis. Let them help you. They are right there next to you, and they **will** help you.*"

It is after I snap out of my trance that I have realize I have been in one. The connection is gone. A bird flies by the window. I don't know if it means that he is gone, or that he is OK, or that a bird happened to fly by the window. Then I realize I have been spinning my wedding ring around on my finger. I tell my sister something happened. She tells me to calm down, that everything is fine. I am calm, but something has happened, something bad. I am just telling her matter-of-factly because I have just experienced it. I call the nurses' station and demand to know what is happening to Curtis. Dr. Richard Head gets on the phone and says they had to intubate him, and they will come talk to me when they are done.

I ask my sister what "intubate" means, and her jaw hits the floor. Then she explains it to me. She starts getting upset. I get teary eyed; this is serious. He has a machine breathing for him. I think of Mexico again. We are following in his footsteps. I am glad Curtis finally got some help, but this isn't fixing him. He isn't going to die imminently because he now has a machine breathing for him, but it is time to get serious and fix whatever is causing him to need a machine breathing for him in the first place. I'll be good and damned if I want to start hearing about tracheotomies, like Mexico. Oh no, we are not going down that road. By now, Mexico is having trouble with his heart.

I also feel a little better because now I know I am not insane, and I know I have a psychic connection to Curtis. At the same time, it occurs to me that knowing you can talk to somebody, and feel them and hear them in your head is left of center, so maybe I am crazy after all.

I call Ginger and let her know they had to put him on a ventilator. I start crying when I say that out loud because, y'know, this is scary. I ask her to look in my Rolodex and call Curtis' boss. I call my mom and ask her to look in Curtis' address book and call his brother Andy to let him know about the change. My sister can't believe I'm calling his family after finally shooing them all away. Well, I tell her, the picture's changed considerably. He's got a machine breathing for him now. I don't believe he's going to die, but I have a duty to inform his family.

Dr. Richard Head came to get us. He, Nice Blond Lady Doctor, Mitzi, my sister, and I all go into a conference room. I'm not sure why Mitzi is here; she is in the doghouse for lying to me about the nurse. I have no use for her. By now she has informed administration that she never told me she wouldn't assign Mean Nurse to Curtis again. I remind her it was the same day she sent Kid Counselors to bend the minds of my children. She denies doing that, too. Karen Vidor was standing right next to me during this conversation.

Dr. Richard Head says the gallstones have blocked Curtis' bile duct, so the bile had nowhere to go but back into his system. This caused infections. *Good reason not to leave it in there for seventeen hours!* It also put stress on his pancreas, causing it to leak, and sent fluid to his lungs. I still don't get the fluid in his lungs part, but I do understand that the trauma in general caused this to happen. Dr. Richard Head says Curtis is struggling to breathe. *It's about time you noticed.* He says that if they had not done this, he probably would have died tonight, during the night shift when there isn't as much staff on hand. *I am terrified to leave him at night.* He says that Curtis would have just tired out and not been able to take another breath. *No shit, Sherlock.* I think about my desperate phone call to Annie to please watch him. Finally, they're getting up to speed. Nothing like waiting until the last minute.

"I told you in the emergency room when your husband was admitted that the number one reason burn patients don't leave burn units is because of infections. Your husband has a bad infection, and he has a bad, bad burn." Well, I dismiss this talk of burns. These burns are never going to stop Curtis. I still believe this, and I still believe they haven't fixed whatever is broken. This doesn't upset me because he just doesn't know Curtis. My sister says, "Whoa, whoa, let me make sure I understand what you're saying. Are you saying..." She's starting to tear up, "I mean, we never expected Curtis may never leave this hospital. Is that what you're saying?" He says, "I'm telling you to prepare yourself for that possibility." My sister is upset and stunned. I'm not crying at all. I am listening to the doctor, but I know better.

My sister starts asking questions in medical lingo and I just wait for her to finish. I know she'll explain it to me later. She is writing down everything he says, and this seems to cause some tension in the room. Dawn explains, "My sister gets precious little information, and what she does get she only gets parts of. His family is upset with her because they think she's withholding information. So I'm writing all this down for her so she can pass along every detail to the family." Everybody relaxes. She finishes with her medical conference.

Dr. Richard Head goes on to explain that when a patient is intubated, they have to immobilize them to get the tube down their throat and so they won't fight the tube. Curtis is sedated, so he is resting comfortably. They have to administer paralytics so he can't move, and his arms are restrained. This sounds sad, but it also sounds like he is finally getting some sleep. I ask, "If he doesn't even know we're here, should I just come back tomorrow?" They all say no, no, there is evidence that patients in comas can hear you talking to them and can hear music. It will be very good for him to have us there. They also tell us where the hospital chapel is. I have another flash of the pickle jar people. This is so odd. Curtis might be able to hear music? Coma? Paralyzed? Chapel? This is whacked! What has happened over the past weekend? We aren't pickle jar people. If our business is concluded, then I want to see him.

Dawn and I get into the room and I am so relieved that Curtis can breathe. What a dramatic difference. He has a garden hose stuffed in his mouth, and it is clear he is off on the planet Mars. He isn't hearing a word we are saying or a tune we are playing, but I am so relieved that he is taking good, easy, deep breaths. I head over to him right away and tell him not to be scared. I tell him that he has a little fluid in his lungs, and they have to put a garden hose in his mouth to help him breathe and get that fluid out, and it is only temporary. I can see by looking at him that he isn't hearing a word I'm saying, but the medical experts said he might. Maybe, but not right now he isn't. He is in la-la land, but he can breathe. They have his arms tied to the bed, I untie them. His arms are still in lots of bandages and heavy splints, and he can't lift them if he wants to.

So, my immediate reaction to seeing him is relief. My sister starts crying immediately, she is so sad. She says she doesn't know how I can be so calm, that I am a stronger person than she is. I tell her I am relieved that he can breathe. She hasn't seen him in six days and to see him now, like this, is a shock. She hasn't seen his rapid decline. We don't spend a lot of time talking about it, and I cluck-cluck her about the tears in his room. They are not allowed. I am thankful that, at long last, he got some help. He can **breathe**. He was so close to taking his last breath. Now we have time to focus on repairing this poor man so he can come home. He wants to so badly.

My sister gives me a lesson on all the equipment. This is his oxygen saturation. When it's at 100, that's 100 percent oxygen he's saturating. That's what you want. She tells me what to watch for, what is bad, what is dangerous, Curtis is at 100 percent. She shows me the heart rate, tells me what a normal heart rate is, blood pressure, everything. All his numbers are good, I can see, which is another indication that he is resting comfortably. His heart rate and blood pressure are elevated, but she says that's expected in his circumstances. A whole new world of communication just opened up. All these monitors and equipment are Curtis talking to us. She explains the central line, how it is different from a normal IV, why it is used, what all his cocktails are—everything. I am armed with information.

Twila shows up. I let her know about the change in Curtis' condition and that the family is probably coming back. We need a meeting.

During my drive home, I do some thinking. The immediate mission is to get him off the garden hose as quickly as possible. I am relieved he got the help, but this is getting serious. Fix what's broken and get him off the garden hose. This is my new focus. I have no experience, but I know enough from watching movies that the longer this goes on, the closer we are to nipping at Mexico's heels, and I may find myself faced with quality-of-life issues. We aren't going there. *Sorry about your luck, Mexico, I feel for you and your family, but you will not have our company in this nightmare. This is as close as we're getting to your adventure.* Get him fixed and off the hose. The hose isn't fixing what is broken; it is just keeping whatever is broken from killing him.

I think about my sister's reaction at seeing him and about his nephew's reactions when he was just burned and in bandages. It occurs to me that it was rude to have my mother call his brother, but it is all I could do at the time. I couldn't call him myself because Curtis' thoughtful mother and sister lost my cell-phone charger. *Mental note: Ask Mom to get a car charger for that phone.*

I get home and update my mother. She tells me she got a housekeeper and shows me all the places the housekeeper didn't clean. She is going to make her come back out and do a more thorough job. Bless my poor mother. I don't care if there is lint under a chair or a dirty rubber seal around the refrigerator. Maybe she just doesn't know what to say. This is all so horrible. I walk around with her, hmm-hmming and ah-haaing.

I call Andy, who is already on his way here, and tell him all I know. I explain to him what Curtis looks like, and that if he thinks anyone can't handle seeing him like that then I don't want them in the room. This isn't a death watch, and it isn't going to be sad. I don't want anything but a positive environment in his room. He seems offended by this, but I don't know why. This is all about Curtis and nothing else. Anything I can do for him—little or big—I am going to do, and I am trying to think of everything. I think attitude makes all the difference, and I don't want any sobbing or sadness around him. Nobody cloaked in black veils. It just seems like common sense to me. I am still operating under the misguided assumption that his family wants to help him get well; they're not just coming to gawk at him. I'm not worried about offending or upsetting anybody, and I am not trying to. I am simply trying to help and protect Curtis. We all should be cooperating and communicating. I want to prepare them for what he looks like.

I call administration again, but Annie isn't working tonight, so I have to repeat the whole family history to a new person and then bring them up to date on the change in Curtis' status. The family is on the way again, and we need a meeting to help facilitate all these visitors.

Kids to school. Off to work. Leave work at ten-thirty to get to the hospital at eleven. I get to his room and kiss his forehead; his fever is 103. Once again, I explain to him the reason for the garden hose in his mouth and tell him not to worry, the most important thing to remember always is to concentrate on taking slow deep breaths.

He isn't as out cold as he was yesterday. I'm certain he can't hear me, but just in case anything is getting through, I don't want him to panic or to be scared of the garden hose. Slow, deep breaths actually do relax you and help with pain, so I feel like this is an important message to get through to him. I tell him I will always explain to him what is happening and that he should always try to stay calm and take slow, deep breaths.

I can't say there are signs of life, really, but it is different than last night. He is restrained again, so I untie his arms. I think it is disgraceful to tie his arms to the bed. He now has a poo bag in addition to the pee bag. There is some poo in it, and I don't think he'll want a whole lot of people seeing that, so I try to hide it behind the blanket. There are little twitches and muscle tics here and there, but they appear to be completely random. He isn't hearing me, but there is more activity, a higher level of awareness than last night, but he's still on Mars. His heart rate is in the high 140s. His blood pressure is 140/90. Kind of high.

He makes some gruesome noise and his chest moves. It spooks me, but I analyze it when he does it again. I try to translate this movement in a normal healthy human, and I think he is trying to cough. I review all his vital signs, and he is clearly...stirred. I know that he cannot hear me. I'm not crazy, and I know when he can and when he can't. I know he is just as much on Mars today as he was yesterday. But he is more... active, based on his vitals. Mind you, he is on sedatives and paralytics. I review his dose of Vecuronium. Not as much paralytic as yesterday. He makes the noise again and his chest moves. After about fifteen minutes of watching him and his vitals, I finally have it. He has to cough and he is uncomfortable, and that's all there is to it. I feel mildly foolish, I go ask the nurse if it is possible that he has to cough. She says she'll be here in a minute. I don't want to be a nuisance or a dummy; these people are busy, but I am certain he has to cough and is uncomfortable. She comes in right when he does that thing with his chest and that gruesome noise, and she says, "OK, Mr. Wright. I'm going to suction you."

She forces a smaller tube down the garden hose and it seems like he's gagging. Then there is a wet, sucking noise, like when you're at the dentist, and up comes a bunch of goop out of the mini garden hose. He *did* have to cough! I can't believe it! I'm getting good at this! It is kind of gross, but what's more troubling is that it doesn't look like Curtis enjoyed that suctioning experience one bit. Maybe we won't have to do that again.

Boy, am I naïve. That was the first of...well, I stopped counting at a bazillion times he had to get "coughed."

She stuffs that mini hose down there a couple more times and gets some more goop out. He doesn't like it, but that nasty stuff has to come out. Hmmm. I figure he'll get comfortable again, I keep watching his vitals, but he doesn't. I repeat the story of the garden hose, little fluid in the lungs, we'll have it out in a couple days. Nice Blond Lady Doctor told me that. Slow, deep breaths. I am like a broken record. It occurs to me that I might be driving him insane by repeating the same things, over and over again. What if he's having an experience like in the movie *Groundhog Day*, where the same day keeps repeating itself? What if he is hearing me? He isn't yet, I just know it, but y'know, the experts said he might.

I always try to put myself in his shoes and think about what this experience would be like and how I can make it better. What if I were lying there helpless? What would help me, what would comfort me, what would I be thinking? I'd no doubt be scared and confused. Having a familiar voice of someone who loved me explaining it to me and reminding me to focus on relaxing breaths would help me a lot. Call it instinct, but it seems like the right thing to do—to keep repeating what I know and to remind him to take slow deep breaths. I never have anything else to talk about, really, because I never do anything but go to work and tell him to breathe. If any little thing is different or new, I tell him about it over and over again. "I am going to have a friend from work come over and teach me how to use the vacuum for the pool. Don't worry about the pool, I'm going to learn how to clean it." Day after day, over and over, until there is something new to tell him. "Penelope from Austin is coming this weekend to stay with the kids. I'm going to learn how to clean the pool later this week. Slow deep breaths, relax. Just a little fluid in your lungs, that's all. My mom and dad are here. My mom is at the house with the kids, and she's going to come see you tomorrow." Over and over again. All day long. All week long.

Mandy, a coworker who almost never goes to church, put his name on the prayer list and the entire church prayed for him. We have relatives all over the country who call and send cards and say the same things. There are churches full of people praying for him. I know how much that means to him. I tell him, "There are churches full of people, across the entire country praying for you, and I know you can feel it." Over and over. People at work say, "My kids pray for him every night, Lisa."

Quite some time later, somebody tells me the sedatives affect his short-term memory. I think back to those early days when my instincts told me to repeat everything, and I have another one of those "I'm pretty good at this; I'm not crazy" moments. The more moments I have like that, the stronger and more assertive and more focused I become. And I become even more certain that somebody or something has their hand on my head, turning me this way and that, because there's no way I can do all this myself. Nobody can. I remember that first day when I just thought, "Surely he has to cough. Can it be?" And I even felt a little foolish bothering the nurse with a cough. It doesn't take long until I don't feel foolish anymore about anything. Nobody can tell me anything because I already know. I know. I become increasingly frustrated when others try to tell me differently. I know this man and I can hear him as loudly as if he were screaming in my ear. I'm not going to ignore my instincts anymore. Curtis wants to come home, and he is putting his life in my hands.

His vitals never settle down to the comfort level they were last night. I know he cannot hear me, but I keep repeating myself. I still believe that all these medical people are the experts and they know what they are doing. I think he is just uncomfortable. He is too warm, so I take the blanket off and put a cool washcloth on his forehead. I want his blood pressure to come down. I want his muscles to relax. I want him to be comfortable.

Dr. Plastic Surgeon comes in. I feel foolish asking, but Curtis' name is on the surgery schedule for the third skin graft. Clearly, he isn't having a skin graft tomorrow, surely not. I ask Dr. Plastic Surgeon about it. Sure enough, he says there's no way; that's tabled until he's more stable. He says they are going to do a CAT scan of his abdomen. That sounds good to me because my mission is to fix him and get him off the hose. What better way than to have a look-see? I am so glad to see Dr. Plastic Surgeon. I haven't talked to him much, but first impressions go a long way, and I'm not usually wrong about people. I put all of our eggs in his basket that first night in the waiting room. Now we're headed in the right direction. No more pillows that get forgotten. Dr. Plastic Surgeon's going to look at his gut and fix him up! I am in a much better mood.

Two administrators, Twila and her cohort, come and summon me for our family meeting. We find a conference room. My mood goes south quickly. Once again, I have to repeat this story about the family. Now I have to start at the beginning, which is twenty days ago. It puts me in a bad mood and the tears start coming again. I point out that I never said he doesn't want to see his parents. I explain the whole trampling business, that he asked his mother to stay home, that nobody ever said he doesn't want to see his family, but he needs a break and some rest. I explain it all to them. I never have any private time with my husband. I describe the chaos, the insanity. He is getting so sick because he is neglected. I can't get into the room. I tell them all of it: Rude Administrator who put words in my mouth, Mean Nurse, Mitzi, who is as useful as a grape, all of it. I am sick of continually rehashing this story for new people, and it takes longer to tell with each passing day. I show them the note Curtis wrote, "I told them not to come." It is exhausting.

Twila says that they can't keep anyone from visiting him. She says that nobody, including me, can stop anybody from seeing him. She says they encourage the families to work out a schedule among themselves. If the family cannot work it out, then they will sit in on a meeting with the entire family and try to help set a schedule.

I am getting panicked. I thought people had rights. My sister seems to think there are laws on this very issue, and that, in the eyes of the law, I **am** Curtis. What does Twila mean, they can't keep anybody out of his room? I tell her that Rude Administrator wouldn't listen to me. I never said he doesn't want to see his parents. He said he wants them to go home right now. There is a huge difference. I'm not trying to get anyone barred for life. What kind of monster do they think I am? All I want is for Curtis to get well and come home. That is also what Curtis wants. That's it. I'm the one who called them all back when he went on the garden hose.

I am feeling helpless again. I have tried talking to his family, every one of them. Curtis told them when he was still able. They will not listen. This is unbelievably violating. Any Tom, Dick, or Harry can come in off the street and ogle Curtis' poo bag, and I can't do anything to prevent it. What if some psycho came in off the street and tried to hurt him? This man is totally helpless and should be provided some protection and safety. Do I have to be on duty 24/7? Is this even America? What the Hell? This can't be right, it just can't be. What if the mayor were a patient here? Same rules? What if one of their husbands were a patient here? Same rules? I doubt it. I call bullshit.

Just then, Calvin comes into the conference room. I start to tell him that they won't help, there's nothing they can do. Calvin says, "It's OK. It's OK, Lisa. The whole family is here, I've gathered them all in the waiting room, and we're going to have a meeting. We're going to sort this out right now." Bless this level-headed, thoughtful man. Curtis' whole family, except Calvin and Ken, make me feel so alienated and hated. They make this tragic, horrid experience a hundred times worse than it has to be. Maybe we can finally gather and speak sensibly. Everything I have to say, I have told them all individually at one point or another. I don't understand all this unnecessary drama. But I am actually hopeful. It will only get better from here. We are all adults.

I am surprised by how many people are in the waiting room. Let me see if I can remember. Curtis' mother and father, Dudley's mother (who is now deceased), his cousin Anthony, minister Bertha, his brother Richard, his brother Andy, and Calvin. Maybe that is it.

Anthony barks, "What's going on with Curtis?" Andy says, "I need to see him before two. I have to leave at two." These people have all driven hundreds of miles and have to be accommodated, you see. Calvin says, "Whoa, whoa! We're going to get to all that. I'd like to speak first, and then Lisa will update us all on Curtis' condition." Calvin goes on to say, "Everyone in this room has touched Curtis'life in a different way. We're all important to him. Curtis needs us all right now and we all need to come together for his sake." His mother sits up straighter in her chair, sticks her nose up in the air, and says, "Well, I should know that, I birthed him!"

Calvin goes on to say that Curtis is very sick and needs us all. He is interrupted by Anthony, "Well, he needs prayer, too!" Calvin says, "Yes, he needs prayer too." Calvin is making a powerful, important speech. His words are giving weight to the seriousness of the situation, but people keep interrupting him. It already isn't going well. Calvin turns it over to me. I tell them how much Curtis appreciated them going to the trouble and expense of coming to see him. It means a lot to him, and I know how much comfort he gets from their company. I look at Anthony, "And your prayers, and the prayers of the networks and churches full of people across the entire country who are praying for him. Curtis has a grueling recovery ahead of him. They keep him busy almost all day. He's taken midmorning to have his dressings changed and have his burned skin scrubbed. That normally takes about an hour and a half, and it takes him several hours to recover from this torture. He has to go through rehab, exercises, physical therapy, and occupational therapy. There are so many of us that want to help him recover that we need to open the lines of communication. We have all these people streaming into the state. They don't know where the hospital is, when visiting hours are, or how expensive parking is. Only two people are allowed in the room at a time. He just can't accommodate everybody. People are developing hostilities toward me, and it's unnecessary. We have a big house and plenty of room, and he and I both need plenty of help. All of you are welcome, but we can't accommodate anybody if we don't know you're coming.

Curtis' schedule here is unpredictable. Today, they are preparing him to go for a CAT scan of his abdomen. It will take them at least an hour to prepare him to leave his room. He's in a bathtub bed that weighs thousands of pounds. They have to disconnect all his cocktails and equipment and make everything portable so he can go have a picture taken of his abdomen. I can't even go in there. Then the whole process is reversed when he gets back to his room and they set him back up on his equipment and cocktails. I can't go in to see him. I can't get his family in there fast enough to pray for him, but it will be at least two hours before anyone can go in there. That is not me keeping people out of his room."

I look at Andy and say, "It's very unlikely that you will see him today. I'm sorry for that, but it is not because I want to keep his family out. He's not going to be in his room. Curtis has a wife, a life, and a home. All these things have been horribly disrupted, and he needs help and cooperation. Why can't we meet at the house? We have a large enough house to accommodate everybody. Nobody tells us their plans. They just show up and expect to be accommodated, and we can't do it. All we've ever asked for is some communication.

I think a realistic plan, at this point, is to meet here in the waiting room at four o'clock every afternoon. I will come update anybody who is here with whatever I know at four every day. I will plan to leave then and not come back until after the night-time shift change. Don't expect me to have daily news, though. It sometimes takes me days and the help of my sister to get any information."

Nobody argues, so I assume they agree. I tell them that by the time they get Curtis back and situated, it will probably be about four o'clock and I want to get his mother and Richard in to see him as soon as he gets back. I know he needs prayer, and he needs the kind where you order Jesus to heal him right now.

"Curtis developed gallstones last Friday that got into his bile duct and created a blockage. Saturday, they made an incision to release the stones. The blockage created some stress on his pancreas and caused his pancreas to leak. The trauma sent fluid to his lungs and created an environment that made it difficult for him to breathe on his own. Yesterday, they put him on a ventilator. He is sedated and paralyzed. They restrain his arms to the bed. If it will cause anyone difficulty to see him in this state, then you don't have to. I personally do not believe it, but the doctors have told me to prepare myself for the fact that he may not leave this hospital. I know Curtis is coming home, but I'm telling you what the doctors have said. He has some bad infections…"

Andy interrupts, "Yeah, that's why you can't go kissing on him," referring to the fact that I always kiss him on the forehead. As if this is my fault. I tell him that he had about a quart of bile backed up in his system for over seventeen hours and that's what caused his infection. He has bacteria in his blood, and that did not come from kissing him on the forehead.

Bertha jumps out of her chair and commands me to drop to my knees and beg Jesus to heal my husband. I am not exaggerating. She says, "The Bible says man and woman are one. If you do not drop to your knees right now and beg his mercy, he will not save your husband." She is bellowing. There are other people in the waiting room. It is embarrassing. I say, "My husband is coming home. If you choose to believe he isn't because I don't make a fool out of myself, that is your prerogative, but you will behave yourself or I will have you removed." She says, "I am a minister of the **Lord**! Nobody is going to remove me!"

I stand up and tell Andy to line this woman out. As I am walking out, I hear Andy say, "Bertha, Bertha, it hurts me to hear you use the Bible as a weapon." Bertha says, "Lisa needs to pray." Andy tells her, "Curtis needs your prayers, and if you want to pray for Lisa, too..." That's all I hear; the door closes behind me.

Andy comes out to the hallway not too far behind me. He is really upset at Bertha's behavior, not for my sake, but for Jesus' sake. A few minutes later, Curtis' mother and her gaggle of hens (Bertha and Now Deceased) come out to the hallway. They probably thought I took off for a secret visit with a doctor. They stand across the hall. Anthony, Calvin, and Richard come out about ten minutes later, maybe to make sure they aren't missing anything. Don't know; don't care. Calvin goes over to Andy, shakes his hand and makes small talk. We are all in the hallway, but not near each other. Little groups are muttering among themselves. I am glad I can't hear them.

They have put splints on Curtis' feet in addition to his hands. The hand splints are to help keep the shape of his hands and prevent contractures from scars as the grafts heal; the leg splints are to maintain the arch in his foot and to help prevent bedsores while he is immobile. I hear the "pshhh" sound and look up as the doors open. I recognize the splint on the partially uncovered foot and say, "That's Curtis." Everybody gets quiet. Real quiet.

A bunch of medical people are surrounding his gurney. One lady has a clear plastic football-looking thing that she is squeezing over Curtis' mouth. She is "bagging" him, giving him oxygen. Another is holding wires and hoses. Another has an oxygen tank. There are four or five people around the head and sides of this gurney. They all have one hand on an instrument attached to Curtis and the other hand on the gurney, pushing it. There is scary-looking medical equipment on the bed with him. And one other thing. They are **moving**, man. They don't stop for the doors; somebody ran ahead of them and pushed the button so they could race through the doors. They are jogging, practically running. This all happens very quickly. It is just like you see in the movies.

As he passes me I say, "They're taking you for pictures of your tummy, Curtis. Your whole family is here waiting for you!" I have to practically shout the last part because they race past me so quickly. He looks red and swollen. He doesn't look good at all, and I wonder what they have done to him. Nobody else says a word. Not a sound. I wish, for Curtis, that he could have heard some of their voices. I think it happened too quickly, and the sight of him is quite shocking. He has deteriorated so quickly. I tried to tell them, but how can you really prepare people for that? You can't. He disappears around the corner faster than you can say "Stat!"

Andy breaks the deafening silence...it is almost a shaky whisper, "I got to see my brother." He has tears in his eyes. "God put me in this hallway so I could see my brother." He is all smiles and tears. Seeing a grown man in tears and strong, vital Curtis as weak as a sickly kitten, begging for mercy—this is raw human emotion. It is uncontrollable, it is powerful, it is exhausting. And it is relentless. Twenty days now. *Geez, is that all? He has to start getting better quickly. Just as soon as they fix him up, he'll bounce right back. I know it.* Andy really felt the hand of God. He now knows the reality of Curtis' schedule and his schedule. It could very well be true that God put them all there in the hallway. It never occurs to any of them, and it never will, that maybe their God put me here to bring him home. The Lord works in mysterious ways. I have had enough spiritual experiences in the past twenty days to believe exactly that—somebody or something put me here. But to them, I am always the devil. Their loss.

I go outside to have a smoke and a Coke, my daily meal. Andy and Calvin come out with me. I have a long, heartfelt conversation with Andy, and go into a little more detail about that day they got so mad at me and had me thrown out of the room. I am very nice about it. I am just trying to explain the whole situation to him. After about three cigarettes and lots of tears from both of us I finally say,

"So, Andy, please tell me what I should be doing differently?" He shakes his head in amazement and says, "Nothing, nothing Lisa, I will speak to the family." I think, after that, that Andy and I are back on track.

But for some reason, he never spoke to me again after that day, and I heard many months later that he doesn't like me at all. I have always known him better than anyone else in Curtis' family, and I have always liked and respected him. I figured it out months later. All those drama queens do is sit around and yap, yap, yap about everybody and their business. The rumor mill in the Deep South was on fire with talk of the devil woman. He got caught up in the lies that were being told about me throughout this ordeal. Pity for him.

Andy heads back up, hoping for another miraculous sighting of his brother coming back down the hallway, as he has to leave now.

That leaves Calvin and me. I know Curtis isn't back and situated yet, so I light up another minty treasure. Calvin says he spoke to Curtis' mother on my behalf. He reiterated how he knows how much Curtis loves me. He saw with his own eyes how I cared for him, and how he responds to me, and basically how wonderful I am and all that. "His mother says she understands," I say, "No she doesn't. She doesn't have a clue," and Calvin says, "Let me finish. She says she understands, but then she goes on about how when she was younger and her husband was sick, she had to stay with her in-laws for a while and she didn't like it because it wasn't home." I look at him with an exaggerated expression, "What is that supposed to mean?" Calvin says, "Well, exactly. She doesn't understand at all." I say, "Well, that's a shame. She's acting like a helpless old woman and that is a crying shame because Curtis needs so much help. She's not a helpless old woman." Calvin says, "I know." He is basically letting me know that he tried and failed to get through to them. He also lets me know she's mad at me for not calling her myself the very first day Curtis was burned. I am being thrown back to the wolves. Oh, well.

I am suddenly overcome by a ferocious fit of concentration. I have to get back upstairs. Curtis is getting worse, not better. I just know their picture will point out what is wrong and they'll have him back on his feet in no time. I can't take much more. *How many times have I said that?* The longer he is sick, the longer it will take him to bounce back and the more problems he is going to have. No dialysis for this boy, nuh-uh. It's only been a couple days. He can still bounce right back, but we are running out of time. There's only so much a human body can take.

I get back upstairs and Dr. Plastic Surgeon says they are going to perform a bronchoscopy. He explains that they are going to go through his mouth—I'm not sure how, since there is a garden hose stuffed in it—with a scope and go deep into his lungs and suck out the mucus. They call it "sputum" or "secretions." I get a lesson on all the bronchi in the lungs and what they do and what has happened to Curtis. His bronchi are full of mucus and his left lung has collapsed. Lung collapse!

Nightmares of Mexico are flashing in front of my eyes. I don't know how long you can live with a collapsed lung, but I don't think very long. In fact, in the movies, I think that means you are already dead. This is becoming the Mexico nightmare that I am fighting so hard to run from. Those poor people have to hear these terrifying expressions, not Curtis.

Now my mission of repair is derailed yet again. We have to get off course again to vacuum out that lung and blow it back up again so we'll have time to fix the real problem. Maintenance issues. Barely even got a look at the engine before a tire blew out and now we have to fix the tire. This is not going according to plan. I sit in the waiting room and answer the Curtis ESP phone. No matter how hard I try,

I can't call him; he always calls me. I can never force it. Maybe we called each other. This is another way I know I'm not insane. When I try to call him, he never answers; but when I'm not even thinking about it, he puts me right into a trance. As soon as I have that thought, it occurs to me that if I ever say that out loud, I would be considered insane. That is just crazy. But hey, it is working for me now, and I believe it. It makes perfect sense to me at the time.

I go into my telepathic trance, "*Look, Curtis, you have to hang in there. They took pictures of your gut. That's where the trouble is, it has to be. But since you've been immobile and have this fluid in your lungs, you can't cough. When they suction you, they really can't get in that far. So they have to vacuum out your lung, all because you can't cough. Get through this, and keep it together so they can fix you. I promise the worst is almost over. People all over the country are praying for you.*" Same old litany. I don't have the heart to ESP him that his lung collapsed, because that scares me to death. Curtis hangs up the ESP phone. He is going in the wrong direction. This is not going according to plan. I need to get him off that garden hose quickly. I am very anxious and distressed.

I go back to the waiting room. I am willing all the people in the whole world who know God to pray for Curtis so he will make it through the night. I can't wait to get his mother and Richard in there to start summoning the spirit. Every minute I can't get them in there is a minute he needs. His mother is on the other side of the waiting room with her gaggle of hens, making small talk about stupid things. They are supposed to be concentrating on Curtis. Praying. Commanding. Instead, they are talking about a soup recipe or somebody's wart or something. They just can't get it right.

I am out in the hallway when Dr. Richard Head tells me the CAT scan detected a fluid collection around his pancreas, a pancreatic pseudocyst. The pancreas contains enzymes that are built to destroy food; they are destructive enzymes. It's best to not stir them up. They are on the fence. They can leave it alone and watch it, as sometimes these things resolve themselves, or they can put in a drain. It is so sizeable they want to drain it, but any time you introduce plastic tubes into the body you're introducing another window for bacteria. They will have to cut through burned skin, which is a further danger of infection. They can wait a couple more days to give the skin a little more time to heal. I don't need to hear any more. This has to be the problem. I don't even let him finish talking. Drain it. Drain it right now. This just has to be it.

I go into Curtis' room to check his vitals. He is pretty calm. I give him the update. "Hang in there, Curtis. Relief is on the way. All the churches are praying for you. I'm going to get your mother and Richard in here right now to pray for you, Curtis. You'll be feeling better in no time. Slow, deep breaths." I am excited and relieved, but no matter how excited, scared, worried, or angry I am, it is always some type of extreme emotional reaction. I'm not saying I'm perfect by any stretch of the imagination, but for the most part I am always so calm when I am in his room talking to him. This is another reason that I say something or someone else is doing this. It isn't me; no mere mortal can handle all this. No way. Not me, not anybody.

I am so glad to finally see a light at the end of the tunnel. I don't want to think that expression because I don't want Curtis to see any lights in any tunnels, but I know he is within hours of turning that corner. I call the waiting room and ask his mother and Richard to come in. I check all his gauges and cocktails. I hide his poo bag and empty his pee tube. I check his temperature. He's too warm. I am so weary of these blazing fevers. I take off his blanket and put a cool washcloth on his forehead.

The garden hose is tied on both sides of his mouth with the straps from a surgical mask. These ties seem to be biting into the corners of his lips, and his mouth is always stretched into a wide scream. It looks miserably uncomfortable. There is a little blood on the ties; they are tied so tightly, they are cutting his lip. Poor thing. I wonder if that is really necessary. *Mental note: Ask Dawn about that.*

His mother and Richard come in. I tell them about the drain; relief is on the way. I show his mother all the equipment and tell her the most important thing to watch is his blood pressure. It can tell her a lot about him. I tell her to watch the top number, the systolic. If it is 100–120, he is sound asleep and resting comfortably. If it's lower than 100, he's probably unconscious and it wouldn't hurt to stimulate him a bit. In the 120–130 range, he can probably hear you. It's a good time to talk to him. If it's any higher than that, he's getting too agitated. Calm him down and soothe him. Keep an eye on his blood pressure. It's like he's talking to you, it can tell you everything. Richard doesn't pay any attention. I ask them to stay and pray for him.

I go back to the waiting room and tell Bertha and Now Deceased about the drain. I am so happy. Curtis calls on the ESP phone, but he isn't saying anything. It isn't working. *"Curtis, your mother and Richard are there with you. They are praying for you right now, can't you hear them?"* It isn't working. Something is wrong. Karen Vidor comes in just then and asks how it is going. I tell her about the lung vacuum and the drain and that his mother and brother are in there praying for him right now but it isn't working. I start crying. Damn these tears again. *It isn't working. Why isn't it working? He is on the line, but he is silent. What am I missing?*

They're not praying for him, I know it. I go back to the unit and gown up. I come out of the gown room and see his mother and brother coming back down the hall. They just don't get it. I stop in front of his mother, put my hands on her arms, and tell her to turn around and go back and pray for him. She says she is. "No, no. Go back in and pray for him right now." She says she's always praying for him and puts her nose in the air.

· I need the "minister of the **Lord**." She doesn't mess around! I go back to the waiting room and ask Bertha if she can stay and pray for Curtis until visiting hours are over. She says, "I think I can handle it." She is snotty, but it doesn't matter, I know she can command the help Curtis needs. If you ever find yourself in dire need of prayer, Bertha's your gal. Trust me.

I go back down to the critical care waiting room pay phone and call Jill. I know she belongs to an emergency phone prayer chain. I ask her, "Please call everyone you know who knows God, and ask them to call everyone they know who knows God, and please pray for Curtis. Please pray for him all night long and pray really hard. I am serious. If you do, then he will make it through the night I just know it." That, along with all his people surrounding his bed commanding Jesus, is what he needs. She says, "No problem, doll. I'm on it."

There is nothing more I can do. He needs mighty prayer all night. I just know if he gets that, he will make it. I need to keep my mind clear, focus on his signal, and manage this whole mess. I am delegating, and tonight Bertha is my Vice President.

Driving home, I am on the ESP phone and Curtis is there, but I get nothing. No relief. No fear. No peace. Nothing. Curtis is alive, but nothing is happening. *"Bertha is going to hook you up tonight and so is the entire country. C'mon, Curtis, turn that corner."* Nothing. It occurs to me again that I am insane, completely gone around the bend. What makes me think I have any control over any of this? I have some, but not really. I can't control the outcome. I am crazy. Crazy people don't realize they are crazy. All this stuff makes perfect sense in my distraught, frazzled, exhausted, dehydrated, starving mind, but I am insane. I am a crazy person. This is pretty depressing.

I have to pass the accident site every time I go to or from the hospital. On the way to the hospital, there is a large billboard advertising caskets right next to the building where he was burned. Every day, no matter how hard I try not to look or think about it, it gets my attention. I wish there were a different route. I am worn out. Depressed. So sad for Curtis. If he were meant to die from this injury, he would have died before he ever got to the hospital. It is so unfair for him to suffer like this and then die anyway. He isn't going to, he just isn't going to. Crazy or not, he is coming home; I just know it. I am worn out. Numb. I am done with all the silly ESP nonsense. My brain hurts. I get home and take a shower.

I go to bed exhausted. I'm so tired, I am going to have no trouble at all falling asleep. For the first time since this happened, I start drifting off almost immediately. Usually my mind has to race for awhile and I have to toss and turn and think and scratch, but not tonight. I am "thinked out." I am more than half asleep. I get cold and pull the blanket up a little higher. I am so tired, I just want to sleep. This cold is in my chest and starts spreading. It isn't like being out in the cold, it is more like a "nerve" cold, like when you bite down on aluminum foil. The blanket is ineffective. It is spreading to down my trunk, to my legs, oh that's cold! I am jarred into awareness. I roll over to look at the clock. I am so tired. It is ten o'clock, I have a brief sleepy thought, oh, it's Curtis, he's getting his dressings changed. *"Hey, Curtis."* It is as if he is lying in bed giving me a hug.

I sit right up, wide awake now. The cold sensation leaves immediately. *That **is** Curtis. He is giving me a hug, and everything is going to be OK.* He is going to make it through the night. I can't believe it. I'm not crazy after all; this really is happening. Wow! I can't wait until he wakes up so I can ask him if that is the cold he's always feeling, even though I know it is. This is unreal. I can't wait to tell him I felt it, I felt the moment when those prayers worked. I sleep like a baby. It is so amazing, but I can never tell anyone because they'll think I am crazy.

I have started asking people at work if I am crazy. I am always asking people that throughout this ordeal because I really just don't know. Sometimes I think I am; these things just don't happen. When I am experiencing them, they are real, no question about it. But it is a constant torment. Am I nuts? Crazy people have "real" experiences that are not real; that's why they are crazy. I am always aware that there is a very good chance I have gone around the bend. That is yet another reason that Curtis just has to live. If he dies, I am insane. It is as simple as that. Everybody tells me I'm not crazy, but maybe they don't realize I am serious. Maybe they really think I am crazy, but they always say no because they're afraid that if they say, "Yes, Lisa, I think you've gone a bit wacko," I'll do some crazy person thing to them. I also know that going days on end without food or sleep and having so much drama and adrenaline really can affect your mental state. I am not myself, that is clear. There is no telling what this is doing to me, Only time will tell.

As for Curtis, I can't do anything other than exactly what I am doing, crazy or not. All I can do is ride out this crazy train until it ends. I know it has only one ending—Curtis is coming home. He is not going to die, he just isn't, and I'm not crazy. It is an exhausting, endless debate with myself.

Get up. Kids to school. Go to work. I plan to meet Curtis' family at four o'clock, and then Curtis is all theirs until after shift change. I take my mother to see him this morning. We get our gowns on and go to his room. I kiss him on the forehead; he is hot. He is in terrible pain. Every muscle in his body is clenched, and he is biting down hard on the garden hose.

He's is in a medically induced coma. Obviously, they have weaned him from some of the paralytics. Tears are running down the sides of his face. He makes that spooky coughing noise again. I call for his nurse and tell her Curtis has to cough. Mitzi comes in to cough him. She is trying to get the mini tube down the garden hose and she can't because he is biting down so hard. She increases his sedative. She calls respiratory to bring a bite block and leaves.

His blood pressure is really high. Every muscle in his body tenses up and then relaxes. Tears are coming out the sides of his eyes. He is obviously in pain. I tell him to try and relax, I know he has to cough and is uncomfortable and they are working on it. It keeps getting worse; his blood pressure is way too high now. I watch it climb from 160 to 180 systolic. I know the nurses can see this on their monitor,why isn't anyone coming? I keep saying soothing, calming things in his ear. Down to 170. Tensing, biting, crying. I go to the other side of the bed and check his arterial line, even though I know this is his real blood pressure. He really needs to cough. I call

Mitzi again. She comes back in and tries to force that tube in there again. Really, she is jamming it in there. Curtis' eyelids slowly open as if he has to work really hard to open them, and he looks at her as if he wants to kill her. I say, "Oh man! I don't want to be you when he wakes up!" She stops trying to force the hose and increases the sedative again. She calls respiratory again and leaves.

I am getting upset; he is in pain. I tell my mom he is in pain; she doesn't know what to do. Up goes the blood pressure again. When it rises over 190, I tell my mom to keep him calm. Alarms are going off like a bank is being robbed. She cradles his head in her arms and whispers to him; I step out to the hallway, Mitzi is on the phone. I watch his blood pressure come down to 180. My mom is calming him down.

175. Mitzi is still on the phone. 200. I tug Mitzi's sleeve and say very pleadingly, "Mitzi, two hundred!" She says she knows, she is calling the critical care team. 240.

I go back into his room, biting back tears. I swear he is having a stroke right in front of our eyes. Alarms are going off. It's just my mom and me. I check all his lines, knowing good and well that it isn't the equipment. My mom and I try to keep him with us and keep him calm. We get him down to 200. Some other lady comes in and says that's not really his blood pressure. *Of course it is*

Mitzi comes back in and says Curtis should be out cold. She can't give him any more sedative or he will overdose. They have to wait for the critical care team. 260. Calm down, Curtis. I know it hurts. They are coming, please calm down. Nice slow breaths. My mom never stops hugging and stroking his head. Down to 240. In walks his mother. I put my finger to my lips to ask her to be quiet. She says, loudly, "Well I want him to know I'm here. Curtis, it's Mother, dear!" Shoots up to 300 like a firecracker. Veins in his fore-head are popping out, I think his head is going to explode right off his shoulders. Right at that instant, a crowd of white jackets swarm into the room and boot us out.

I get to the gown room ahead of them. When they come in, I ask his mother, "What happened to four o'clock?" She says, "I never made any promises to you!" I say, "You should have made a promise to Curtis. You almost killed him!" She rolls her eyes up and says, "Oh, Jesus, help this poor child!" I explained the blood pressure to her in great detail last night, she ignored it and just walked in there bellowing. He's critically ill. Emphasis on critical. She ignored everything I told her I need to get away from her before I say something I might regret.

His brain exploded, I just saw it. It is horrible. He surely had a stroke. No, not Curtis. I don't know what that is all about, but it is very disturbing. It is scary. I kid you not; it was 300 systolic. I wrote on the calendar for that day "300" with an arrow going up. It was terrifying.

A short while later, Dr. Plastic Surgeon comes to talk to me. My mom comes with me, and Curtis' mother and one of her hens follow us. I tell Dr. Plastic Surgeon I want to talk to him alone. Curtis' mother objects, as does her hen, "This woman is 75 years old; she can't handle this." *That's exactly why she should be at home.*

Dr. Plastic Surgeon says he is not going to referee any family fights. I don't think there is anything to referee. I thought people had rights or there are laws, I thought it was solely up to me who he speaks with.

Curtis' mother, Dr. Plastic Surgeon, and I go into a conference room. Dr. Plastic Surgeon starts back on Friday with the gallstones, and runs through everything that has gone on, up to the ventilator. Well, we already know all this. He says almost word for word what I told the entire family in the waiting room yesterday, but his mother keeps saying, "Hmm, Uh-huh. Oh, I see," on and on. She keeps interrupting him, and none of this is news to anybody. Finally, Dr. Plastic Surgeon says Curtis'blood pressure has become unstable and they have started him on blood pressure medication. I thank him and leave. As the door is closing, I hear his mother start to say something about the eggs he had for breakfast last Friday morning and maybe he has indigestion.

What a minute! Eggs for breakfast! They serve breakfast at eight o'clock. What is she doing here at eight o'clock? It suddenly becomes crystal clear. All those times Curtis had begged me, "Why aren't you here? I need you. Where have you been? I've been watching the door waiting for you to come through it." I had to constantly tell him that they won't let me in; visiting hours don't start until eleven. All those times. No wonder he didn't seem to understand me. He must have thought I was lying to him because his mother had been sitting right there the entire time.

My mom and I go back to Curtis' room. His blood pressure has stabilized. He must have been coughed because he is a little better. In come the Wrights again. My mom and I leave. I drop my mom off and go back to work.

I go back in the evening and still have to squeeze around Wrights. I give up on the "two people at a time" rule. I squeeze my way in there and update the calendar and worry that Curtis might have had a stroke. I stand against the wall and keep an eye on his vitals. His blood pressure stays elevated, but there are no alarms or crises of any kind. His Foley tube needs to be drained, his poo bag is in plain view. I feel so bad for him to have no dignity in front of his mother and her gaggle of hens. I figure he is too warm, but there isn't anything I can do about that either. All I can do is stand flat against the wall or be trampled by Wrights. I am starting to hate them all.

I get home and update my sister. I tell her I hate that place. I tell her about the family again. She tells me somebody at that hospital can help me; I need to keep going over people's heads. No they can't, I've spoken to administration repeatedly. They're not going to let him have any peace, and I have no authority whatsoever. She says that is absurd, that my husband is incapacitated, and the law says I'm him. I told her Memorial Hermann is above any law that may exist on this issue. This really sticks in her craw, because she is a hospital administrator and she knows what I am telling her is not correct. She figures I am talking to the wrong people, and she's frustrated with me for not trying hard enough. She just doesn't believe me.

I go to bed, toss and turn, and don't really get any sleep.

Day 23: Thursday, March 27, 2003

I take the kids to school and go to work. I stay at work until ten-thirty, then head to the hospital to see how much better Curtis is doing. I know he is coming home, I know it. But I also know what I saw, and I am very afraid his brain is now Swiss cheese. Surely not, not Curtis; he can take it. He can take whatever they throw at him; he's coming home.

He is worse. I don't know how much a human being can take. Blood pressure is unstable. I check his flow sheet and see that he still has raging fevers. They have to put an ice blanket on him. This isn't right. He was supposed to start improving after that drain went in. I check the drain bag; it is still draining. *C'mon, Curtis, what is wrong with you, why is this happening?* Something is still broken. This is not Curtis. This is not all Curtis is capable of. There is something going on that the doctors have missed. They just don't understand. Those burns are never going to take his life, not even close. I ask Curtis to tell me what is wrong. His mother, sitting in my chair again, says, "I like to see you correspond with him." I ignore her.

I stand against the wall and start thinking. *What if it isn't the gut at all? What if the lungs caused the gut? The only thing they ever said is the leaking pancreas 'sent a little fluid' to the lungs. That never did make sense to me. What if there is something unrelated in the lungs? Something else is wrong.* I check all the numbers and graphs on the ventilator. I soon realize that he isn't on very high settings at all. He's getting 30 percent oxygen, and a really low pressure. That makes me feel better. I ask to see his chest X-rays, but nobody has time to show them to me or they can't find them or something. It's not like I know how to read X-rays, but I'm riding the crazy train, y'know, doing whatever comes to mind. I ask a lot of questions of every nurse or doctor I see. I never really get any answers other than "I dunno" or assurances they are doing all they can and time will tell. They don't want to go cutting into all that burned skin. *Cutting into it to do what?* The best thing to do is wait and see. I ask his nurse, surely they've seen sicker people than him, huh? She points to the ceiling and says it is in God's hands, but they've seen miracles before. *Miracles? We are already at miracle stage? Oh no, we are not. This is wrong.* Curtis needs help and I am desperate to get it to him. *Lungs and gut, huh? Well, then, he needs a lung specialist and a gut specialist.*

On my way home, I fish out Karen Vidor's card. There is finally something she can do for me. I call her from home and leave a message, "All I've been hearing from is burn doctors about his gut and his lungs. I want a lung specialist and a gut specialist to see him pronto if they haven't already done so, and if they have, I want to hear from them right now."

Fifteen minutes later the phone rings—*Wow, I'll be calling Karen again*—and it is Dr. Gut. He's been seeing Curtis since last Friday. He starts with the stones. I pace around the pool impatiently while he speaks; I already know all this. I have something to say. He finishes with, "The body tends to wall off injured organs and protect them while they heal. Everything is functioning in his gut. It's best not to go stirring up those destructive enzymes leaking from the pancreas, and it's best to let the body heal itself without intervention. Everything's good in the gut, no worries. I'm keeping an eye on him."

Finally, it is my turn to speak. "I've been watching my husband deteriorate rapidly for the past week. The man in that bed is not my husband. He can take everything you can throw at him if it gets him home. He's ready to go. Those burns were never going to stop him. I keep hearing 'if he gets any worse we can sure step in and save him, but for now everything's fine and we're going to watch him.' I'm telling you I know that man and everything is not fine. Whatever extreme measures you have available to take, now is the time to take them, **right now**. If it's not the gut, then it must be the lungs, but something is very wrong and he needs help. That's all I wanted to say, I appreciate your call."

He needs to be cut open from stem to stern or he needs to be nuked. It is time for desperate measures. This is crystal clear to me. I need to make it crystal clear to the experts. I am glad I got that off my chest. Now I need to say the same thing to Dr. Lung. It must be the lungs because Dr. Gut said everything's groovy.

Dr. Lung never calls. These doctors make their rounds early in the mornings. I am starting to wonder how I'll ever get hold of them since visiting hours don't start until eleven. I idly wonder if this is intentional. *Surely, they aren't trying to keep families away from the doctors?*

I call the hospital at eight o'clock. I want to give his day shift nurse time to settle in and take care of his business. Some guy comes to the phone. He is Curtis' nurse. A new nurse, I don't know this guy. I tell him it is very important that Dr. Lung call me when he makes his rounds. I make sure he understands how important it is to have Dr. Lung call me. I never leave my desk. I don't even go to the bathroom because I might miss his call. He never calls. At ten-thirty, I call again and speak to his nurse. I ask if Dr. Lung has made his rounds. "Yea, but he left. He said he doesn't have anything to say to you, but Dr. Gut is here. He's clearing out an OR, stat. He's taking your husband to surgery." I ask, "For what?" "Gallbladder." "Why didn't anyone call me?" "Well, his mother's here. I told her." "I thought visiting hours didn't start until eleven!" "She's just sitting here." I slam down the phone and grab my purse. These people are starting to piss me off.

I race to the hospital. Dr. Gut introduces himself and says, "I took a look at the ultrasound from last Friday myself. The gallbladder is dead. It needs to come out, there's no need for another ultrasound." I tug his lapel and say, "See, I told you!" I am so happy.

Doctors usually read the radiology report. They don't look at the films themselves. My call must have caused him to take a look with his own eyes. *God bless him. Now here's a world-class doctor.*

He starts going over consent forms and explains he will be drilling holes in Curtis' abdomen and removing the necrosed (dead) tissue. The procedure will take about ninety minutes or so. They can't take him away and cut him open fast enough as far as I am concerned. Off he goes. I didn't see Curtis or check his vitals or anything.

I sit in the L-shaped waiting room ready to answer the ESP phone, but it never rings. I am on the opposite side of the L from the gaggle of hens. After about thirty minutes of listening to them, I go out to chain smoke. After about two hours, I go back up to the nurses' station. He isn't back yet, so I go back to the waiting room. Curtis' mother starts talking about how lovely somebody's funeral was that she just attended. *Geez! All the moons, and stars, and planets need to be in perfect alignment. Curtis wants to come home. He needs all the help he can get, and the word "funeral" shouldn't be used within a thousand miles of him. Bad karma. She is going to kill him with bad juju.*

I go sit in the hallway, use my backpack as a pillow, and shut my eyes for a few minutes. I sit there until my legs go to sleep. He's been gone for three and a half hours. Maybe he is in post-op and the doctor isn't going to come talk to us. I check with the nurses' station. He isn't back yet. "Could he be in post-op?" Oh, no, he's an ICU patient. He will come straight back to his room. I am mildly alarmed. I go back to my post on the floor.

After about another thirty minutes, Nice Blond Lady Doctor appears out of nowhere and sits on the floor next to me. She says she checked on Curtis. *What a nice blond lady doctor!* He is tolerating the surgery really well, but it is taking a long time because they had to cut him open. The gallbladder is dead and has become infected with gangrene. They have to clean all that goop out of there. It is pretty soupy and nasty. It is going to take a long time to clean it up, but he is stable and doing well, and there is every reason to believe the surgery will be successful. Probably a couple more hours to go. I thank her and tell her I am going home. Then I update the Funeral Forecasters.

I can't wait until tomorrow. I no longer expect him to jump back out of bed. He took a pretty hard hit, but he for sure will be off the garden hose within a week. I secretly think less than that, but give him a longer timeline so we won't be disappointed. I expect to see some immediate improvement, though. You can only get better after having your soupy, infected, gangrenous guts taken out.

What a stressful week. Thank goodness that's over!

My mom takes the kids to my father's for the weekend, then she has to go back home. Penelope will be coming next weekend. My cousin Jackie is scheduled to come on April ninth and stay for a week, so I have this weekend and the next two covered. Maybe I won't have to worry beyond that because Curtis will be home. My sister is going to meet me at the hospital this evening after her classes.

I get to the hospital promptly at eleven and his room is already full of Wrights. We are kicked out shortly, as Curtis has to get his torture. I wonder why they have a rule that no visitors are allowed before eleven. I don't see anywhere in small print, "except for Wrights," or "unless you really want to be here" or "unless you just don't respect rules put in place to benefit burned people," or anything like that. I wonder why they even have that rule. I'm still waiting for an answer to that question. If rules are not enforced, then there are no rules. All the doctors do their rounds before visiting hours, so good luck ever speaking to a doctor. About 95 percent of the time they wait until after visiting hours start to change dressings, so most often I get kicked out as soon as I get here.

I get a Pepsi and chain smoke. I steer clear of his family. They make constant phone calls to Priscilla, his employer, and Karen Vidor, the case manager for the insurance company, looking for money or for updates on Curtis. They don't realize that Karen finds out everything she knows from me, and I leave all the same updates on his brother Andy's voicemail. Priscilla was getting updates from

Karen, but she finally told Karen to stop giving her updates because she couldn't listen to any more. She can't sleep at night. It is terribly upsetting to her.

His family accuses me of not telling them about Curtis' condition. I tell Andy everything I know, but it isn't always easy for me to get any information. I tell Dawn everything I know, and she tells me everything she knows. Dawn calls my mother, and my mother carries on the phone chain. I don't talk to anyone except Dawn, Ginger, and Andy's voicemail. It is all I ever have time for. I'm convinced, though, that nothing his family does will surprise Curtis because he knows them better than I do.

I head back up to his room. All I can do is stand against the wall because there are Wrights everywhere. His vitals are stable. I know he has a fever, but there is nothing I can do about it. At about two in the afternoon, I tire of standing against the wall. I can't take care of him. I can't visit with him. I can't even sit down, for Pete's sake. I will come and pick him up when he needs a ride home; that is all I can do. I leave.

I notice Mrs. Mexico outside Mexico's room putting on a plastic gown and hat and mask right there in front of the door. That is new, but I don't know what it means. She is getting all dressed up in plastic-wear from a cart right outside Mexico's room. Looks like a hassle.

I'm nearly home when I remember my sister is planning to meet me at the hospital later. I call her and tell her not to bother. "Put a fork in me, I am done. I am not going back to that place until he needs a ride home." She says, "You can't do that to him. He needs you, and you know his family can't take care of him." I tell her I can't take care of him either; they aren't going to let me. She says, for the millionth time, that **somebody** at that hospital can help, and I have every right to keep people out of there for whatever reason

I want to—it is the law. I tell her again that nobody on the floor and nobody in administration is familiar with this law, and nobody cares. She tells me I am wrong. "Call security and have them thrown out." I tell her, "I can't do that. Curtis would never forgive me. He would never do that to them, so neither can I. There is nothing I can do." She tells me to turn right back around and call administration, and she will meet me at the hospital at seven o'clock.

Well, she is right. I can't leave him there alone with his family; they are hopelessly incapable of taking care of him. She is right about everything except "somebody in that hospital can help." I turn around and go back, call administration again, and wait in a conference room. I feel really bad. *Why, oh why, does it have to be this way? Why can't we just all be adults?* Bertha walks by and sees me in the conference room; she asks me what is wrong. I told her it is nothing that concerns her. She actually is really nice and encourages me to talk to her. I tell her briefly, again, that these people need to let me visit my husband; this is insane. She says she can't take this anymore. She has high blood pressure, and she isn't getting involved in this. I tell her that would be best. She leaves.

Two new people from administration show up. I have to start at the beginning again, all the way back to March fifth. I tell them about all the conversations Curtis had with his family about his parents going home. About him being so sick and everybody missing it; I couldn't see him, so he is neglected. I show them the paper where he wrote, "I told them not to come." About us being trampled. The two-person rule. The visiting hours rule and all those times he begged me, "Why aren't you here," and I have to keep telling him visiting hours don't start until eleven and it turns out they are letting his mother in the whole time. They don't follow the rules, the rules aren't enforced, and the end result is that this man thinks his wife, who he wants the most, just doesn't want to be with him. I tell them about the family meeting we already had and how poorly that went. His mother and the blood pressure. Everything. I have to repeat everything, and this is wearing me out.

They tell me neither they nor I can keep people from visiting, but they see this type of thing all the time. They can gather the family and try to set a schedule. I tell them I'd like to be alone with him in the evenings from seven-thirty until nine, and that I would like to be alone with him the rest of tonight and all day Sunday. But if I can just be alone with him from seven-thirty until nine, I can live with that. They write this down and look at me expectantly. "That's it. That's all I want." They seem surprised that this is all I want, and they think this can be easily accommodated. *Ha!*

They summon the family. Bertha, his father and mother, and I don't know who all else come into the room. The table is full. I think Now Deceased is there, too. I feel really bad for Curtis' father. I know he doesn't like getting mixed up in all the fuss created by his wife. One of the administrators starts speaking to his mother. She is really nice. She sympathizes with her and her critically ill son. She expresses how important it is for her to be there. *No. it isn't, but whatever.* She spends a long time placating her and being really nice and understanding, and then, "It's also important that his wife have time with him..." At that, his mother stands up and says "When I see my boy rise up from his bed I will go home, and not until then," and she rides out on her cane like it is Gene Autry's horse. *Drama queen. And it isn't true, anyway. She has seen her son out of his bed, and he told her to stay home, and she came out and stayed anyway.*

The administrator looks at me and I say, "See, I told you." Bertha says, "Let's finish the meeting, I will speak to her." The administrators tell them I'd like to be alone with him tonight, tomorrow, and in the evenings from seven-thirty until nine. His dad says, "Is that all you want?" "Yes, that's all I want." He asks, "Why didn't you just say so?" I tell him, "I've been saying so since March fifth." He says, "You never asked me. I'm ready to go home," and leaves. Bertha says she'll go speak to Mrs. Wright.

After they leave, I comment to the administrators that as long as he is in that room, this is our home. They commiserate with me, either because that's what they're trained to do or because they now see how obstinate and hostile Curtis' mother is.

Bertha comes back and says that schedule won't work for his mother because she gets a ride to the hospital in the mornings and isn't picked up until nighttime. The administrators suggest that she come every other day. Bertha leaves again and comes back and says absolutely not, that won't work for her. The administrators suggest that his mother wait in the chapel or cafeteria when I want time alone with him. It is only ninety minutes in the evening. Bertha leaves and comes back, nope that isn't going to work for her schedule. This goes on for over an hour. Now it is seven-thirty and shift change is over. *This is ridiculous.* "This is ridiculous, I'm going to visit with my husband and we want to be left alone!" I get gowned up and go back into his room. My sister is there. She's already removed his blanket and put a washcloth on his forehead, and now she's brushing his teeth.

I give Dawn the update on the family meeting with the hospital people that can't do anything. She is incredulous. She's been giving updates to her coworkers at her hospital, especially the ICU nurses, and they all tell her the same thing—that I have every right under the law to keep them out. But Memorial Hermann is lawless. She says, "So, are you alone with him tomorrow?" I reply, "I doubt it. Nothing was resolved, and his mother is totally unwilling to commit to any schedule." She says, "I'm not speaking for Curtis, I am speaking for myself," and leaves the room. When she comes back, she says she told the Wrights, "Lisa has someone watching her kids tomorrow so she can spend the day with Curtis. Alone. I'm going to be here and I better not see a single one of you here."

Day 26: Sunday, March 30, 2003

Of course, the room is full of Wrights when I arrive at eleven. Surprisingly, they don't stay long. They tell Curtis goodbye, and they make sure I hear them tell him that they'll be back later. They are all acting so dramatic.

Mexico is still on the trach and on dialysis, and now he has a machine pumping his blood because his heart doesn't work. Mrs. Mexico has to wrap herself in plastic before she enters his room. I don't have the heart to make small talk with her anymore.

Curtis is now up to forty percent oxygen on the ventilator and the pressure has been increased. He isn't better. If anything, he is slightly worse. I tend to him all day, except when I am kicked out. Raging fevers, ice blankets, unstable blood pressure—he keeps me busy all day. I play the CD that Calvin brought, BeBe and CeCe Winans. I turn on the news and tell him he is missing the war, he needs to wake up and see this. His hair is starting to get nappy. He always keeps his head shaved really close, darn near bald, but now he is growing a 'fro. His lips are sliced and bleeding from the ties to the garden hose. It looks so miserable.

Dawn meets me at the hospital this afternoon. We have a lot of questions. One of them is, "Has Infectious Disease seen Curtis yet?" No, burn doctors are prescribing his antibiotics.

My sister has her back up about this family visitation. She is determined to prove me wrong. She tells Twila all the same things I have so eloquently communicated myself. She reminds them of my rights and the law. She finds out the same things they've been telling me. There is no law at Memorial Hermann. Patients and their next of kin have no right to privacy at Memorial Hermann, none. I have become used to being called "next of kin." Dawn is furious. She still is, to this day. I am, too, but not as much as Dawn. I need to keep my energy for Curtis. She picks this ball up for Curtis, though, and carries it for months. She is incensed that they so blatantly disregard our civil rights.

Dawn tells me she's getting concerned about Curtis' eyes. They are always open, and they will dry out. She says she puts drops in his eyes and massages his eyelids every time she's there, and he likes it. She encourages me to do the same. She says they should have something thicker and greasier than Visine. She has asked about it. We both start asking about his eyes.

HIPAA day. Today HIPAA goes into effect. Well, Dawn says HIPAA goes into effect on April 14, 2003, but this fine hospital decides to start our punishment early. My sister takes the day shift. She calls me at work to tell me she happened to be in the hallway when Dr. Lung was briefing the new residents on all the patients. This is a teaching hospital, so once a month they get another new round of residents. I don't realize this means I'll never see Nice Blond Lady Doctor again. That sucks. Anyway, talking about Curtis, Dr. Lung says, "He has the liver of a chronic alcoholic, and I blame radiology."

It's been a hellish week. Curtis has been battling with his blood pressure all week. I know the longer he is on the garden hose, the closer I come to facing quality-of-life issues. I am still concerned about the episode last Wednesday when his blood pressure shot up to over 300. He must have surely have had a stroke. What is to become of this poor man? We have to get him off the hose. Now the liver!? They love to 'wait and see' Curtis get sicker.

My sister asks them about brain activity tests. They can't talk to her. HIPAA. It's the law. They can't talk to Dawn. *Oh, so there is some law here.* Dawn keeps up with the eye drops, but nobody knows anything about doing anything else for his eyes. Nobody will tell her anything because of HIPAA. She is reduced to lurking around corners and eavesdropping, hoping to hear a crumb of news about Curtis. Sneaking a peek at his flow sheet when the hallway is clear. This is insane. You have to commit a crime to find out what his temperature is. This place is nuts, it's a joke.

My sister meets me at home in the evening with more bad news: Mexico died today.

Dawn has signed up for every kind of benefit, and insurance, and disability offered through her job. She is scared to death after seeing what has happened to Curtis. She has told me and everybody in our family that if she's ever brain dead to unplug her, no hesitation about it. I think everybody in my family is reviewing their wills and insurance by now.

Back at the hospital, I am in a mood. I am not crying; I am fed up. Mexico's death hit me really hard. We're getting much too close. My head is throbbing, and my chest hurts so badly that I think it's possible I am having a heart attack. The next person in a white jacket who gives me a bad answer or says anything that sounds like HIPAA is going to get karate chopped in the throat and dropped like a bag of rocks. I am done being nice. I march to the gown room and think surely I am going to drop dead from a heart attack at any moment. I make it to the gown room, I gown up and battle motion sickness while I wash my hands. Do I have to paint it on the wall in his room? "You are allowed to talk to Dawn. You have my permission! Tell her everything."

I turn the corner and purposely avert my eyes from Mexico's room. There is Curtis...lying there as calm as can be with his eyes wide open. *Wow, that's creepy, he looks wide awake.* He looks right at me. *No way.* I kiss him on the forehead, notice that he's running a fever, and get him a washcloth. He looks right at me. He is following me with his eyes. *No way man, he's in a coma!* "If you can hear me, blink your eyes." He blinks his eyes. *What! He* **is** *awake!* I say, "Blink once for yes." He blinks. I say, "Don't blink for no." He doesn't blink. *It is all him. His brain isn't Swiss cheese; he* *is perfectly fine. Get-outta-here! How did this happen?* His vitals are all stable, peaceful as a lamb. I am so happy.

He lifts his heavily bandaged, splinted arm in some sort of gesture. I ask him if he itches. He doesn't blink. I put his arm back. I explain again about the garden hose and everything else that is going on. He blinks. I am so pumped! I explain to him about the cocktails they have him on, and that he always has to stay calm—*He apparently already knows this, as he is very calm*—because every time they try to get him off the cocktails, he fights it and they have to knock him back out again. He is doing really, really well and he needs to remember to stay this calm always and forever.

As a family, we always watch *Fear Factor*, a tv show that offers contests disgusting and scary challenges to complete, like eating cockroaches. We get disheartened when somebody is supposed to eat three roaches, but quits after eating only one. Why even eat one? Why even put it in your mouth if you're not going to see the finish line? Well, I explain to Curtis that he's eaten half the roaches and he is halfway home. Don't give up now; you can see the finish line! He lifts the arm again.

"OK, Curtis, just be patient with me. I know you want some-thing, but I don't know what it is. I'm going to start at your feet and go all the way up. Can you move your right foot?" He moves his right foot. "OK, when I get to the right spot, move your foot." I start with his feet, "Are the boots too tight? Too cold? Too hot? Itchy?" His arm rises again. I ask him if he can move his right foot. He moves his right foot. I thought I had hit on something with the itching, and maybe he forgot to move his foot and moved his arm instead. No, he knows to move his foot. "You understand to move your foot when I'm right? Blink once for yes." He blinks deliberately. OK, he gets it.

I continue, legs, knees, thighs. "Too cold? Too hot? Wee-wee? Do you want the light off?" I keep going up his body. Periodically he lifts that arm again. I know how heavy that arm is, why does he keep lifting it? Every time he lifts it, I think I've hit on something and remind him to move his right foot if I am right. The foot doesn't move. Can you move your foot? He moves his foot. I know it is frustrating for him. It is for me, too, but we just have to be patient. I work my way all the way to the top of his head. Nothing is wrong. The arm keeps coming up. "Do you need pillows under your arm?" Nothing. "Do you want to turn your whole body?" Nope. *Darn it all, why does he keep lifting that arm?*

I get to the very top of his head, but never get it right. I don't see how I missed anything, I have covered every possible thing. "I'm so sorry Curtis. I don't know what you're trying to tell me, but I'll keep at it until I get it right." Up comes that arm again. If he could have kept it going, it would have gone around my waist.

"Curtis, do you want a **hug**?" His whole right leg shakes like a dog getting a belly rub. *Aww, poor baby!*

I lay on top of his chest and he gets that heavy arm against my side. He can't get it all the way around me. We stay that way until his nurse comes in. I forgot all about karate chopping someone to the floor. I am happy as a clam. I don't even notice my chest doesn't hurt. I am starving!

The nurse explains that they have moved his central line. It has to be replaced with a new one, in a new location, every couple of days so it won't get infected. Every time they move it, they have to X-ray it before they use it. The sedatives he is getting are not the type that wear off slowly. Once they are turned off, it is like a light switch—he is wide awake. "Yes, I can see that. He's fine. Why can't he stay awake?" She explains it is better for him, as he is on a ventilator, to stay sedated so he doesn't fight the hose. Well, I have seen how fine he has been over the past week, with tears streaming down his face and blood pressure sky high. This is the finest I've seen him, off the cocktails.

They kick me out to X-ray him, I just stay in the hallway. Mexico's room is stark and empty. All the papers and instructions that have been taped all over the windows are gone. All the equipment is gone from the room. It is a scary reminder of where we almost went. My sister said the family had no doubt chosen to stop treatment, as he was hooked up to enough machinery to keep him going forever. I cry for his family. I feel their pain.

Curtis is coming home. I know it.

They finish with the X-rays and a few minutes later, Curtis is in a coma again. This is really disappointing, but I am peaceful. I leave the hospital a different person than the one who arrived. I cry all the way home. Curtis took care of me tonight, no doubt about it. He isn't a vegetable; his brain isn't Swiss cheese; he isn't going to die. I am so sad that they have to put him out again. He is fine.

I am overjoyed to have seen him and talked to him. I feel lucky to have been there right when I was. This is so important. I decide to ask that they always change his central line while I am there. Well, that never happened again. I guess that's just too ridiculous a request to accommodate. Not in the best interest of the patient.

I am exhausted beyond description. It is getting harder and harder to get out of bed in the morning. When the alarm goes off, I have to let my legs slide off the side of the bed until they hit the tile floor. Ouch! I am so tired. I go upstairs to get the kids up, and I tell them to ride the bus to school. Coming back downstairs, I can't really see straight. I am so tired. I slip on the stairs and wrench my back. I catch the rail before I fall all the way down. I call Elmer and let him know I am going back to bed. I wake up at two and wonder if the kids made it to school. I feel disoriented. *A shower will help.*

I get out of the shower, comb my hair, and pick up the blow dryer. *I really don't care what my hair looks like. I always have to cover it in the hospital, anyway, and it gets sweaty. I could save ten or fifteen minutes every day if I didn't have any hair.* I put the blow dryer down, go across the street to a salon, and tell them to cut it all off.

Curtis went for another CAT scan of his abdomen. I don't know why, and nobody else seems to, either. I tend to him all evening. No family around, nothing eventful other than he has a new nurse taking care of him during the day, and another nurse I've never seen before taking care of him tonight. I update the night nurse on everything to watch for and everything going on with him. It is scary to leave him in the hands of someone who's never seen him before.

I ask the nurse if he's seen people as sick as Curtis get up and go home. I ask everybody this all the time. I never get a direct answer like, "Oh yes, much worse than him, sure." Well, they are going to see it this time, I can tell you. His vent settings are going up as the volume of air in his lungs and his oxygen saturation are declining. I don't get ESP phone calls from him anymore, so I know he has left the spirit world behind for good and has come back to the land of mortals.

They have determined that he needs blood pressure medication because of all his blood pressure events. They also switch him to a different sedative, Ativan. It is much friendlier. I never saw tears streaming down his face again after they switched to Ativan. I like Ativan. It sounds so peaceful, like a sigh.

Other than continued raging fevers, increased vent settings, a new nurse every shift, scrounging for a crumb of news from a doctor, and my sister sneaking around eavesdropping, nothing is going on. I go to work in the mornings and take care of Curtis in the evenings. That is enough; trust me.

I meet my sister at the hospital after work. Curtis is now getting 100 percent oxygen from the ventilator and the pressure support is on maximum settings. This is not good. His fevers are blazing for days on end. It's never under 102. This man has been burning up for days. We constantly put ice blankets on him or ice or cold washcloth on his forehead. Fever, fever, fever. They changed his central line earlier today. Dawn and I both missed it.

We ask if we can see his Curtis' chest X-rays. Dr. Doom and Gloom takes us to the nurses' station and brings them up on the computer. By now they have taken dozens of chest X-rays. Up on the screen appear some clouds. These clouds are today's chest X-ray.

As soon as they appear on the screen, my sister says, *"Damn!"*

"What? What?" What were they looking at? My sister points out a small black circle, not too much larger than a golf ball, in the upper left-hand area of the screen. She explains that this is what a normal X-ray should look like, two black lobes full of air. She starts to trace the outline of the lung and I can see it taking shape. It is full of clouds. I blurt out, *"F---!"* Curtis' left lung is full of clouds. There are no black spots of air anywhere. No wonder they had to vacuum his lungs. This is much more than "a little fluid." He has raging pneumonia. He has inhaled every cloud from the sky.

These become known as the *f---/damn X-rays*. We look at earlier X-rays. They aren't improving at all. Every time either of us gets to look at his X-rays, we update the other. He always has *f---/ damn X-rays*, for months. The left lung is persistently troublesome.

Dr. Doom and Gloom also shows us Curtis' CAT scans. My sister is impressed that they can call this all up on their computers. This is what she is getting her Master's degree in, and she is seeing it in action. The CAT scans look like lava lamps, but according to the doctor, they are normal. There are plenty of dark circles of air in Curtis' gut. *I wonder if they can drill holes in the bottom of his lungs to let the clouds drain out and run a hose to the life-saving air in his gut.*

He is still burning up with fever. His abdominal incision is oozing. His abdominal drain bag is still draining, although not a lot. His blood pressure and heart rate are still high. He is really sick, probably the sickest man at Memorial Hermann. But he can take it; he doesn't know how sick he is. His third skin graft is still tabled for the time being. Dr. Gut is still watching him, but he can't find anything else wrong with the gut. Curtis now has a lot of infections and a lot of possible sources of infections.

There is a sign posted in his room now: "Arm and leg splints to be worn at all times." Almost every time I arrive, his splints are off. I finally asked the occupational therapists, "When is he supposed to be wearing them?" That's when they posted the sign. I still have to put them on almost every time I get here. He is now wearing Isotoner gloves on his hands, turned inside out. The grafts have taken, and these gloves provide compression so he won't develop debilitating scarring. I can now get a look at his hands every so often.

The entire backs of both hands are covered in skin from his calf. It wraps around to his palms and all ten fingers. Poor thing, his hands were severely burned. I am vigilant with the lotion, gloves, exercises, and splints. He is going to need his hands when he gets home. I don't know if he still has nerves in his hands, or what. I've done a little reading about burns and I know that he doesn't have sweat glands where he suffered third-degree burns. I wonder how he will ever be able to regulate his body temperature. I'll always have to watch him closely so he doesn't overheat like he's doing now with these relentless fevers.

I never stop telling him, "Slow deep breaths. No matter what, just stay relaxed, Curtis." They try to wean him from the cocktails, but he gets overly agitated and his blood pressure goes up. I have nothing else to talk about.

Day 31: Friday, April 4, 2003

Smitty from work comes over in the afternoon to teach me how to clean the pool. He hooks up the vacuum and shows me how to do it. It seems easy enough so far. He starts to vacuum, but he can't get any suction. He keeps fiddling with dials on the pump and explaining what they are and what they do. We don't have a lot of time. He suggests that I throw some shock in it and try again later. It is nasty. He comments that he didn't know fungus and mildew came in so many colors; shock may not be enough. It is full of leaves, and snakes, and three-eyed frogs. And it is a big pool. "Good luck to ya!"

Mandy comes over to babysit for me. I leave as soon as she arrives. The shock has started to change the color of the pool, but it has a long way to go.

Let's see, what's new with Curtis today. I check his flow sheet before I enter his room. Still relentless fevers. That isn't new. Elevated blood pressure and heart rate. That isn't new. I ask a few more questions of Dr. Doom and Gloom and start learning about his blood gases. They look like crap, and that also isn't new. They moved his central line again. That isn't new, either; they move it every few days. Abdominal drain still oozing. That's not new. I sure thought it'd be done draining by now. It doesn't drain a lot. I wonder why they leave it in there. His abdominal incision is packed with gauze and healing nicely. That isn't new. His gloves are on and his splints are off. That isn't new. He has another new nurse. That isn't new, either.

Aha! At last, here's something new and significant. His vent settings have increased yet again. He is requiring more and more pressure and support from this machine. This is new. *Another revoltin' development.*

Curtis, come on. You can do better than this! This man, my husband, is rotting in this miserable pit of suffering. He is not meant to go like this. I don't know that anybody is, but surely not him. If these burns were meant to kill him, he would have died in the ambulance.

Curtis doesn't keep me too busy tonight. I play BeBe and CeCe Winans on the radio Calvin brought. I like all types of music, but this isn't normally something I would choose. I soon discover I like the entire CD. I play it over and over to accompany my repetitious, one-sided conversations with Curtis. I never play anything else; eventually, I take all the other CDs home. My favorite is "I'll Take You There." I always play this one on repeat and turn it up a little louder. He has to hear this! Sometimes I sing to him

When I get home, Mandy stays and waits with me for Penelope to arrive. Penelope shows up late, after eleven. I update her on Curtis and the events of the past month and finish with the grim and depressing day that today has been. This takes us well into the night. When I am finished, she just sits there with her mouth agape for several minutes. She finally says, "Lisa, I'm so sorry. I just don't know what to say. I haven't stopped and won't stop praying for you both." There is nothing you can say. The three of us have a hen party, talking well into the wee hours of the morning about things unrelated to the burn unit.

I arrive promptly at eleven and am immediately crestfallen. Curtis is dying. There is no avoiding it. The Grim Reaper is pulling him by both ankles. It isn't Curtis' fault. He tried. I don't even bother to look at his vitals. *He looks like a human being who's in his final hours.*

A short while later, Dr. Doom and Gloom tells me they called for a kidney consult, as his kidneys are failing. Dr. Kidney Specialist explains that his kidneys are only functioning at fifty percent, but a person can live a normal life with just one kidney. There is no reason to intervene at this point. They will continue to watch him. His kidneys may improve on their own, or they may worsen. He asks for family kidney history, and I refer him to his mother.

I am not emotional at this news. I am numb and so sad. He is dying. I watch the life slip out of him. I play BeBe and CeCe. What a tragic waste. There is nothing I can do except continue my *Groundhog Day* speeches, try to lower his fever, put lotion on his dry skin, and keep him comfortable until he leaves.

Dr. Doom and Gloom comes in a couple hours later and says his blood gases have improved slightly. He might as well say, "His teeth are nice and white." Nothing he says matters because Curtis is dying. Anybody can see it.

Later in the afternoon Dr. Soap Opera comes in and asks if I have any questions. My sister has mentioned that there's some type of device that is placed on the chest to vibrate the lungs. I ask about that. He says they don't have anything like that, but there is a type of ventilator that oscillates the lungs to keep the mucus moving so the lungs won't deflate. I ask why Curtis isn't on that. He said it's a desperate, last-ditch effort; it only treats the symptoms, and it can damage the lungs. I think maybe it would keep the mucus moving so his lungs won't collapse. We have a lengthy discussion about moving his lungs, but in the end, the wise doctors decide to leave him like he is. You can't get any closer to needing extreme measures, but they aren't going to take them.

I keep in Curtis' ear all day, telling him to pee. I help him visualize a full bladder and say anything I can think of to get him to pee. "You just drank a six-pack of Bud and it's cold out. You're jumping up and down, you have to pee so bad!" Any time something comes down the hose, I let him know it. I tell him to keep it coming, "Pee, pee, pee. Your kidneys need a little help, Curtis. Keep peeing, don't stop." He sure is starting to pee a lot. I keep telling him all day. Of course, they are giving him Lasix, but I can't help thinking some of it is because I am telling him to. If he wakes up and tells me he saw the light, but turned away because he heard me telling him to pee, I will be shocked. But if I didn't know better, it seems like that's exactly what is happening. We do this all day long. He fills the hose and I dump it in the bag. I report to him his every drop. I come up with as many descriptive circumstances as I can to trigger his brain into firing up the bladder.

I mention this to Ginger when I am kicked out and smoking cigarettes. I am 99.99 percent certain that I am witnessing another miracle. (I have to leave 0.01 percent on reserve, in case I am insane.) When I arrived in his room this morning, he was dying. Tonight, he actually looks a little better and is peeing like a race-horse. This is more than a coincidence.

Curtis' name keeps appearing on the surgery schedule for his third skin graft to his right thigh. Dr. Plastic Surgeon schedules him, so it'll be in the OR rotation, but he always gets rescheduled. He is now on the schedule for next Wednesday, April ninth, but I know it doesn't mean anything.

When I get home, I give Penelope an update. I had given her my credit card and a shopping list this morning. She bought groceries and supplies, and she refuses to let me pay her for them. I really want to pay her. I don't want to be on a pickle jar. She refuses. She sure is a nice lady. I thank her for that and for taking care of my kids, who are becoming strangers to me.

To be honest, I have no idea whether I am broke or not. I stopped paying bills on March fifth. I am not paying attention to any of that. If I see a cutoff notice for electricity or something, I'll pay it. If I had bothered to pay any bills, we would probably be broke. But my whole world is Curtis. Bills and money are just never on my mind.

I no longer think Curtis is going to die. The nights are the worst, though. If he does die, it will happen at night when nobody is watching him. It is so scary, I can't even think about it. I hate to leave him there at night. If I think about how neglected he is, and about all the things that can go wrong, I will go out of my mind. I never get calls on the ESP phone, and I'm not sure what that means. I lose an hour tonight because we turn our clocks ahead.

As soon as I get to Curtis' room, they kick me out so they can torture him. I am always looking for a silver lining, and this is one. At least he is now "sleeping" through most of the pain. I will never have to hear those screams of pain again from Curtis. I still hear them from other patients, though.

I check his flow sheet when I get back from my eviction. He is still putting out copious amounts of liquid gold. His kidneys have improved. The doctors are still watching him, but his kidneys have come way up. That's my husband. The vent settings have come down slightly. Finally, finally he is going in the right direction. The abdominal drain bag isn't draining any more. I wonder why they are leaving it in. I ask the nurse, another new nurse. I know before I ask that she won't know, and she doesn't, of course.

I'm concerned about all these new people taking care of him. At least he is starting to get better. It is a pretty quiet day. Lots of BeBe and CeCe. He keeps me busy, to be sure, but it is a pretty peaceful day for him. I keep repeating my lessons to him, "Relax. A little fluid, that's all. Come back to us, Curtis, please. Rest and get well." Over, and over, and over. My cousin Jackie will be arriving in two days, and the pool looks like a swamp. It is important to me to get it clean, as I know she will want to use it. So will the kids, for that matter. I am like a broken record, "I'm going to clean the pool, Curtis!" I hope I'm not driving him insane.

My sister calls to tell me that Curtis' vent settings have come down. Ever so slightly, but they've come down. *Oh yeah! That's what I'm talking about. See, I told you so. I told you he is coming home. I knew it, I knew it, I knew it!*

Dawn asks what happened to Curtis' cell phone. She calls it sometimes just to hear his voice, "Hi, this is Curtis, please leave me a message." When she called it this morning, there was a generic greeting. What I had done? Nothing. Some buttons got pushed when it was in my purse, but I didn't do anything to his message. I panicked. I may want to hear his voice sometime. That is all we have left. I call T-Mobile. Trying not to sound hysterical, I explain the situation and why it is so important to get his greeting back. The T-Mobile lady has me push a few buttons and she does a few things, and then she tells me to try it. I almost do , rather than sound like a complete fool, but I just can't. I tell her that I will fall apart if I hear his voice and I have to stay focused. Can she please call it and check it? She does, and I hear Curtis' phone ring. I am holding my breath. What if I screwed up his phone? My sister and I, and who knows who else, won't get to hear his voice anymore. How could I be so careless? After a long wait, she says it's fine, she got his greeting. I thank her and almost start crying. She God blessed me and said she'd pray for him. I used great caution with his cell phone from that day forward. That was a close one!

I can't wait to get up there tonight. My neighbor is babysitting and won't get here until between five-thirty and six. Well, that will put me at the hospital just in time to be tossed out for the "secret ritual" of shift change. No point in sitting there. I have things to do at home. I can leave at seven and be there at seven-thirty. I have two hours to clean the pool, at long last. I told Curtis I was going to, and who knows when I'll have another two hours at home. It takes every bit of the first hour just to get the pump primed with good suction. Once I finally do, I have to empty the reservoir by the pump with almost every pass because there is so much ooze in the pool. I make a big dent in it. I have to drop the pole and turn the pump off at seven sharp. It is nowhere near ready to swim in, but I am halfway there and quite proud of myself.

I can't wait to see Curtis. I've been sending him "pee ESP" all day.

By now, he's probably spitting the garden hose out of his throat.

Well, not quite, but he is holding steady. He still has a high fever and unstable blood pressure, but this is now the norm for him. These days I'm keeping an eagle eye on the ventilator. That is my barometer. He is hanging in there and has successfully kicked the Grim Reaper out of his room. I'm not falling into any comfort zone, though. We play the "pee game" all evening. I'm excited about every drop I see, and I share my enthusiasm with Curtis and beg for more. I try to get him to fill the bag before I have to leave. I never would have guessed that taking a leak is so important, but these days, every drop is a step closer to home.

Dawn calls me at work; she is not happy, Curtis' room is trashed, and she gets after the nurse about it—another new nurse, who also knows nothing about caring for Curtis' eyes. Dawn is very upset that Curtis' eyes are so dry. I really wish she would be nice to his nurses, and she knows I feel this way, but she couldn't keep her mouth shut about his messy room.

Dawn says she doesn't know how I can be nice to these people. I explain it to her again. I am so afraid human nature will kick in when we are not here. I do not want to bicker with anybody, particularly his nurses, and have them take it out on Curtis when we are gone.

I also tell her I am worried about all these new nurses taking care of him. She asks why. "He has issues from head to toe. How can somebody notice something different from one day to the next if they've never seen him before? How will they know what is normal for him? How can they keep up with all the medications and doses?"

She tells me she's had the same concerns, and she is glad I noticed because she wasn't going to say anything. She doesn't want me to have more to worry about, but now that I have noticed it on my own, she is going to say something. "Thank you." She goes on to say that having consistent caregivers is an important factor in healthcare.

She still puts eye drops in his eyes and continues to wonder why they aren't putting a thicker ointment in his eyes, and she makes sure I know to put eye drops in his eyes and massage his eyelids when I am there. He loves it.

She stays at the hospital until shift change. That gives me until seven to mess around with the pool again. I have so much suction that I can barely move the vacuum. The shock has already eaten up a good bit of the algae. While I am vacuuming, every two passes or so, I have to shut the whole thing off and drain the basket on the pump because there is so much debris. I spend every minute of the next two hours cleaning the pool. I am so proud of myself.

I get to the hospital at eight and tell Curtis about it all night long. "I cleaned the pool." I leave the pump running all night, but there is nothing to agitate the water, so it doesn't do much, other than run up my electric bill.

Those garden-hose ties are really tearing up Curtis' face. They're so tight that they're scraping his skin away and splitting his lips open. His mouth bleeds almost spontaneously, and it is hard to stop. My sister started asking about blood clotting tests. Have they done any? Well, in the lawful world of Memorial Hermann, HIPAA forbade her answers to those questions.

I always have a long list of questions to ask doctors when and if I see them. Sometimes it will be days before I see a doctor, so the questions always pile up—blood clotting tests, the eyes, the bloody mouth, the torn up face, it never ends. In the absence of any doctors, we repeat our concerns to the nurses. There is a new face every twelve hours. Some of the nurses say they'll tell the doctors. Some offer their opinions. "Oh, his eyes are fine; Visine is all you need." We get conflicting answers every time we open our mouths. You'd think, by now, we'd learn to keep our mouths shut, but we just can't help ourselves.

Now, I don't want to give anybody a bum rap. Dr. Doom and Gloom and Dr. Soap Opera are nice young men and great doctors. Dr.

Doom and Gloom just got stuck with this unfortunate nickname because he drew the short straw and happened to be on the floor when I was, and he got to answer all my questions. It isn't his fault that this always happened on grim days. Dr. Soap Opera is gorgeous; he looks like he just stepped off the set of General Hospital. Both of them were very tolerant; they seemed amused by my nicknames for them.

And they both talked to my sister. They are intelligent, reasonable people. Never did either one of them stab our hearts with HIPAA. They were never caught up in the politics and the fracas. If it were just my sister, Dr. Plastic Surgeon, Dr. Doom and Gloom, Dr. Soap Opera, Dr. Gut, and Drs. Infectious Disease, this would be a different book. I like Dr. Soap Opera and Dr. Doom and Gloom, and I wish Curtis could keep them forever. Dr. Doom and Gloom is going to specialize in Urology and I can't remember what Dr. Soap Opera is going to be when he grows up. They are both residents on the burn unit at Memorial Hermann during April 2003.

My sister spends the night at the house. She'll pick Jackie up from the airport in the morning. Then Jackie will drop Dawn off at her class, and Jackie will find her way to our house in Curtis' truck. Jackie's friend will fly in later tomorrow to stay at the house, as well.

Dawn will take the bus to the hospital after class, and I will drop her at her car when we leave tomorrow night. Parking is expensive everywhere in the Med Center. The lot she uses at the university is free after nine o'clock at night, so she leaves her car there, takes a free bus to the hospital, and I take her back to her car when we leave at night.

Curtis is scheduled for his third skin graft today, and they are going ahead with it. To me, this means he is back on schedule. He is back to where he was supposed to be in March. He should have been having this surgery March twenty-seventh, or thereabouts. That means we are only thirteen days behind schedule. Instead of thirty-five days in the hospital, he'll be here forty-eight. Let's throw in an extra five days, since he's in a coma. Fifty-three days and he'll be home. That puts him home the last week of April. Only three more weeks to go. No problem. We can make it. I can see the finish line.

Curtis leaves at two for his skin graft. My sister gets there late in the afternoon after her class.

When I get home from work, some woman I don't know is vacuuming my floor. I say, "Oh, no, please don't do that! You don't have to do that at all! Relax and enjoy the pool!" Jackie's Friend says, "Absolutely not, I came here to help," and turns the vacuum back on. Now you see, that's how a Yankee does things! There is no getting around the fact that we are pickle jar people. I would do exactly the same thing if I were Jackie's Friend.

I once again have to ponder what is wrong with Curtis' family. If this had happened to one of Curtis' brothers, I would be at his brother's house, mopping his floors and watching his children, so his wife and brother could take care of him.

My parents dropped everything on a moment's notice and drove all through the night to get here, simply because I asked.

Dawn postponed her education and graduation by dropping classes to help me with Curtis, and I never had to ask. My cousin bought a round-trip plane ticket and left her life for a week to help me. Jackie's Friend did the same. They came over fourteen hundred miles; that's a long way. What if the tables were turned, and I were in the hospital? How would my family be different than they are now? They wouldn't.

I often ponder the behavior of Curtis' family. What did we ever do so wrong to them? You can no longer excuse them with, "They don't know what to do." I asked them, and when Curtis was able, he asked. We asked and asked. It's never too late to do the right thing. This has been going on for over a month.

I give Jackie my credit card and tell her where Wal-Mart is, then I head for the hospital. Once again, I am so glad Curtis is sleeping through this. His right thigh is all bandaged in that red dye stuff, and the lamp is on it. I don't even know where they took the donor skin from. It doesn't seem as though there is anywhere left to get it from. Some came from his chest.

Dr. Lung decided to vacuum his lungs again at eleven in this morning. They removed a lot more "thick, white secretions" and no doubt sent them to the lab. He is on all manner of cocktails at this point, including broad-spectrum antibiotics. The ventilator is now on what they call "bi-level" settings, which I understand is a higher level of support. He is getting 100 percent oxygen, but this does not surprise me, given the day he's had. He still runs fevers. I always check his flow sheet, to see how much he's been peeing, and I'm ever hopeful that his fevers are abating. I can understand blood gasses by now, I can understand most everything on his flow sheet, and it means the world to me.

Another new nurse sees me reviewing his flow sheet. She tells me I am not allowed to look at it, and she turns it face down. I tell her I look at it every day. She *harrumphs* about how they may do things differently on the burn unit, but not while she is on duty. She tells me that I can't look at it unless a doctor shows it to me. HIPAA.

Dr. Doom and Gloom is at the nurses' station, trying to look small. I ask him to stand next to me so I can see how much Curtis has peed. This is just a record of his vitals throughout the day. *I can stand in his room and watch his blood pressure on the monitor, but I'm not allowed to see what it was five minutes ago. That is a crime. According to the experts at Memorial Hermann, once something is written down, I am not allowed to see it. HIPAA.*

HIPAA, HIPAA, HIPAA. Every single person who says they "can't because of HIPAA" is wrong almost every time. HIPAA is nothing more than a common-sense guideline to protect a patient's privacy. It doesn't have a line item that says, "Sister-in-law of co-matose patient is forbidden any access to his status or condition, even with permission of next of kin."

However, HIPAA does state specific requirements like, "Identifying patient information shall not be displayed in public areas." What about that huge dry-erase board in the hallway next to the nurses' station? It isn't even *behind* the nurses' station. It is on display with every patient's name, room number, their doctor's name, when they are having an operation, and what kind of oper-ation. Now that is a blatant HIPAA violation. My sister is forever nudging my elbow and pointing and mouthing, "HIPAA." All over the hospital, she spots violations. They never get it right. Almost every time hospital personnel quoted HIPAA, they were wrong.

They took Curtis' photograph off his door—HIPAA violation. I'm not sure about that one, but that just sucked because it is there for the medical staff. I already know what he is supposed to look like. It is there so they will know when their job is done. It is their road map.

We've seen no improvement in the staffing situation. Curtis has no consistent caregivers at all. They don't think it's a serious issue, like it doesn't matter if he never has the same nurse two shifts in a row because they are all qualified nurses. I don't care what they say. I can see the problems it's creating for Curtis and the resulting breakdown in his care. I want him to have a regular rotation of nurses, and I expect them to take this seriously. He is critically ill, and this is creating setbacks for him. I can't let it continue. Tomorrow afternoon, Dawn and I are going to meet with Mitzi, the useless grape, and her boss, Lorna*, the unit director.

Several weeks later, I get a nursing publication in the mail with a lengthy article about all the benefits to the patient when they have consistent caregivers. I think of a couple things they missed. I should've written that article. I'll bet I can Google right now and find some articles about it.

When this is over, I am writing a book.

When I get to the hospital at eleven, Curtis is gone. His nurse—another new one—says they've taken him for a HIDA scan. "A who-da-what?" And he says, "A HIDA scan, a nuclear test to examine the abdomen." I ask, "What for? What are they looking for?" I have my own suspicions about housekeeping issues in the gut. He says he doesn't know what they are looking for. "Which doctor ordered it?" He doesn't know. He looks in the chart, but he can't make out the handwriting. At least they are taking a look at the gut. Maybe they'll finally take that drain out, since it isn't draining any more.

Dawn comes over on the bus. We have our meeting with Mitzi and her boss and express our concerns regarding all the new nurses. We point out how sick he is and how a new person who's never seen him before won't know what is normal for him. They won't know something is different from yesterday. Our concerns are never passed along to the doctors because the nurse is only working for twelve hours and then they're outta here. It is a huge concern for us and we expect them to at least make an effort to get him a more regular rotation of nurses. A new nurse every shift is unacceptable. They assure us that our concerns are important to them. They are doing the best they can, but that they are all qualified ICU nurses and it actually helps to have a "fresh set of eyes."

We present a list of fourteen nurses, more than enough to cover a week of shifts. Dawn and I have spoken to several trauma float nurses who indicated they would like to care for Curtis because they would know from one day to the next when they are working. This is a problem with an easy solution. Dawn and I present the solution, and we are ignored.

At shift change, I take Dawn back to her car at the university parking lot. She can't find her keys. Earlier in the day, she walked along all the street-front businesses, trying to get donations for a school event. She thinks she might have left them on a counter or something. They aren't in her purse, they aren't in her backpack, she has no pockets. My sister is notorious for locking her keys in her car.

She calls her insurance company to send a locksmith. She gives them precise directions—the tenth floor of this university parking garage, one of dozens of parking garages in a city block. We wait an hour. She calls to check for an update. The locksmith is on his way. It's another hour before he shows up. I tell Dawn as soon as he gets it open, the alarm is going to go off, so she should check the trunk, and I'll check inside the car. He opens it in two seconds. The alarm goes off. She checks the trunk while I check the glove box and interior. It is really dark in the garage, and even darker inside the car. I feel more than I look. She has a ten-pound key ring, the style that was so popular in the eighties. It'll be hard to miss. No keys. They aren't in the trunk. Should we call our brother and have him bring us her spare set? That will take two more hours. It is almost nine, and the parking garage is going to close for the night. She has no choice but to come home with me. We'll figure it out tomorrow. It is too late to go back and see Curtis. We head home. The alarm turned itself off, eventually.

She talks about her keys all the way home. What could she have done differently? She should have had our brother bring her spare set to begin with. She is so sorry to have kept me there in the parking garage. All the way home, she talks about her keys. We get home and sit on the couch, and I get to hear the key story again because Jackie has to have an update. Where can her keys be? I tell her to turn her entire backpack upside down. Out fall her keys.

I call the nurses' station to check on Curtis before I go to bed. He has another new nurse who won't tell me his vitals or anything, just that he's "stable." Mitzi or Lorna didn't bother to call and let us know that he has another new nurse tonight. They probably knew right at that meeting he was going to have another new nurse tonight. They just wanted us to shut up and go away.

I have to take Dawn back to her car, so I leave work early again. When I get to the hospital in the late afternoon, Curtis has another new nurse! The floor is full of nurses we know, but none of them are taking care of Curtis.

Curtis' vent settings have increased over the past couple of days. Nothing too dramatic, but he is supposed to turn that corner and start running. This is not going according to plan. This has been the history of his hospitalization. Two steps forward and three steps back. His fevers haven't been as steep lately. He always throws me a little something like that, like a little wink to let me know he'll be home soon enough. These reduced temperatures are a wink from Curtis.

I tell Curtis the key story. I finally have something new to say to Curtis. I write "keys" on the calendar for yesterday. This is a bona fide event. I never have anything new to tell him, so this key story is added to the play list of events to repeat to him. Dawn lost her keys, but it turns out she really didn't, and I know how to clean the pool.

I hang a picture of the pool, sparkling like a diamond, above his head. I also have a picture of the living room taped to the ceiling. In case he opens his eyes, I want him to see home. And I am pretty proud of the pool. You can ask Smitty. He thought it was lost forever. We have been surrounded by miracles, and turning that filthy pool into an inviting swim is another miracle.

Dawn comes over after classes, Dr. Doom and Gloom comes to give us an update. They cultured the secretions from Curtis' lungs. He has acquired a bacteria called *acinetobacter*. Another uninvited guest. They have to repeat this several times. I write it on the calendar, "ass in knee toe bacter." Otherwise, I won't be able to pronounce it when I tell Andy it is in his lungs.

In itself, acinetobacter is not a harmful germ. If we had it in our lungs, we would simply cough it up. Curtis cannot cough. Problem number two is that it is a "resistant" bacteria. In other words, this bacteria just keeps growing and multiplying in his lungs. It's suffocating him, and antibiotics will not kill it. They took cultures and tested different antibiotics against it in a Petri dish in the lab. Curtis has a very resistant strain. Dr. Doom and Gloom lists the types of antibiotics they are trying to use against it. I ask if Infectious Disease has seen him. He says no, the burn doctors are prescribing his medications.

Curtis is now on "contact isolation." We have to gown up in hefty bags before entering the room. *Just like Mrs. Mexico!* We have to remove all hefty-bag clothing before we leave the room. *Oh no, not again! Here we are, following in Mexico's footsteps all over again.* I rack my brain trying to remember how many days I saw Mrs. Mexico in hefty bags before he died. They all ran together. It wasn't very long

Curtis is coming home. Why are they making him work so hard? The end result is going to be the same: I'm taking him home. The more grim things get, the more I dig my heels in. Curtis is coming home, he is coming home alive, and he will be just fine. They try their darndest to prove me wrong. I know him best and he's coming home. I'm realistic enough to realize there is only so much a human body can take, but Curtis has yet to tell me he's had enough.

They take him for another CAT scan of his abdomen. His belly is puffy. There are issues in his gut. I know it, but nobody can figure out what is wrong. Curtis is septic, which means he has bacteria in his blood. He has been this way for a while, and who knows what else is infected. He's been on antibiotics and had non-stop raging fevers for weeks. Now acinetobacter is in his lungs, suffocating him.

They have started him on Amikacin, the only antibiotic that their lab tests show to have any effect. The whites of his eyes are getting yellow again. He is down to fifty percent oxygen on the ventilator, saturating ninety-eight percent, so he is doing well, but if they can't wean him from the hose very soon they will have to put a trach in. I am no longer afraid of a trach; his poor face is a mess. Those ties have sliced his lips multiple times, his chin and cheeks have pressure sores on them and are bleeding. I am ready to get that hose out of his mouth. If it has to go into his neck, so be it. I'm sad because I think that means he'll have a mechanical voice for the rest of his life, but Dawn says, "No. Once he's off the trach, that hole will close, and you'll never know he had it."

Well, that has been the reason I've been scared of this trach business all along; I thought it was permanent. I sure wish somebody had told me this a long time ago. It might have spared him some face destruction, thank-you-very-much. But they wouldn't have put a trach in just because I told them to, anyway. They never do anything I suggest.

Heck, yeah! Put the hose in his neck. Look at what it's doing to his face!

It isn't going to happen over the weekend. Nothing ever happens over the weekend if they can help it. We don't ask our usual litany of rapid-fire questions. This acinetobacter and hefty bag business has pretty much swept the world out from under our feet. I have long since trained myself out of exhausting crying fits. Often, though, the tears will flow on my way home. Instead of a runny nose I have runny eyes. Tears stream down my face like rivers. I have to lift up my glasses and wipe them so I can see, but they just keep coming. I often drive home with tears streaming down my face. Tonight is no different.

"Must get off garden hose" is still at the top of my list. *Yeah, we need to get right on that.* I get home and update my cousin. I run through the entire nightmare from day one. She's another listener. All she can do is sit there with her mouth open for several minutes. She clamps it shut with her hand, and says, "I had no idea. I don't know what to say."I said,

In a popular movie, the dad thinks Windex cures everything. By the time I catch Jackie up, it is late and we are a bit punchy. I ponder, "Why don't they just pour Windex in his lungs?" We laugh until we cry. But seriously, why can't they just put antibiotics right into his lungs?

She asks, "How long he can live like that?" I'm sure the whole thing sounds pretty grim to her, and in a very delicate, roundabout way, she is wondering if it is getting close to time to unplug him. Well, I "get" where she is starting to go and cut her off immediately. I know those kinds of questions might be lurking in my future. I've known it since hose day one. I knew it on stroke day. It is a sore subject, a sleeping beast that is never going to be awakened. I tell her he is still Curtis, and he is coming home. He will be just fine. He isn't trapped by the hose forever. Another sleepless night. I study a photo of Curtis and me in Las Vegas. I try to remember the sound of his voice. I try to remember what he is like as a healthy person, his mannerisms, the way he walks, something. I can't remember. Nothing.

He isn't going to die there like this, he isn't. This is not going to be my last memory of him, rotting away in that bed.

They moved his central line again. I'm sad that I didn't get to see him awake. I wish they would move that line while I'm there. They also flushed his abdominal drain. I guess the CAT scans must've shown there is still something in there, but I haven't seen anything come out of it for several days. I keep asking why they keep it in, but it is up to Dr. Gut to remove it and nobody else knows anything.

He has a couple more X-rays today. I am starting to worry he is going to get cancer from so many X-rays. I've lost count. Bags of blood are almost always hanging with all his cocktails. I ask how many bags of blood he's had. Nobody knows. *Mental note: Ask Karen Vidor. I bet she can find out. Somebody has been paying for it.* My sister gave blood, more than once. My coworkers gave blood, and I'm sure his coworkers did, too. These are things that happen to the pickle jar people, not us quiet, low-key folks. This is not my world. This is not Curtis' world.

Dr. Plastic Surgeon crosses my path outside the burn unit. He says his current course of action is to dry Curtis out. They've been infusing him with fluids frequently to stabilize his blood pressure, but they are not going to do that anymore. They will treat his blood pressure with blood pressure medication only. He says he can support the kidneys but he can't support his lungs, so his plan is to sacrifice the kidneys to save the lungs. They'll dry him out to try and kill all this bacteria.

OK, bring on dialysis; I am not worried about the kidneys. Curtis can take whatever they can throw at him. His desire to come home is much more powerful than his sickness. He can take it. One of his family members can finally do something useful and give him a kidney if he needs one, and that is that. So long kidneys, you've served us well. Curtis has no idea how sick he is, he hasn't a clue. He just wants to come home.

Priscilla and her husband stop by with a basket of goodies for the kids and another parking pass. I give them the update. They don't stay long. It seems it is never good news.

He was doing better earlier in the week. What happened? It has to be the gut. What was I thinking? You can't just get gangrene scooped out of your guts and get back on your feet. No telling what kind of damage that did. But they have been taking X-rays and CAT scans on a regular basis. Dr. Doom and Gloom shows me the CAT scans. Still looks like a lava lamp to me. I can't tell anything. His tummy is puffy. Sometimes it is hard, sometimes it is soft, but it is always distended. There is something in that gut, there just has to be. Non-stop fevers. F---/damn X-rays. It is relentless.

Dawn tells me not to worry about dialysis. Most people who are as sick as Curtis wind up on dialysis long before this, and sometimes they even lose limbs. Dawn is very proud of Curtis and his kidneys for toughing it out this far. I tell Dawn I'm not worried about dialysis, and Curtis isn't going to need it. I still keep up my usual mantra of relaxing, taking slow deep breaths, the pool is clean, the funny key story, you're missing the war, my cousin Jackie is here, she came all the way from the other side of the country. Over and over. I am getting a pretty good repertoire of stuff to repeat. His room is full of cards and picture the kids have made him. I hang another picture of our house on the ceiling with all the others. Just in case he opens his eyes, he'll see something familiar.

There are four nursing shifts this weekend; two of them are nurses we've never seen before.

My sister calls me at home tonight. She's done some research on acinetobacter. When Dawn started her nursing career, she specialized in pediatric infectious diseases, so I'm all ears. She reads it all to me. She says she'll leave it in the room for me to read. It is all over my head, but what I understand from her is that she thinks Curtis should be on Imipenem. She thinks he surely must be already. She also mentions that this bacteria is very common in burn units and ventilated patients, so Curtis is like a five-star hotel for acinetobacter. I can't help but wonder why isolation precautions weren't taken before he ever got it. Obviously, other patients had it—*Mexico*. I soon find the answer to this question. They don't really take isolation precautions that seriously in this facility.

The vent settings are always up and down. They are trying aggressively to get him off the hose, but in general, he isn't improving. The fevers will not stop. It is a quiet weekend as far as traffic goes, but Curtis wears me out; he kicks my ass. You wouldn't think somebody just lying in bed could keep so many people jumping, but he sure does. I work my tail off.

It hurts me to look at his face, but there is nothing I can do about it. I don't understand why they have to keep his lips tied so tight in that grimace. The paralytic is always up and down, too. They want him off of it, but he just won't cooperate. This is another repetitive task, "Get off the cocktails, Curtis. They keep trying to wake you up, but you have to stay calm. Let them wake you up."

I keep asking how many pints of blood he's had, but nobody knows. Karen doesn't know. I sure would like to know, to be able to tell Curtis. I know it's a lot.

Curtis has another crappy day. His head is turned towards the window when I arrive. There is a huge knot on the back of his head, like a baseball. I ask his nurse, "What is this lump on his head?" She says, "Oh, nothing, that's just his head." I say, "No, it's not. Look at this!" She looks and says, "Oh, yeah, that's just his head. See, feel mine, mine's the same way!" I show her the 'before' picture of Curtis. "You see how he keeps his head shaved? I'm intimately familiar with the back of my husband's head, and that is not his normal head!'' Again, "Oh, yes it is. See, here, feel mine!"

My sister is meeting me at the hospital this afternoon. I leave work early again and get there in the late afternoon. Curtis had his lungs vacuumed again. This time, Dr. Lung has left a photo for me, a photo of the inside of his lungs. Dr. Soap Opera shows me a pink spot and tells me that's what his lungs should look like, but Curtis' are pretty much all red because he has "hemorrhaging bronchitis." That's on top of the raging pneumonia and incurable bacteria. And that's just the lungs.

I have long since come to the realization that I am paying for my sins. There is no doubt about it, and I am as sorry as I can be for everything I've ever done to anyone, intentional or not. But what did Curtis ever do to anybody? Nothing! If he were meant to die from this accident, he would have never made it to the hospital. No human being is meant to suffer like this, to rot away in every grue-some fashion you can think of. Curtis doesn't have a bad bone in his body. I am going to make it right, and he is going to come home.

My sister arrives and we summon Dr. Doom and Gloom. While we wait, she shows me all the stuff she's found from the Centers for Disease Control (CDC). I really appreciate her doing the research because it is certainly over my head, but I just don't understand most of what she is saying. She also has an ample supply of litera-ture about the importance of continuity of care. Well, I don't need to be convinced about that! I don't need to read it—the experts do.

I ask Dr. Doom and Gloom again if the Infectious Disease doctors have seen Curtis yet "No. The burn doctors are prescribing his antibiotics." My sister asks him to supply more eye drops. She doesn't think drops are enough. I don't remember a conclusion other than getting more drops.

Dawn asks about Imipenem. Dr. Doom and Gloom says that Curtis' strain of acinetobacter is resistant to Imipenem. I don't understand most of what she's saying about all this, but I know she has her hopes pinned on Imipenem. It is a deflating meeting. It gets really quiet when he says that Curtis is resistant to Imipenem. You could hear the nail going in his coffin.

My sister has to go to class, I walk her out to the bus stop. We pass Dr. Gut in the hallway. "Hey! Hi Dr. Gut!" He stops and says he just returned from vacation today. He checked on Curtis and determined that the pancreatic pseudocyst was infected, so he got right in there and removed 280 cc of pus.

We've just come from a meeting with the residents, getting an update on Curtis, and nobody bothered to mention this. This is pretty significant. I am trying to wrap my mind around 280 cc. It sounds like a lot, but know it can't be that much. Dawn tells me that 280 cc is more than a can of Coke. I tell Dr. Gut to give me his cell phone number, so I can call him the next time I think something is amiss with Curtis, and he can cut him open immediately. I knew there was something amiss with that darn gut.

That thing stopped draining weeks ago, and all this time there was more infection just festering in there. I am going to write a book when this is over.

I get a call this morning at work. They need to vacuum Curtis' lungs again and I have to give consent. Another bronch. This is two days in a row. They call again, less than an hour later. They are taking him to OR immediately to put in the trach. He is too unstable; if they don't do it right now, this minute, they might not get another chance. I give consent. They have to do it right now. OK.

When I arrive several hours later, I am anxious to get a good look at his poor face and see just how much damage has been done by the garden hose. I turn the corner from the gown room and a bunch of people are outside Curtis' room, all looking pretty busy. I get scared. I lean against the nurses' station. I don't recognize any of these people, and they don't recognize me. I try to look like I have some sort of business and listen and watch. All sorts of strangers are in and out of his room, but none of them are putting on the hefty bags before they go in. This must be an emergency. I guess "droplet precautions" and "contact isolation" don't apply during emergencies.

Equipment is being wheeled into his room. One lady has a package of hoses and stuff. She doesn't seem familiar with some of the parts. She goes into Curtis' room. *No hefty bag!* She comes back out, pointing to something in her kit and asks another stranger, "What is this for?" Another woman explains what the parts are and where they go. Whoever that lady is, I don't want her near my husband. She doesn't even know what the parts are for. They are having quite a conversation about the bag of parts. I want to go tackle Stupid One to the ground so she won't go near Curtis. Nobody is in a hurry, so it can't be much of an emergency.

Somebody finally notices me twitch and asks if she can help me. I feel like I am going to vomit. I tell her I am the patient's wife and I want to know what is going on. She says they are getting ready to perform a tracheostomy. I look confused, so she starts explaining what it is. "I know what it is, but it was supposed to have been done hours ago in the OR." Her only answer to this is for me to go to the waiting room and they will call me.

I don't mention the infection control procedures—I don't want to piss off the people who are about to cut his neck open. It's bad enough that they don't even know where the parts go. I am a nervous wreck.

I guess if you are only going to be in the room a little while and then go to another part of the hospital and carry the bacteria to another patient, then it is OK to enter his room without hefty bags. That must be OK as long as you are leaving the burn unit. Or maybe if you're only there to cut open a patient's neck, isolation precautions don't apply. I guess if you haven't been around any other burn patients, you don't have to follow the rules. Well, I am never around any other patients, and I have to follow the rules.

I guess I must be pretty ignorant about "isolation procedures" and "droplet precautions" because, based on the behavior of the medical staff, I can't tell when you are supposed to abide by the rules and when you aren't. There's no consistency. I keep trying to figure out the logic and the only logical answer is that isolation precautions apply to anyone entering the room.

I go out to chain smoke. I am starting to itch. No more ESP calls from Curtis. Maybe his brain is mush. Maybe he doesn't know who I am. At least his poor face will be able to start healing. I need to buy stock in Newport and Pepsi.

It is more nerve- rattling and terrifying to see all those strangers and their equipment in a flurry of activity around Curtis' room. I am scared of the lady who doesn't know what to do with all those parts. I am pissed they are ignoring infection control procedures— really pissed because this isn't the first time I've noticed it.

I keep thinking about Curtis, telling him to stay calm and relaxed, not to be scared. I know I can't call him on the ESP phone; he can only call me. Maybe I finally am crazy. Itch, itch, itch. Scratch, scratch, scratch. I don't want to go back up until those people are gone; it is too scary knowing they are all there to cut his neck open and put a hose in it. I'm going to vomit if I think about it. Scratch, scratch, scratch. Second day in a row they have to vacuum his lungs. I am losing count of how many times they've done that to him.

I'm glad I've been noting things on the calendar so I can tell him all about it. That was Dawn's idea. By now, the March page is taped to the wall next to the calendar, and April has Xs through it all the way to today. April 15, 2003. Tax day. The digital pictures I've taken of him periodically are all on my wall at work. I framed the picture of his lung and put it on my bookcase. I think those pictures disturb some of my coworkers, but it is all I have of Curtis. I can look at him while I am at work and send him good ESP. This has become the Curtis I know. He is still my husband, and I still love him. I am starting to forget how he is as a healthy person, the sound of his voice, his mannerisms. This is all I have left. These gruesome pictures, in some twisted way, bring me a comfort.

Everybody is gone when I go back up. I put on all my hefty bags and go in. I am no longer allowed to take my backpack in. I live out of my backpack. My digital camera is still in it. Dr. Soap Opera tells me how well Curtis did with the trach. His numbers actually look pretty good. I can get a good look at the destruction to his face now; the hose and all the ties are gone. He has pressure sores on his cheeks, and his lips are cut, bloody, and dry. It looks so painful. I ask if they can do something about his face. He sure seems to bleed a lot.

Dr. Soap Opera says they have ordered a rotating bed. It will rotate him from side to side and keep the secretions from plugging his bronchi. Hopefully, that darn left lung will quit collapsing all the time. This is another frustrating moment. Dawn and I have asked both him and Dr. Doom and Gloom on several occasions what the options were to keep his lungs in motion. All we were ever told is that there is an oscillating ventilator, but it can damage his lungs and is only a last ditch effort. It is not a good option. All this time, they've had a rotisserie available to them and we've been asking since April fifth to keep his lungs moving. Ten days.

I get kicked out again when the rotisserie arrives. I call my sister and tell her about the rotisserie. She asks why nobody mentioned it on the numerous occasions we've inquired about the different methods available to keep his lungs moving. Dunno

After a while I head back up. That rotisserie is huge. They've never had a patient in this type of bed in the history of the burn unit. Curtis is making history. *He is going to be full of surprises. Wait until you see him get out of it!*

His legs are parted and confined by bumpers. His arms are splayed out to his sides and held in place with padded bumpers. His head is surrounded by padded bumpers. He isn't going anywhere but back and forth, side to side. It takes a good half hour for his nurse and me to catch all the IV lines and find a spot for everything so his bed can move from side to side without yanking anything out. It isn't easy. By now he is on so many cocktails, there is no more room on his IV pole for any more pumps, and several bags of stuff just hang from the ceiling. He still has a fever. It is quite a sight. It is a photo op.

They are trying to wean him from the sedative, Ativan, so periodically his nurse comes in and dials the pump down. *Blip-blip!* It is another wink from Curtis, "I'm coming, Lisa." I keep talking to him, more excited with each visit from the nurse that he might be able to hear me. More importantly, I want him to wake up while I am still here to explain everything that is going on, so he will stay relaxed and not be scared.

Shift change. Time to get kicked out for an hour. I still don't understand this. If I were a nurse, I'd sure appreciate having my help. By now, many of the new nurses ask me if I work at a hospital. They all gather at the nurses' station during shift change. Nobody is in the patient's room. Why can't I stay? What is so secret and important? It sucks.

I go outside to chain smoke again. I have so much to do. I still have children, a job, a house, chores to do, and errands to run, and none of it ever gets done. This always eats at me when I am kicked out. I waste so much precious time just milling around the hospital and its grounds. This is just another frustrating consequence of our circumstances.

When I came back from shift change, Curtis has another new nurse!

The night is quiet. I notice that his blood pressure goes up whenever he rotates to his left, and it goes down when he rotates to his right. I mention this to the new nurse and he says I am incorrect; his blood pressure goes up when he rotates to his right because it is the opposite side from his heart. I've been watching Curtis go back and forth for an hour and I've noticed the consistent pattern of his blood pressure. I never take my eyes off of him. I record his every moment. I watch this with my very own eyes, but I am wrong.

I decide it's because he has to work harder when he is on his left because that is the lung that keeps collapsing. Maybe it's filling up with clouds right now as I'm watching him.

At my first opportunity, I glance outside in the hallway, ever careful to not actually leave the room as to infect the whole ward, even though the staff does it all the time. It is a quiet night. I can just reach the strap of my backpack with my foot. I drag in my contraband. I drag it all the way over by the bathroom, away from Curtis. I take out my digital camera. I stand at the foot of his bed and take a picture. He will want to see this history-making bed. I slide my backpack back out and change my gloves. I am scared to get too close to him after this, in case my disgusting backpack might kill him. But I keep up my broken record of instructions for him, in case he wakes up when I am not here. I haven't heard from Dr. Kidney Specialist in several days. An ounce of prevention is worth a pound of cure, so I still make Curtis pee frequently.

I have to give the new nurse the endless list of instructions and things to watch for before I leave for the night. If I were Curtis' nurse, I might be a little intimidated. He has a lot of medical issues. He now has what they call a "complicated course." I sure would appreciate hearing from somebody who knows him and who has seen him everyday. They are never interested in anything I tell them, but I still keep it up. You never know what might sink in.

My sister takes Jackie to the airport. I don't remember how we got my sister's car from the university. At work, I get a call from the hospital first thing. They are going to vacuum Curtis' lungs again. This is the third day in a row. I ask them to have Dr. Lung call me when he is done. My husband has been on a ventilator for over three weeks, and I have never had a conversation with his pulmonologist. I've never even seen him, as they do their rounds several hours before the families are allowed in. I always ask to speak to Dr. Lung—every day—but he can never spare the time.

All my questions will have to wait until I can get there, so they can be answered by people who don't know the answers. It is maddening. Is the goop they are getting out of his lungs more or less than before? Is it a different color? Is there more from one lung or the other? I am always full of questions that I can never get answers to. I am still convinced there are gut issues, but I guess nobody can figure out what they are.

Curtis actually looks a little better today. He looks better cared for and more comfortable. Somebody has taken great care in bathing him and shaving him and cleaning his face. There is ointment on all his pressure wounds. There isn't blood all over his mouth. His nurse comes in. It is Sonny. We had her a couple times early on, but it is only now that I realize she's an angel straight from Heaven. All his splints are on. She is pointing things out and telling me she has done this and she has noticed that. Yes, I can see that she notices. She actually cares. Can it be that somebody actually cares? I love Sonny. I want her to be his nurse twenty-four hours a day. What a difference.

She has put Lacrilube in his eyes; it's a thicker, greasy-type ointment that looks like Vaseline. I don't like it because I can't read his eyes as well, but his eyes are starting to get really red. His lids never close. I can tell a lot about him by looking at his eyes. They really are a "window to the soul." This is the thicker grease that Dawn kept asking about. I tell Sonny that my sister and I have been concerned about his eyes for days, but she is the only person who has done anything about them. I love Sonny. It's been a long time since I walked into Curtis' room and could see instantly he is well cared for from head to toe. There was only one other time, and it was so remarkable that I took a picture. I hope a lot of good things come Sonny's way. I can never give this woman enough praise. She's a healer.

I realize a couple hours later that the whole floor seems quieter and more peaceful. It is usually a mess of yelling and screaming and alarms squawking. Lydia is the charge nurse today. I hear Lydia and Sonny talking and I realize they are running the floor. That's why it is so peaceful and quiet. I love them both.

Sonny tells me they are trying to wean Curtis from the paralytic again. I am glad they are doing it while I am here, so I can give him his relaxing instructions. He is still running a fever, but it doesn't go over 102.

After a while, it looks like Curtis' cheeks are inflating and then the air that is trapped in his cheeks blows out his mouth with his lips flapping like he is snoring. I watch, analyze, and think. If a machine is forcing air into his lungs, where is this air in his cheeks coming from? Is the air being blocked on its way to his lungs? I watch the vent. All seems well, but something isn't right. He hasn't done this before. I call for Sonny, and she comes in and "inflates his bag."

Apparently there's some sort of wire or small tube attached to a small bag, and this bag has to be inflated. I'm not sure what it has to do with anything, but that's why his cheeks are inflating and his lips are flapping. I had actually hoped, momentarily, that he was trying to breathe on his own, but that is not the case. This cheek inflation occurs more and more frequently over the next ten days or so.

There is a hard plastic tube going down his neck and a small bag of air outside his neck. I still don't understand what one has to do with another, but whenever his cheeks blow up, it's time to inflate the bag. It has become a bigger and bigger problem, so they eventually changed the cuff, the tubing in his neck, to the Cadillac of cuffs, a Bivona cuff. Instead of having a hard plastic tube in his neck, this Bivona is spongy and forms to his neck, like a custom fit, and it's more comfortable. The Bivona stops the ballooning cheeks and flapping lips.

I'm kicked out for shift change. Again. I go out for my Pepsi and cigarettes and I call Dawn to tell her about the wonderful angel named Sonny. I am pretty relaxed and content. But I know it won't last. I return from shift change and Curtis has another new nurse! Another new person we've never seen before.

Why do they keep doing this to him? Especially on the night shift, when I have to leave him alone. That eats at me like you wouldn't believe. I feel so helpless.

New redheaded night nurse comes into the room to tend to her charge. She has her hefty bag and gloves on, but she has no mask and no hat. You have to put on a hat before you even enter the burn unit. That is not specific to somebody on isolation, so it is doubly important to cover your bacteria-filled hair before you come into Curtis' room. She smiles and says hello. I can't take her to task—she is going to be left alone all night to care for Curtis. I can't make her mad. I know that anything I say is not going to be friendly, so I just have to keep my mouth shut, for his sake. I will say something to the charge nurse when she is out of earshot. I sit in my chair fuming, hoping she'll stay away from him and leave quickly.

She takes a dirty stethoscope out of her dirty pocket and puts it on Curtis' chest. She returns it to her pocket when she is done. *Now she can transfer all that bacteria she just got off Curtis' chest to the next ailing victim.* This is the third violation. Curtis has his own stethoscope that stays in the room because they are trying to control the spread of bacteria. That's why there are signs on the door, "Infection control precautions in place" and "Droplet precautions." These people are supposed to know better than to pull a stethoscope out of their pocket, use it on Curtis, and put it back in their pocket to use on somebody else. If Curtis had a regular nurse, this would not have happened.

It gets worse. She unwraps a new tooth sponge and hooks it up to the suction machine. *Here we go, his mouth is going to start bleeding again.* I know how to brush his teeth and clean his mouth and keep the bleeding to a minimum. She probably doesn't even know how raw the inside of his cheeks are. She doesn't know that what she is doing is going to cause his mouth to bleed for the next hour. She stands over him, brushing his teeth and cleaning his mouth, and yammering about how important dental hygiene is. I don't say a word. I am just hoping she will shut her unmasked mouth, quit breathing on him, and quit dropping droplets of death on him. I can almost see her Miss Clairol #45 drifting into his open mouth and morphing into a new bacteria.

I can't stand it anymore. I jump up and remove all my infectious barrier clothing. Nothing can leave this room. It has to be thrown away in the biohazard can by the door. I find the charge nurse and tell her what red hair is doing in there with no mask and no hat. I start crying before I get three words out. Damn these tears. "Why is she assigned to him if she doesn't know what infection control means? Why do they keep doing this to him?" She says she is sorry, she understands and she will speak to her. I make sure she understands that I'm not mad at Red Hair, and I'm sure she is a great nurse. I don't want to make her mad because Curtis will be alone with her all night. She says she understands, and that she will speak to the Red-haired Killer and bring her up to speed on the classes she missed regarding the spread of bacteria from one patient to the next.

I never go looking for trouble. I head to the hospital almost every day in a positive mood, hoping to see some improvement in Curtis. One thing after another just smacks me in the face every time. This is supposed to be a top notch facility. Why does an uneducated housewife from the suburbs have to keep reminding them to put a mask on? Signs are posted in the room "Arm and leg splints to be worn at all times," yet I still have to constantly put them on myself. If they don't think the splints are important, and they don't think a mask is important, what else don't they think is important? You have to wonder. It causes me a tremendous amount of anxiety to leave him at night. I have to watch every little thing. Whatever I miss, my sister picks up.

I update Dawn on the new nurse and about her trying to kill Curtis with all those germs. Dawn finds it inexcusable that we don't get any kind of effort to provide consistent caregivers. We never even get a call from anybody, "Hey, we had Curtis scheduled with so and so, but then something happened. I'm so sorry, Mrs. Wright, but he will have a new nurse tonight. I can assure you she is a very qualified ICU nurse." Nothing.

My sister, as a hospital administrator, also looks at it from the revenue side. Curtis is not an indigent case. They are billing thousands of dollars a day for his care. They can afford to throw a few nickels at the problem and get him a regular rotation of nurses. She is finally starting to understand what I've been telling her all along. Nobody cares. Curtis has been here a long time and somebody needs to start treating us better. They never do. Dawn is disgusted for her profession.

Curtis has been lung vacuumed again first thing this morning. Dawn doesn't have any information about it, other than he got vacuumed again. HIPAA. This is the fourth day in a row they've Hoovered his lungs. Curtis has another new nurse, a guy named Jason*. Dawn hopes I don't mind, but she tracked Mitzi down. She told her, "We are no longer asking, we are telling you that you **will** provide Curtis with a consistent rotation of nurses. We demand it."

I sure hope that made her feel better, but I know it isn't going to accomplish anything. They'll bring out their smooth talkers to twist us into crazed, hysterical women. But there is no excuse for this.

Twila calls me at work later in the day and asks if she can do anything. "No." I don't even want to talk to her. She is useless, and I am pissed. She keeps prodding me. She understands there was a problem last night with a nurse. I tell her, "The problem with the nurse isn't the problem, it is a symptom of the problem. And no, you can't help me. Nobody in your empire can help me because nobody really gives a damn about fixing any problems, they just want me and my sister to quit our bitching." She assures me that isn't the case, and she is here to help in any way she can. Well, that finally tears it for me. All I ever get out of this woman is words, words, words—never any action. Now I'm on a slow burn.

I remind her that I've asked her for help almost since day one with the whole family issue. "You can't even help him get a **nap!**

How **dare** you call me!" I remind her about our repeated requests to the unit manager and the unit director for consistent caregivers. I tell her all the reasons why it is so important. I tell her about the splints never being on, and about the educated world-class staff that keep coming into his isolated room without the proper attire, pulling stethoscopes from their pockets and breathing all over Curtis.

I remind her about all the times I've left messages and asked somebody to have Dr. Lung talk to me. "I still to this day have never had a conversation with Dr. Lung. I can go to the doctor with a sore throat and have a lengthy chat with him, but the man who has my husband's life in his hands can't find the time to speak to me, not once in over three weeks, and I've asked **every single day**. I want to talk to Dr. Lung!" Dr. Plastic Surgeon always answers as many questions as he can, but when it gets to the lungs, he always defers me to Dr. Lung, who I can never speak to. It is an endless circus. "My sister is trying to help me get Curtis home, and nobody will speak to her at all. They throw HIPAA in her face. It is hostile, insulting, and downright cruel. What is **wrong** with your hospital?"

I remind her about the unit manager assuring me that Mean Nurse would never be Curtis' nurse again and then denying she ever had that conversation with me. "That woman is the manager of a **f---ing burn unit**. The whole floor is full of people who are burned, maimed, and scarred for life, if they even live. Why are we constantly being treated like we are annoyances? Curtis is going to **die** in that hospital because of something stupid that somebody neglected or was never aware of. I can see it as clearly as I can see the shoes on my feet, but nobody will listen and nobody will do a thing to prevent it. How **dare** you call me and tell me you can help, you are **worthless**!" By the time I am finished, I am in my office yelling.

I have nothing else to say. Twila says she will speak to Mitzi about the nursing. I tell her that she is wasting her breath on that useless, heartless woman. Mitzi will never lift a finger to help Curtis. She has no business being within a hundred miles of caring for burned people. She is a bureaucrat. Twila says she will speak to Lorna. I remind her that we've already spoken to Lorna and we've provided a list of fourteen nurses that she can rotate for Curtis. Several of these nurses would be grateful for the steady work, yet Curtis keeps getting new nurses! Not a word to us, just a steady stream of strangers every twelve hours. She says she will make some calls and if I ever feel the need to yell at anybody again, she is here for me, okay?

Oh, why do I even bother? I don't feel the need to yell at anybody. I am tired of repeating the same stories that are so upsetting. It is getting so old. I am sick and tired of people telling me they can help when I know they won't or can't. She doesn't get it at all. I'm not looking for a friend; I am looking for results.

I don't feel any better. I am just angrier because I know the problems will never get fixed.

About an hour later, Dawn calls again and says the Infectious Disease team is outside the room reviewing Curtis' chart. Finally, somebody called for Infectious Disease. My sister asks me if I want her to talk to them. "Hell, yes!" She says, "That's what I thought. I've been waiting in the hallway for them to finish their rounds. Mitzi told me I have to wait inside Curtis' room because of HIPAA. I told her I am staying in the hall because I don't want to miss them." Mitzi tells her that HIPAA dictates she has to wait inside the patient's room, and says she will send them in to talk to Dawn when they are done. Well, this is when Dawn calls me, because she knows Mitzi will not send Infectious Disease into Curtis' room. Dawn tells me to call administration and make sure somebody there knows that she has permission to talk to the Infectious Disease doctors before they leave.

I call Twila back. Here is her big opportunity to put her money where her mouth is. This should be an easy task. I tell her everything Dawn just told me. I tell Twila that if she really wants to help she will call up to the burn unit and make sure my sister speaks to the Infectious Disease team. She starts to say something about HIPAA, and I retort, "HIPAA, my ass! I'm the wife of a comatose man, and I'm telling you to let them talk to my sister! You have my permission! Fax me something and I'll sign it!" She says she'll see what she can do.

Dawn calls me a short while later and says that Infectious Disease left without talking to her. We are both boiling mad. This man's life is in their hands, and we want to talk to them!

Dawn and I make a row about it with administration all day, but to no avail. Neither one of us gets to speak to Infectious Disease. My sister's specialty is infectious disease.

The case manager for the insurance company gets to sit down once a week with all Curtis' doctors, Mitzi, Lorna, and everybody involved in his care, but I am never allowed in these meetings. I am never even given the opportunity to speak to all his doctors, unless I am lucky enough to be in the hallway to trip over them. I have to beg and plead and pester, and I still can't talk to his doctors. My husband has a machine breathing for him, his lungs are so full of clouds they had to be vacuumed on a daily basis now, and I have never even said hello to Dr. Lung. It becomes a running joke. Nurses ask if I've spoke to the elusive Dr. Lung today. Nope, I've never had the privilege. I'm never quiet about my desire to have a conversation with Dr. Lung, I tell anybody who will listen to please have him call me. I've thought he is a jerk ever since the day his nurse told me, "He left. He said he didn't have anything to say to you." He reinforces my opinion with each passing day of silence. I don't care what kind of superstar pulmunologist he is; I think he is a crappy doctor.

My sister leaves the hospital at three-thirty to meet the kids at home. I come home after work, and she repeats pretty much everything I already know about the day. I am fuming.

I get to the hospital to start my evening shift. Curtis' vitals all look good and they stay stable. He seems to have picked up some momentum over the past couple days. Maybe it is all the lung vacuuming. Dr. Lung has left three-color photographs of today's vacuuming. I don't know what the inside of a healthy lung is supposed to look like, but I can guess this isn't it. It doesn't look good. But these pictures went into frames and onto my bookshelf at work.

I never hear about the kidneys. I haven't for days. I don't know if Dr. Kidney Specialist has stopped seeing Curtis or what. I always check his flow sheet, and he keeps putting out liquid gold like I always tell him to. His fevers have come down, but he still has fever. Not ice blanket fever, though. That is another of the many questions to ask if I ever come across anybody who knows anything. What is the deal with the kidneys? I don't find that person tonight.

I take the day off work. I just know Curtis is on his way, and we are going to spend the entire day getting better. Ken is coming tomorrow and is going to stay for the weekend and cut the grass again. It hasn't been cut since the last time he was here. Any extra minute I have at home is devoted to the pool, and I don't have much time for that.

I get to the hospital at eleven. As soon as I open the doors to the burn unit, I can hear the angels singing. Lydia and Sonny are running the show again. What a difference. Lydia is his nurse today. What a lucky man he is. We are on our way home today!

Curtis has been vacuumed again first thing this morning. Again, none of my questions can be answered. The illustrious Dr. Lung has no time for that. I have been assured all this time that he is the best pulmonologist west of the Mississippi. Even my sister has heard of him. I take some comfort in that, but he isn't the **best** lung doctor because part of being a good doctor is talking to the family. I think he is highly skilled because everyone says so, but he is an arrogant asshole as far as I am concerned. It's not like I want to talk to him ten times a day. Just once per bronch will suffice. Is that too much to ask? Yes, yes it is. Whenever I see a doctor, I better really pick his brain and ask anything and everything I have been storing up because it might be days or weeks before I talk to them again.

I tend to Curtis and start with all my instructions about relaxing and breathing. I yap about cleaning the pool, tell him that

Jackie has come and gone, and that Ken is coming to see him and is going to cut the grass again this weekend. His blood pressure stays on the low side, lower than usual, especially for Curtis because his is always higher than normal. I keep an eye on it, and it becomes worrisome.

It drops to 90 systolic. This is very low for him. I keep trying to stimulate him. I lift his recently grafted leg a little and it rises to 110. His vent is at 50 percent oxygen and he is saturating 98 percent, so that is doing well.

Dr. Soap Opera shows up. I fire all my questions at him, asking the next one before he even finishes answering the last one. He updates me on Infectious Disease. Guess what? Infectious Disease has decided to double his Amikacin and start him on Imipenem! My sister asked about Imipenem on Monday, and we were told it would do him no good. Infectious Disease hadn't even been consulted then. Oh boy, wait until Dawn hears this. They started him on Imipenem, and he is going to get better. She has saved his life. He suffered all week needlessly. She was right. I can't wait to tell her.

I ask about the gut again. I just can't let go of that gut. He says they all think the same thing I do, that there is persistent trouble somewhere, probably in the gut, but he is too unstable to leave the room. They can't even take him for a CAT scan. He's been having frequent onset episodes of rapid oxygen desaturation, not getting enough oxygen, which is why they have to keep vacuuming him. His left lung keeps collapsing with very little warning. If that were to happen on the way to a CAT scan, he would die in the hallway.

Curtis is hovering on the brink of death. There are no two ways about it. He has raging pneumonia with resistant acinetobacter. Sepsis. All kinds of infections. He's recovering from severe burns, cholelithiasis, an infected pancreatic pseudocyst, and some sort of bleeding disorder. His blood won't clot. He just bleeds, and bleeds, and bleeds, mostly from his mouth. And his eyes are really looking foul.

They have signs up around the unit announcing the date that they are moving to the new burn unit in another part of the hospital. How will they move him? Are they going to put him in a plastic bubble to keep germs off him? Now, I am really worried about this move. He will just have to stay put. I don't want him to die while he's moving to another part of the hospital. It is going to be something stupid like this that kills him. I have worked myself ragged to prevent it. I try to stay one step ahead of everything and everybody. I have my sister's CDC printouts and I point to something Dawn circled and ask Dr. Soap Opera if they've tried this word I can't pronounce. He says he'll look at the labs, but that is really something I should discuss with the Infectious Disease team. Well, I'm not allowed to talk to them because of HIPAA, so this is quite a dilemma indeed.

I tell Dr. Soap Opera that Curtis doesn't know how sick he is and that he wants to come home so badly he is going to surprise everybody. They'll see. *Please, Curtis. C'mon, show them what you can do!*

I ask about his eyes, and tell him that Dawn and I put drops in them, and that some nurses put Lacrilube in them and some don't. There is no consistency, and his eyes are getting worse. I ask if Ophthalmology can come and see. He says he'll mention it to Dr. Plastic Surgeon. I finish with my observations of his steadily declining blood pressure during the day. I tell him that when I lift Curtis' freshly grafted leg, his blood pressure comes up a little. He says stimulation is good, and pain is stimulation, every little thing helps. I ask about the kidneys. He reports that they are still watching him, but the kidney's have improved slightly and are holding steady. *That's my Curtis.*

Dr. Soap Opera leaves. Over the next thirty minutes, Curtis' blood pressure keeps dropping. I slap his cheeks. I yell at him. I take the washcloth off his forehead and put the ice bag directly on his head. I am trying everything. It helps a little bit, but not for long. His blood pressure drops to eighty systolic and keeps going down. I don't know at what point bells and whistles are going to start ringing, but I know it will be soon. I pick up his grafted leg and start to bend it at the knee. Now, I know this has to hurt pretty badly, but his blood pressure just holds steady at seventy-five to seventy-seven. This isn't good.

I don't want to tear up his skin graft by bending it too much, so I put his leg back down. Just then, Dr. Soap Opera comes into the room again. I tell him Curtis is losing his blood pressure. He checks the arterial line and says they'll watch him. As Dr. Soap Opera starts to leave I say, "Get ready. The alarms are going to start lighting up. It's coming." I can tell by looking at Curtis that he is drifting away. It isn't condensation in his arterial line or anything like that. He's been sliding down all day.

Dr. Soap Opera no sooner leaves the room than Curtis' blood pressure drops to sixty systolic. The games have begun. An alarm I've never heard before starts going off. On the monitor, a digital heart is flashing and that thing is beeping, just begging somebody to come running. I can't tell you how many times I've wished someone would come running.

Long ago, I naïvely believed that all this equipment comes equipped with alarms, and bells and whistles, and beeps and bongs and quacks because all that noise is meant to get someone's attention. I believe these alarms are going off because something **alarming** is happening and it requires immediate attention. I was so naïve. They never come running, and I don't expect them to now.

I am scared. This is a new sound. I have been watching this all day, and I know something bad is coming. I pick up his freshly grafted leg again and quickly bend it as hard as I can. Just then another floor nurse, comes **running** into the room. I can't believe it. I wish Curtis could see it. They finally come running. Floor Nurse didn't gear up for isolation precautions, either. This is an emergency, and thank the heavens, somebody here knows it. He is at the equipment side of the bed in one giant leap like he's Batman. I sit in my chair and get out of the way before they kick me out.

Batman turns off the alarm, checks the arterial line and starts wrapping the blood pressure cuff around Curtis' arm. Dr. Soap Opera arrives. I know there isn't anything wrong with the arterial line. That is Curtis' blood pressure, what precious little of if it there is. But, they gotta do their thing. The alarm goes off again. The little heart flashes again. Batman turns it off, wraps the cuff around Curtis' arm, and pushes the cuff machine to start inflating to read his blood pressure. The alarm goes off again. Batman turns it off. Dr. Soap Opera leaves to get something, stat!

The cuff machine stops inflating without getting a reading. The alarm goes off again. Curtis' blood pressure is between fifty-five and sixty systolic now. Batman resets the cuff machine and starts inflating again. Alarms go off again. Batman turns them off. Dr. Soap Opera comes back with a bag of new cocktail. The cuff machine stops inflating again. They have a quick meeting of the minds and decide to go find another cuff machine because this one isn't working.

I want to scream at them, "Don't fix the equipment—fix the patient!" But I know if I open my mouth I will be evicted. I am really quiet, sitting in the corner. Every move they make is seared into my brain so I can tell everybody. I am going to watch him die while they worry about the cuff machine.

Dr. Soap Opera must subscribe to the same ESP service that Curtis and I do because he determines that a new cuff machine is not necessary. They have to get this bag of cocktail into him, stat.

Open it wide up and gush it into his veins. Yeah, Good, do that do something quick. To Hell with the no fluids rule. This is a bona fide 911.

Alarm. Reset. Alarm. Reset. It is not going to stop alarming no matter how many times they tell it to. Batman is tracing all the lines coming off Curtis' body, following them to their host cocktail. This goes on forever. Alarm, alarm, alarm. Cocktails on six or eight dual pumps and bags hanging from the ceiling. He follows them all. He finally tells Dr. Soap Opera there are no open ports. There is no available IV to flush him with lifesaving cocktail, I'm no doctor, but I would pick just about anything, unplug it, and plug in the lifesaving fluid.

More people come in the room and I am excused. I go out to chain smoke and scratch my many itches. It is so nerve racking. I am getting no ESP at all. Poor Curtis, it just isn't his fault. He is working so hard, and they make him work so much harder. I go back up after a while, and they have him magically stabilized. My hair must be white by now.

The rest of the evening is fairly quiet. I update the calendar again. Good Friday ends on a quiet note. Eliza is his night-shift nurse. I ask her about the magic potion from the papers my sister has left from the CDC. Elisa shrugs her shoulders. Of course she doesn't know, but I never stop asking.

The kids are at my dad's. I get to the hospital at eleven. Lydia is Curtis' nurse again, so he isn't going to die today because of something stupid. As soon as I arrive, I see that his face and eyes are swollen again and his color is very red. His oxygen saturation and volume are very poor. The ventilator is back up to one hundred percent oxygen. Dr. Doom and Gloom comes in and says he paged Respiratory. Dr. Pinch Hitter is covering for Dr. Lung. As soon as they arrive, they are going to vacuum his lungs again. It is a Saturday, so they have to page people and wait for them to get here.

Dr. Plastic Surgeon arrives in his jogging shorts. This is my biggest clue that this is very grim. Dr. Plastic Surgeon is Curtis' treating physician, but he has nothing to do with actual pulmonary procedures. For him to come in on his day off and not even take time to dress tells me how serious this is. He is chipper and upbeat and doesn't stay long. Maybe he just has to say it is OK to do the procedure, since Dr. Lung is off improving his golf game.

They have stopped the rotisserie bed, so Curtis has finally stopped moving. I put my head on his chest and one arm across him. With the other, I stroke his nappy hair. Give him another one of those hugs that he wanted so desperately eighteen days ago. I can't believe it has only been eighteen days; it seems more like eighteen years. I tell him for the zillionth time, "Stay relaxed and try to take big deep breaths. They are coming to vacuum your lungs again because you can't cough. You have to get rid of the bacteria, Curtis. It just keeps growing. It's just a little dirt. Get it out and you can come home." I stay on his chest, stroking him and talking to him, until some people come in.

It is Ken and some lady. I say hello to Ken, introduce myself to Some Lady, and thank them for coming. Some Lady is Ken's wife. I tell them they are about to vacuum Curtis' lungs again.

Dr. Pinch Hitter shows up. She wants to talk to me. Now we are just waiting for the respiratory techs, who have to be summoned from the softball field. She takes me out to the nurses' station and starts explaining the vacuuming to me. All the risks. She goes on quite a bit about it. She is starting to scare me, but then I realize that this is the seventh or eighth time he's had this done. Maybe she doesn't realize that. I have never realized that this is a really invasive procedure. It has never been explained to me so graphically. She is a good doctor. I am terrified. I sign the consent. I think it is a little late to start having me sign consents for bronchs, but then again, there's no time like the present to start doing things right.

She seems receptive to chatter, so I think about those CDC papers again. I don't want to gown up again to go back in the room just to grab papers, so I briefly explain it to her. She says she can get all the labs they have done on him. "Really?' She says yes, and asks somebody behind the desk to print them out. Five seconds later she has them all. I'm instantly irritated.

I've asked dozens of people for this very information, and I got shrugged shoulders. It took five seconds; everything is computerized.

She explains what everything means. All the drugs they have tested against his bacteria. We get to the most recent one for the acinetobacter. There are about a dozen different drugs in a column. The next column over is a MIC number. I have no idea what this means. In the last column, across from every drug, it says

RESISTANT. Over and over, in big capital letters, RESISTANT. It doesn't take a rocket scientist to figure out what that means—it means that the drug does not kill this bacteria. The very last drug on the list says *Intermediate*. I ask if that means it will kill it. She says no, and shows me some other labs from some other bacteria that say *Susceptible*. Susceptible with a low MIC means it has a good chance of killing the bacteria. I get the feeling that Intermediate isn't much different than RESISTANT.

Bacteria are very smart, and they adapt quickly to their environment. One of the reasons we have these strains of bacteria that drugs can't kill is because we have become a nation of people who don't finish their antibiotics. If you have bacteria and start taking antibiotics, after a few days you've beaten that bacteria down to the point that you don't feel sick. Maybe you forget to finish your prescription. Maybe the antibiotics upset your tummy too much, and you feel better, so you don't take them anymore. We've all done it. Well, you didn't completely kill the bacteria. It's still there. After a couple days, it's figured out how to adapt to its environment and it's made the appropriate adjustments. So the next time it sees Amoxicillin coming down into your belly, it can just smile and wave as it passes by. No effect. Now the bacteria continue to grow and eventually make you sicker, so you have to try a stronger antibiotic. Are you starting to see the pattern? These bacteria are smarter and faster than our best scientists. They can't develop the drugs as fast as the bacteria can overcome them, and if we're not going to finish them anyway, it's a never-ending cycle.

Now, this acinetobacter in itself is not a harmful bacteria. It is also what's known as a "nosocomial infection," meaning that it originates in a hospital. Just a couple days ago, I heard a story on the news about this very topic. There are some nasty, deadly bacteria that are killing people within days. They are attacking major organs, and they are resistant to antibiotics. A significant one has started showing up in locker rooms and health clubs. Microbiologists are starting to see healthy people who are infected with strains of bacteria that they used to see only rarely in circulation in hospitals.

I'm sure there are some technical errors here, but this is my story, this is the information I've been able to glean from my experience, and I am sharing it with you. I'm pretty sure I'm getting the gist of it right. Finish your antibiotics because this could happen to you. It happened all to easily to Curtis.

The respiratory techs arrive with some scary-looking equipment. Mr. and Mrs. Ken come out of the room. We walk to the gown room and Mrs. Ken is wiping tears from her eyes. Ken says she is going to take the kids to the zoo across the street, and he is going to come over later and cut the grass. I tell him he can take the family to the house and the kids can enjoy the pool.

Mrs. Ken heads to the zoo with her kids. Ken and I head for my office, the smoking area. I let him know how much I appreciate him mowing the lawn. Things have been pretty quiet with Curtis' family. I leave messages for Andy when I have an update on Curtis; he never calls me back. I hear from the case manager once in a while about calls she is getting from his sisters, looking for money, trying to intervene in any way they can. I pretty much ignore all that. I don't have the time or the interest.

Ken tells me his aunt, Now Deceased, said she was here one weekend and that they tried to have a family meeting, but I refused. Baloney! Ken's brother, an attorney, has gotten a bunch of phone calls from Curtis' relatives wanting to know if they can hire a lawyer in their state to sue somebody in our state. They want to sue Curtis' employer. They want to have Curtis moved out of this hospital and into their state. Ken says that he heard I've been telling folks, "Ken and I are getting a lawyer." *That never happened*! People have been telling Ken's wife that Ken and I are having an affair. That's why she came with him on this trip—she thinks he and I are having an affair!

I tell Ken to stop talking, I don't want to hear another word. This nonsense is so unnecessary. I guess that Mrs. Ken, after seeing me laying on Curtis and seeing his condition, got over her suspicions real quickly. Those tears in the hallway were probably guilt tears.

I tell Ken that the next time he hears this foolishness he should ask them, "How is getting a lawyer going to help Curtis get well?" They will not be able to answer that because they have never been focused on Curtis getting well. I tell him to go back there and tell all those people to start praying for a miracle and stop all the drama. They are digging themselves a very deep hole. Curtis is going to wake up and find out everything,

There is no telling what else they're up to. I don't want to hear about it. It is a waste of time and energy.

We go back up to see about Curtis. Normally after a vacuuming, his oxygen saturation improves, his volume improves, his blood pressure stabilizes, and everything improves dramatically. Now, even with one hundred percent oxygen, his numbers look poor. He is only saturating eighty percent. His volume is five hundred. What have they been doing all this time? I tell Ken they haven't vacuumed him yet.

Dr. Doom and Gloom comes in and updates us on the kidneys; they are declining again. I say, "I thought they were going to vacuum him." He says they did, and they got a lot of secretions out. "You can't even tell." He tells me, "I know. I wish I had better news for you. We've done everything we can, but he's just not responding, I'm sorry." He leaves.

Ken and I don't know what to say. *No, no, no, this isn't right. It's the gut.* I suddenly need another cigarette really, really badly. I tell Ken I'll be right back. *See, I wasted that time giving pause to all that gossip when I should keep my focus on Curtis.* I go out and smoke, and scratch, and think.

They doubled his Amikacin and bathed him in Imipenem and that was only fifteen or sixteen hours ago. That should be kicking in any minute. If it is going to work, it should kick in at any minute. OK, OK. Curtis took a hard hit and he isn't himself. If it's going to work, we will see improvement by Monday. I'll give him until Monday before I give up hope. I secretly think this is too long, I really figure those drugs will take no less than thirty-six hours but I'm not ready to let him go, so I give him until Monday. Just to be on the safe side, the end of the day Monday. Just to be on the really safe side, 11:59 PM Monday night. Please don't let me be crazy. Why can't they just pour that Imipenem right into his garden hose? Right into his lungs? At this point, it sure can't hurt.

When I get back upstairs, Ken is in the hallway with tears in his eyes. He says he can't take any more; he's leaving. I ask him if he is going to the house. He said he was going to cut the grass. Where else would he be going? They just drove a long way out here. He says, no, no, he is going back home. He can't take it.

If there were ever a man who needed somebody to mow his lawn, it is Curtis Wright. I am very disappointed with him. "OK, 'bye, thanks for coming." Ken never came back to Memorial Hermann.

I stay with Curtis the rest of the day. He isn't getting worse, but he isn't getting any better. I check the cocktails and make sure they are dousing him with Amikacin and Imipenem. You never know, maybe somebody forgot to turn the pump on. No such luck. They have done everything right. I update his calendar. Vacuumed six days in a row. I write "Doomsday," as this is the day Dr. Doom and Gloom said they've done everything they can and he's going in the wrong direction. I want to be sure and tell Curtis about this when he comes home.

At shift change, I head to my lounge. I need to take time to put some lotion on because I sure am itchy. I go through my smoking, scratching, thinking ritual.

OK, I've long since given up on the gut. Everybody in a white lab coat knows I have concerns over the gut. A lot of them agree with me, but nothing can be done about it now that he can't leave the room. We have to clear out those lungs, lickity-split. I'm no doctor, but all I can come up with is to pour Imipenem into his lungs. If we don't see improvement by 11:59 PM Monday night, I am going to insist that they pour Imipenem in his lungs. It isn't going to hurt him. If it kills him, well, 11:59 PM is the deadline, and he is going to die anyway. This is my plan of action.

Curtis declined during the shift change. Dr. Doom and Gloom says he thinks it is time for the oscillating ventilator, Level 5, their last ditch effort. If it is their last ditch, then I know this is really, really bad because I am always so far ahead of them. They always want to wait until it is practically too late. So to say I am getting desperate would be an understatement.

He calls Dr. Pinch Hitter and she recommends some changes in his vent settings. I thought he already had that machine maxed out and red-lined, but they fiddle with it some more. I go to get the CDC papers to compare to the labs and ask Dr. Doom and Gloom about our Windex. The papers are gone. Somebody has thrown them away. No doubt it was another new nurse. They suddenly seem so important. Forget waiting until Monday; he needs help right this minute.

I am desperate. I don't know what else to do, so I finally "take off the gloves." Curtis doesn't know how sick he is. I've never lied to him, but I have conveniently omitted significant statements. Until now.

I get in Curtis' ear and tell him what's going on. I tell him he has some bacteria in his lungs. It keeps growing and creating more and more mucus, and it is suffocating him. I tell him he keeps getting so much mucus in his lungs that his lung keeps collapsing, and they have to suck all the mucus out. I tell him it is just one little germ, invisible to the naked eye and it is killing him. I tell him they have no drugs in the world that can kill this bacteria. I tell him to quit screwing around and stop making mucus. Stop it right now! And get rid of that bacteria.

"It is just a microscopic piece of dirt, when you get right down to it, and it is up to you to get rid of it. Wish it out, will it out, pray it out, spit it out, **make it go away**. Stop making mucus. Open your lungs. Get that bacteria out! It's going to kill you, Curtis and it's just a little piece of dirt you can't even see. It's not worth it."

I keep telling him this, over and over. No more relaxing, no more clean pool, no more nothing. I am whispering in his ear, but it isn't the usual loving, soothing whispers. I am pissed and I expect him to snap to and pay attention and get that bacteria out of his lungs. "Make those drugs work, Curtis. **Get it out!**"

His temperature rises to 101. The fever has begun again. I am glad. That means he hears me and is trying to kill the bacteria. Another wink. There are so many coincidences like this. I swear he hears me. Either that, or I am crazy. There's only one way we are ever going to know for sure.

At eight-thirty, they bring up the oscillating ventilator. It is like an ugly monster sitting in the hallway. This is Level 5. There is no Level 6. All this ugly monster does is treat the symptom, not the problem. I don't want it. It is the most vile-looking thing I've ever seen in my life. In reality, it doesn't look much different than the vent he is on. It's the symbolism. Suddenly those CDC papers seem really critical. There is no way I can stand to see Curtis go from Level 4 to Level 5, because that might mean I'll have to see him go from Level 5 to Heaven, and that is not going to happen as long as I have breath in my body.

I get in Curtis' ear again and remind him this bacteria is killing him. "Don't let it get you Curtis. All we're talking it a microscopic piece of dirt. Wish it out. Will it out. Pray it out. Get it out of your lungs, Curtis. Work on it all night long. It better be gone when I get back tomorrow. Stop making mucus, Curtis, stop it **right now**! Tomorrow is Easter Sunday, Curtis, and churches are going to be full of people all over the country praying for you. Work with them!"

I go home. I don't even call Dawn with an update. I have to stay focused. I can't get on the internet fast enough. The computer keeps crashing. I suddenly wish I had paid a lot closer attention to all the medical and technical details my sister told me because this is all Greek to me. I search for anything I can find on *acinetobacter baumanii*. I don't really learn anything new. Burned and ventilated patients are its favorite places.

It takes forever to get to the CDC website. I really have to spend some time reading carefully to get to where I want to be. They have case studies and statistics on successful and unsuccessful treatments of acinetobacter. The people that died were older than Curtis, but it is definitely a popular bug in burn units and in intubated patients. It's probably the most popular. Finally, I find information about the drugs. I learn about the MIC number and what it means. If a drug isn't effective, that is the end of the story. If it is effective to a certain degree, that has something to do with this MIC number. The number tells you how well the drug will work. Figuring out this MIC number is clearly a factor. There isn't just a list of drugs and MIC numbers like I saw on his lab paperwork at the hospital. I want to look for Cipro, for example. I know this drug as Ciproflaxin. Well, it isn't listed like that. It is listed in families, or types of antibiotics, so I have to do more research to determine what family of antibiotic Cipro is to see how it performs. It is very, very technical, and completely over my head. But I am a desperate woman, and I have to keep plugging away.

After many hours of this and many scribbled notes to myself, I am actually getting a crash course in microbiology. I glance at my scratch pad and am impressed. It looks like something my sister would write while working on her homework. All these big impressive words, and I have a vague idea what they mean. Back to business. After all this, I come up with only two that, as far as I can tell, they haven't tried on Curtis. Both are pretty much guaranteed to destroy his liver. One has a better MIC than the other, and I've also seen it on a few other websites. I've found his Windex. It is Doxycycline.

I call Dr. Doom and Gloom. I am so excited. I ask him why they haven't tried Doxycycline. He says it won't work. But he said the same thing about Imipenem. I tell him, "They haven't even tested it! This could be our Windex!" He wishes he could tell me it will work, but it won't. The hospital has seen this bug before, and Doxycyline is not going to work. He is sorry, but they have done all they can.

"Well, there's still the chance that the new antibiotics can kick in within the next twenty-four to thirty-six hours, right?" He says, "There is always that hope, but we have to make it that long first."

I am stunned. Nobody ever actually came out and said Curtis was within hours of being dead. Yeah, you have to spell it out for me. I thought machines could keep people alive forever. No way. I hang up the phone, speechless.

The house is quiet, yet I hear a deafening roar. I see Curtis' guitar on the wall, a picture of us in Las Vegas. There is no way he is not ever coming back to this house. Of course he is coming back.

The roar gets louder. I start crying. I start chain smoking. I have to get out of our room and all these reminders of an alive Curtis. I pace around the house with a box of Kleenex, talking right out loud to Curtis. Everywhere I go, I see reminders of him and I just can't believe he isn't coming back. I'm not crying frustration tears, I am bawling like a baby. Sniveling and muttering and everything. I am a mess. He caught me totally off guard with this. I pace, and cry, and smoke. My ears are still roaring.

"They're wrong, Curtis, prove them wrong. Stop that mucus and come home. You have to come home." I am talking right out loud through my tears and snot. "I'm not crazy. I know I'm not crazy. You are coming home." I am saying this right out loud, crying like a baby, when I have that thought again, *You may not think you're crazy, but if anybody saw you right now they'd sure think you were.*

I try to stop my sniveling. I've started to itch again. I need to talk to somebody. Bless my sister, I know she sees the writing on the wall. I know she will be kind, but that she will gently prepare me for his death. I can't listen to that. I don't want to listen to anyone, but I need to talk to somebody.

I call Ginger, the only other person I've talked to daily. She is ever the optimist—not just about this—she's always positive about everything. I tell her what Dr. Doom and Gloom said, and start crying again, "I just can't believe, cannot believe, Curtis isn't going to come home." She says, "The only time to give up hope is when hope is gone, and that's when he's dead. He's alive right now, and he'll be alive tomorrow, and he'll be alive the day after that."

That snaps me out of my blubbering. Of course Curtis will be here tomorrow. Dr. Doom and Gloom just doesn't know him. Curtis will still be here tomorrow. She is right. I should have known better than to give that statement a second thought. I tell her I expect to see these new drugs kick in by the end of the day Monday. I can't tell her 11:59 PM Monday—she might raise an eyebrow and think I'm wacko. I have been thinking that all day anyway, and I am sticking with the plan. We chat a little about Easter. I have to make my children's Easter baskets so I get off the phone. Now I am excited again.

End of the day Monday, pour the Imipenem in his lungs. Stay with the plan, Lisa.

I have forgotten what his voice sounds like. I have a hard time remembering a lot of little things about him. I stare at pictures of him and try to bring back something—his voice, anything. I still have his cell phone. Dawn calls it all the time to listen to his voicemail greeting, "Hi, this is Curtis, please leave me a message." She encourages me to call it, too, but I just can't. I am afraid it will make me sad and get me off track.

Once I finish the Easter baskets, I am exhausted. The crying episode wore me out. I head for bed, feeling numb. What a waste of precious energy. I start to fall asleep almost immediately.

As I'm drifting off, I hear Curtis say, in his gentle voice, as clearly as if he were lying next to me, "I'll see you tomorrow, Sweetheart."

He is going to be fine. I heard his voice. I had forgotten what it sounded like. I couldn't have made that up. *I can't wait to tell him about all this psychic stuff.*

I call the nurses' station. I ask Elizabeth, his nurse, how he is doing. His volume is 700 and he is saturating 98 percent. Wow, that's a big difference. I don't even ask about fever because I expect him to have one. He has a lot of bacteria to kill. I say, "Wow! Level 5 kicked right in, huh?" She says no, they never had to hook it up!

Today sucked, but it sure ends on a good note. Curtis is on his way home at long last. I'm not insane, after all. That's a relief, too. I have to keep this good momentum going, so I send him ESP about getting the bacteria out until I fall asleep. I'm sure I send it in my sleep, as well.

Day 47: Sunday, April 20, 2003 — Easter

I arrive in Curtis' room at eleven. Lydia is his nurse and she has no other patients. Curtis looks wonderful. His vent is at 100 percent oxygen. Lydia says they've had it down to 70, but they had to turn it back up because they were moving him around. His fever stays below 99 all day. It is a pretty quiet day; I even get a nap. We listen to BeBe and CeCe all afternoon. I watch him and I just know I am witnessing a miracle. You can feel it in the room. He has a good day.

For the first time in a week, they don't have to vacuum his lungs. There is talk of it, but it never happens. The drugs are working; I knew he could do it. I am very, very proud of him. That vile Level 5 machine has been rolled into Mexico's empty room. I hope they'll move it back to the dungeon. Easter Sunday 2003 is a blessed day.

The only bad thing is that his eyes look like they are crying blood. I take a Q-tip and try to get the blood off, but it is attached to a string of tissue. I finally realize it is the insides of his lower eyelids oozing out of their cavities. His eyes are really getting bad. The whites of his eyes are brown, like coffee, and his eyeballs look like melting Jell-O. They are starting to ooze out of his head. It is gruesome. I no longer want to put drops in them; this is beyond drops.

When Dr. Soap Opera comes by, I ask him about the eyes. He says he'll mention it to Dr. Plastic Surgeon. I tell Dr. Soap Opera that when Curtis wakes up, which is going to be any day now, he is going to want to see, and he sure can't see with these! I also make him look at Curtis' face. This has to be more than just pressure sores. His face had second- degree burns that are nearly healed, with no scarring. But now he has terrible, bleeding wounds all over his chin and around his mouth. They need to be treated. He'll mention this to Dr. Plastic Surgeon as well.

At 8 o'clock, I call to speak to Curtis' nurse. I ask how Curtis is doing. She says, "I don't know. This is my first time taking care of him
so I don't have anything to compare. But his night nurse said he's
doing well!" I take a deep, relaxing breath and inquire about Curtis'
vent settings. She's not able to tell me this over the phone because
of HIPAA. I ask if Sonny is working. Sonny comes to the phone and
tells me they've turned his vent up to eighty, and he has no fever.
I ask if he is getting his lungs vacuumed. She doesn't know; they
are changing his dressings right now. I ask her if Ophthalmology is
coming to see him today. She doesn't know about that, either, but if
she sees a resident she will have them call me.

He never gets vacuumed today. His vent comes down to sixty.
It comes down to fifty. It is a very exciting day. This is finally it. At
last he has turned that corner, just like I knew he would.

Dawn is with Curtis for the day shift. Nobody knows anything
about Ophthalmology examining Curtis' eyes. Dawn is fed up;
somebody needs to examine his eyes. She says she stomped her
foot and told Curtis' nurse, "Do you understand what I'm saying? I
demand that you send an ophthalmologist to examine this man's
eyes, without delay." My sister is mighty angry about those eyes.
So am I, but I am so happy he's turned that corner, I am trying
not to let anything rain on my parade. We have been mentioning
our concern about his eyes for weeks now and have requested an

Opthamologist for at least four days now, that's eight shifts. Nobody followed through.

My sister and I meet at my house in the late afternoon. She is going to stay with the kids, and I am going to take care of Curtis. She gives me my Ophthalmology battle instructions. I am not to take no for an answer. She's right, but I am running out of energy. Everything is such a battle; I just want to celebrate his victory.

There are new white lab coats surrounding Curtis' chart when I get there. I hang back and listen. I try not to act like I am hanging on their every word, committing a federal crime by listening to their thoughts regarding my husband's condition.

There is a small, young, Korean man; another Soap Opera guy; a woman; and a gray-haired, bearded Grandpa. Grandpa is flipping though Curtis' chart, and they are discussing all Curtis' cocktails. I hear *acinetobacter*. Grandpa starts flipping pages and says, "If I'm not mistaken, this patient also has a fluid collection in his pelvis." He continues to flip pages, and I finally speak up, "It's a pancreatic pseudocyst." Grandpa says, "Yes, yes, I know about that, but there is something else in his pelvis." He finds what he is looking for. Yep, there is another fluid collection in the pelvis! That's news to me. Grandpa tells his underlings he thinks they should remove that fluid, to draw as much fluid off Curtis as they can get.

Yeah! I knew there were gut issues; I just knew it. I'm with Grandpa. Drain away. Drain, drain, drain. Grandpa is on the ball. Oh Grandpa, where have you been all this time?

They finish their meeting and Grandpa introduces himself to me. Guess who these mystery coats are? Infectious Disease. They already saved Curtis with Imipenem just in the nick of time. Once again, they save the day. I love Grandpa. They load Curtis up with Lasix again. Another cocktail added to the bar.

When Dr. Plastic Surgeon shows up later in the day, I ask him what he decided to do about Curtis' eyes. "What about them?" All these nurses and residents we've talked to about his eyes have all said they'll let Dr. Plastic Surgeon know, yet this is the first time he knew there was any concern about Curtis' eyes. Do these doctors even look at their patients? Dr. Plastic Surgeon comes into the room, tells Curtis' nurse to tape his eyes shut, and leaves.

We've always admired Dr. Plastic Surgeon and have been grateful to have him. He, he really disappoints me with this one. It breaks my heart to see Curtis with his eyes taped shut. They are the windows to his soul. Now I wish I had never said anything.

I never heard another word about the foreign pelvic collection. I know there was never a drain put in. I don't know if it corrected itself. I don't know if it was a tumor. I don't know if it became infected. Nobody I asked about it ever knew, either.

My daughter has developed a sore throat and now she is running a slight fever. I've seen this before; I know it is strep throat. There is no way I can take her to the doctor. I tried to get them to prescribe antibiotics over the phone, but they won't do it. Dawn is assigned this chore as well; take Amy to the doctor and get her prescription filled. Amy has to stay home from school for a couple days, so my sister will stay at our house with her. I get to the hospital in the afternoon and find that Curtis' vent is down to forty, low fever, and good liquid gold production. I notice a piece of paper next to his flow sheet. It has some scribbles on it, "Dr. Stranger... wife... verbal order per Dr. Richard Head." It looks like gibberish, but "wife" catches my eye. What are they up to now?

Karen Vidor is at the nurses' station, faxing Curtis' records somewhere. I tell her about Curtis' eyes and Amy's strep throat. She says they have to figure out how much money to put on reserve to pay for Curtis' care. There really is no way to tell, but they put the number at 1.7 million dollars.

Just then, an ophthalmologist shows up to see Curtis. I go into the room with him. He darkens the room and examines Curtis' eyes. He explains why he is darkening the room, what he sees, and what he is looking for. He has a bottle of something, and puts some of it in Curtis' eyes. He explains every little thing. I am starting to worry because I'm not used to so much information, but then I realize he's just doing his doctor thing the way it's supposed to be done.

He makes some notes and says, "It's a good thing you called for me when you did." I tell him, "We've been asking for an Ophthalmologist for at least four days." He says, "He's lucky to have people who care about him so much." I almost start crying. I have never been praised before. Really, this is Dawn's doing anyway.

He says Curtis' eyes have dried out due to exposure and they are permanently scarred. The scars look to be in a spot that will not interfere with his vision, but it is tough to say at this point. He is ordering Lacrilube to be applied every four hours. *That's the thick Vaseline-type stuff that Sonny used last week.* He is also ordering ophthalmic Bacitracin to be applied every four hours. He says he wants his eyes covered alternately with Lacrilube and Bacitracin. He says every six hours is sufficient, but orders aren't always followed, so he is ordering every four hours. And whenever I am here, I should put a bead in each eye. *It's like he knows Curtis is going to keep getting new nurses who won't pay attention.*

When he leaves, I explain to Curtis why we're greasing his eyeballs. This is another tidbit for my list of things to explain to Curtis over and over again.

I update Karen on Doctor Eye's report. "Make that 1.722 million." Ha-ha! The fax machine jams. Karen is tugging at paper and pushing buttons, "Oh, shoot! I think I broke the fax machine." I say, "Now it's 1.7223 million!" *Ha-ha-ha-ha! I crack myself up.*

She asks me how I feel about Curtis' condition. I say, "Are you kidding? He's doing great!" I tell her all about the fever coming down, the vent coming down. "He is kicking ass and taking names, are you kidding?" She doesn't have anything to say, and I know she has just come from her roundtable meeting with all of Curtis' doctors. I ask her what she thinks. She crinkles her face and says, "It doesn't look good, but I'm on the fence, hard to say which way he's going to go." I tell her Curtis is going to surprise her.

They arrive to torture Curtis, so Karen and I go downstairs to grab a Coke and smoke cigarettes. I yammer about Curtis and some of the highlights and miracles I've seen. I rant and complain about all the issues with the hospital. I give her a laundry list of items that the insurance company shouldn't pay for. I express my frustration about feeling as if I'm two steps ahead of the doctors. She says it's good that I keep speaking up. "It gets them thinking." Well, that is scary.

It made me nervous, the way she was acting at the nurses' station, so I finally ask her what makes her think Curtis isn't coming home. She says she's changed her mind. He is coming home, and she doesn't doubt it for a minute. She believes me. She really does. Something in my thirty minutes of yammering has convinced her, I'll never know what. She starts telling me all the things I need to think about and get ready for his homecoming. He will need rehab, blah, blah, blah. She is on board. She is on the bus. He is coming home.

I think about the scribble that said "wife," and ask her if she knows who Dr. Stranger is. She says, "Oh, yes. He's a great guy. He can really help." I say, "What kind of doctor is he?" She tells me, "A psychiatrist." Dr. Richard Head issued an order to send a psychiatrist after me!

How dare he! The hospital staff is always spinning everything to make me appear crazy, which is what makes me crazy. If they would spend all that energy fixing what is broken, instead of denying that anything is wrong, it really would be a world-class facility. At least I now know what they are up to.

Karen says, "Maybe he **can** help." I shoot back at her, "Oh, please! I have plenty of people to talk to, to vent to. He can't do a thing. I am sick to death of trying to talk to an understanding soul in that building who can fix problems. There isn't one; they are all helpless politicians. Besides, Curtis is the patient and the insurance company isn't going to pay for care for his wife. I don't want to talk to him." Karen has to go. I go back upstairs, chewing on this revoltin' new development.

I know Dr. Richard Head didn't just wake up and decide to sic a shrink on me. I hardly ever speak to him. Somebody put him up to it. How dare they! Curtis is coming home.

One of the nurses says Dr. Stranger came by to see me and that he will come back later. I let her know I have no interest in speaking to Dr. Stranger and to keep him away from me. I ask her who sent him. She says Dr. Richard Head gave a verbal order. I ask her who put Dr. Richard Head up to it. She doesn't know. It is my mission to find out.

A short while later, Respiratory comes in. This time, he hooks up a small cup-type thing to Curtis' garden hose. "What's that?" Antibiotics that Curtis will inhale; they'll go straight into his lungs.

At long last, our Windex. Yeah, I'm crazy like a fox. He is on a new regimen of inhaled antibiotics. About time! I'm pretty hyped by the time they kick me out for shift change. Curtis is on a roll.

After shift change, Curtis has another new nurse. I'm not a bit surprised, but I'm pretty pissed, nonetheless. I give her a history of Curtis and tell her about his eyes. I tell her to be careful with his mouth because the inside of his cheeks will bleed if you so much as touch them, and the blood won't stop coming. I tell her all the little things I can think of. *Geez! I just hate leaving him there alone with another rookie.* I'm in for another sleepless night. I remind her that his splints have to be on at all times. There is a sign plastered to the wall that says the same thing, but they don't read the signs.

By the time I leave, his vent is down to forty. He really is on a roll. I figure he'll get at least one more vacuuming before all is said and done. He hasn't had one for three days, so one is probably coming soon. The move to the new unit has been delayed, which suits me just fine. It's still too risky to move him.

My office is closing for lunch because it is Secretaries Day. I don't plan to go. Time is too valuable; I need to spend it at work or with Curtis. A lot of people have mentioned that I am losing weight. I'm not paying attention, but I do notice my clothes are getting baggy. They talk me into going with them. It wouldn't hurt to eat and just relax for the first time in seven weeks. Is that all it has been? Seven weeks?

A lot of people ask about Curtis' condition. I never have time to chat with anybody except Ginger. I start yammering about ventilators, and tracheotomies, and cysts, and pus draining, and collapsed lungs....and suddenly I notice somebody putting a fork down, looking a little pale. It dawns on me that this isn't polite mealtime chatter. I remember how horrified I was when I first heard Mrs. Mexico using the same vocabulary. I shut up, feeling isolated from the normal world.

I no longer know what normal is. I don't want to live this life anymore. I want to go home after work and sit on my couch and watch TV. I want to do laundry, go to the grocery store, cook dinner for my family. I want to sit on my own toilet, for crying out loud! This just has to be over soon, I can't take much more. Lunch was a bad idea.

My brother Mike is at the house with Amy. I'll meet Dawn at the hospital during shift change. Curtis' vent has hovered between forty and fifty since I left last night. His chin and face are all greasy and bandaged. No real changes. He is just resting up to get out of that bed. I grease his eyes and explain what I'm doing. I tell him they are trying to get him off the cocktails so he can wake up, to stay relaxed and take slow, deep breaths.

The remarkable thing today is his tongue. I wish I had snuck my camera in for a photo of this. It appears to be completely outside his mouth. It is the size of a baseball and looks like cowhide. It has clearly been outside his mouth for some time and has dried out. His nurse comes in, and I tell her that when he wakes up, which will be any day now, he is going to want to eat.

"What is wrong with his tongue?" She says there is no way to get it back in his mouth. She has tried, but his tongue is too swollen. "There's nothing you can do?" She says, "No, sorry." I ask her if I can pour some water on it, so it won't dry up and fall off. She says no. Well, this is unacceptable, but there's nothing I can do about it. Blood is always running out of his mouth. I always suction it, but I have to do very carefully because if I touch anything inside his mouth it just bleeds even more. We are always sucking blood out of his mouth. Where is all that blood going now?

Curtis' nurse tells me some of his family has been around. They always come and go, but they aren't so much of a nuisance now. I'm far too busy to take any note of them. Shift change. The secret club is meeting and I have to go.

I get my Pepsi from the cafeteria and head out for a smoke. I meet my sister and tell her about Curtis' tongue. She lets me know that I am wrong, there is something they can do about it, and this is unacceptable. There's nothing we can do but wait until seven-thirty when we can go back up.

When we get back to the room, my sister takes care of Curtis' tongue immediately. She gets it back in his mouth and holds his mouth shut for a while so it won't pop back out. Nothing to it. Over the next couple days, we'd see his tongue trying to sneak back out of his mouth, and we'd put it back in before it could swell up like a baseball again.

I open the doors to the burn unit and hear the angels singing. Sure enough, Sonny is his nurse today. His vent is down to forty. Curtis has gauze packed in his mouth and he looks so much more comfortable. There isn't blood everywhere. His face is clean and treated. Sonny tells me that his mouth bleeds and bleeds. "I know, it's been like that for weeks!" She says, "That's not right. I told the doctors." In the meantime, she rolled up this gauze and packed it in each cheek to wick the blood up. As the gauze fills with blood, she puts in fresh gauze. She has soaked the gauze in a solution that was created by Dr. Plastic Surgeon to help blood clot.

She points out the wounds on his face. "I know, I know, Sonny. It's been like that for weeks, and it keeps getting worse!" She says, "That's not right, either. I told the doctors, and I'll make them look." I like the gauze. It is so much better than having blood running all down his face and the never-ending, delicate suction dance.

They get him off the paralytics completely today. He is still sedated with Fentanyl, which is a powerful painkiller. He's still on Ativan, an endless array of antibiotics, blood pressure medication, Lasix, and who knows what else. By now, he has developed yeast infections, as well, from all the antibiotics. He now has yeast in his lungs, to keep the acinetobacter company. But a big one is down; he's off the paralytic. I'm seeing a lot of muscle twitches as the drug is wearing off. It is pretty cool watching him come back to life.

I have to leave shortly after shift change; the babysitter can't stay late. I get home early enough to see my children and to clean the pool. Although I have learned how to use all this equipment, I soon realize it is a never-ending battle, like digging a hole in sand. On a slope. As soon as I vacuum, it needs to be vacuumed again. I'm in a pretty good mood, though. Curtis is getting off the cocktails. If he could see me now, cleaning the pool....

Amy brings the phone to me and says it's Memorial Hermann. My heart jumps. It's only Twila, nothing to worry about. I go back to cleaning the pool with the phone on my shoulder.

She says Dr. Stranger has been trying to get in touch with me. "Is it OK for him to call you at home?" "No." "Do you want to set up a..." "No!" "He can really help..." "No!" "...deal with the psychological trauma..." "No!" "You've both been through a lot..." "No!" I know I am being rude, barking "no" at her every other word, but I am in a good mood and I am having some immature fun.

If I had been none the wiser, and some doctor appeared on the burn unit asking to talk to me, I would have leapt into his arms. I am always so desperate to get news about Curtis and ask my many questions. And you know, once those mind benders have you within eyesight, they've got you man. There's no escape. Everything you say gets analyzed and your head gets shrunk. Oh, I am so proud of myself for escaping this fate.

Twila continues to dig herself deeper. I know that everybody in the hospital expects Curtis to die. Nobody ever speaks of discharge planning. She is just saying that to placate me, to try and trick me, I do not want my head shrunk, and I don't need this kind of help. She finally gets the message loud and clear. "No, I do **not** want to talk to Dr. Stranger. Stop wasting your time. Who set this up?" She says it is her idea. I think she is lying, but I don't know who else it can be. I hang up, still amused, and finish cleaning the pool.

If you could see me now, Curtis, I'm cleaning the pool. Who could it have been? The only other person I can think of is Karen, but I really don't think she would involve herself in this. It is a bona fide mystery.

After I put the kids to bed, I call Dawn to fill her in on the amusing mind-bender story. I pick her brain to help me figure out who could be responsible for this. My sister is really quiet. She is usually just as animated and worked up as I am, if not more so. What the heck...?

Finally, she says very quietly, "Lisa, I'm going to ask you something. It hurts me to even ask you, but I have to ask. I promise I will never, ever bring it up again." "What?" She says, "Just in case—I'm not saying this will happen or that I think it will happen—but just in case things don't turn out the way you expect them to, it would-n't hurt to spend time planning for...planning for...Lisa, have you thought about what you'll do if he doesn't make it? A funeral?" She is crying now. I snap at her, "Of course I did. I spent all of forty seconds thinking about it weeks ago. If he doesn't make it, I will donate any viable organs, have him cremated, and bring him home in a jar. He's coming home one way or another." That's the truth. I did think about it. I did make a plan, and then I never thought about it again. Everybody knows what the outcome might be and whoever wants to can have a final moment with him. I see no need for a funeral. His family can do whatever they want, but my plan is to bring his ashes home and be done with it.

She stops sniffling, and her voice sounds stronger, "OK, OK, it's good that you've thought about it. I doubt they'll be able to use his organs, but I'm proud of you for thinking of that. I won't ever mention it again."

She sure sucked the wind out of my happy sails. I ask her if she is going to 'fess up about sending the psychiatrist after me. I can't be mad at my sister. I suddenly feel guilty for all the "useless moron," "dumbass" thoughts I had about whoever had done this.

"Actually, that is my fault, but I didn't ask for a psychiatrist. I asked if they could send someone from Hospice to talk to you." I ask, "H-h- hospice? Why would I want to talk to somebody from Hospice?" She is crying again, "Well, Lisa, Hospice... They can help... They help whenever people are...are dead or are...dying."

Now that does hurt. It hurts really bad. A knife in my heart. All this time, every day for over seven weeks, I have fought so hard to bring Curtis home and she fought right alongside me. She's the one person who stood by Curtis and was as determined as I am to save his life. Now she is giving up. I thought I felt alone when Willy checked out. I thought I felt bad when his family turned on us. I thought I felt isolated when I tried to have a normal lunch with normal people in the normal world. I had no idea what alone and isolated felt like until right now, at this moment, when those words came out of her mouth.

"Dawn, how could you do that? How **could** you? I have a hard enough time trying to talk to the people who are supposed to be keeping him alive! I have no time to waste on people who are going to help him die! How do you help somebody die anyway? Once he dies, he's dead, gone, it's over, nothing else to do, that's it. I don't want to talk to anybody from Hospice." She says she's sorry, she didn't do it to be mean spirited, she's only trying to help.

Well, I know she's trying to help, but somehow she's gotten off track and I need to rein her back in. Somehow, those medical folk in that hateful place have gotten to her. I have to re-establish her focus.

She's invested a lot of her time, she's postponed her degree, she has become as consumed in saving Curtis' life as I have. It has disrupted her life almost as much as it has mine. She stays at my house a lot and takes care of my kids when she isn't in school or taking care of Curtis or working. We are living the same life. She's picked up so many balls for me. When I just can't carry anymore, she always picks them up. It's not that I take her for granted. Since day one, I've been so grateful to have her.

This is her world and she helps guide me through it. We have often talked about how this experience really rounds out her re-sumé. She's had years of experience as a health care provider, and years in hospital administration. She's had some experience with loved ones in the hospital, but being on the patient and family side of an ICU event like this one is a real eye-opener for her.

I have always assumed that this is her thing, she is used to it. Maybe this is taking a greater emotional toll on her than I've thought. Maybe she needs to talk to a psychiatrist. I need to keep a closer eye on my sister and handle her a little more carefully. She is losing focus and getting off the bus, and Curtis needs her.

Dawn's friend, Violet*, works in the Med Center; she also lives near my dad. So I meet her at the emergency room, and she takes my kids to my dad's for the weekend.

When I get to Curtis' room, the angels have stopped singing. It is a circus. I check Curtis' flow sheet. Wow, he is doing great: vent at forty, no fever, peeing just fine, blood gasses are good. I watch the vent for a while and his volume is incredible, in the seven hundreds with peaks over eight hundred. I start jumping up and down and do a little jig of joy as I am getting my hefty bags on and watching the vent. Every single breath is powerful and he isn't working hard at all. I am so excited I jump up and down again. I forget myself for a minute and shout to him, "You **go**, Baby!" One of the nurses looks up at me. "Sorry." She smiles at me and says I can dance all I want; they are excited, too. We are watching another miracle.

I catch sight of Dr. Plastic Surgeon going down another hallway. I stay outside Curtis' room so I can talk to the doctor. I watch his vent. It is so exciting, it's almost indescribable. I notice a line on the screen that follows every breath in and out. When Curtis inhales, this line comes to a sharp point at the top and when he exhales, the line goes back down. Some of the breaths don't have a sharp pointed tip, they have a double humped, rounded tip. Hmm... It must mean something, but everything else looks good, really strong. Maybe it means something good. It is just so exciting to watch, I can't stand still. It is every breath. This is no fluke. *You go, Baby.*

Finally, Dr. Plastic Surgeon comes by. I forget all about asking him about Curtis' destroyed face; I am ecstatic at what I am witnessing. He updates me on everything I already know, Curtis is doing great. They want to start weaning him from the sedatives and wake him up. *Yeah, yeah, that's great.* I ask, "Hey, see those lines that go up with every breath?" He starts to remind me, again, that he is Curtis' treating physician and he can tell me what he knows, but my lung questions really need to be directed at Dr. Lung. "Are you kidding, that guy is a ghost. He will never call me."

Dr. Plastic Surgeon says that Dr. Lung told him he has tried repeatedly to contact me without success, so he is getting a different story from each side. "Are you kidding me? There are three phone numbers on Curtis' chart: one of them has voice mail, one has an answering machine, and one has live people taking messages. If I'm not at one of those numbers, I'm in this building. Please! Nobody **else** has a hard time finding me. I'll take what I can get from you. What are those lines?"

He says they measure him inhaling, or something like that. "OK, but watch. How come sometimes they end in a sharp point and other times they're double rounded, like a camel?" He says they watch the trend over a course of hours, not every breath. "I can't help watching every breath." He says, "I know, and I feel for you." I ask again, "What do those humps mean?"

I understand that they mean there's a disruption in the breaths allocated by the machine, like he is trying to take his own breath. Over-breathing the vent. *Yeah, Baby, that's what I'm talking about.* I am done talking to Dr. Plastic Surgeon. I want to get in there and watch for double humps all night long. Curtis is trying to breathe all by himself. Leaps and bounds.

When I get into the room, I see we are back to the all too familiar bleeding mouth and face. The comfortable gauze is gone. I ask his nurse, another new one, why she doesn't put gauze in. She says she's never heard of such a thing. I tell her his nurse yesterday did it and it worked great. She won't do it, so I do, but I can't do as good a job as Sonny. His face is so badly damaged you can see fat tissue in his chin. At least, that's what it looks like to me. The wounds are bloody and are turning white. It looks like fat tissue. It is disgusting.

But more importantly, his vent is still at forty, the pressures have come down, and his volume and saturation are fantastic. All I write on the calendar today is "Go, Baby, go!" Maybe he will never need another vacuuming. I express my concerns about his face, as usual, to anyone who will listen. I keep a constant watch for isolation violations, and put his splints on when I get there. I can't wait to get him out of here.

The move to the new unit is scheduled for the following Wednesday, April 30, 2003. I am no longer concerned about moving him; he has stabilized considerably.

I get to the hospital and take care of Curtis' needs. Grease his eyes, explain why he is moving from side to side, the usual litany. After he is all situated, I start BeBe and CeCe, with a repeat on my favorite, "I'll Take You There." I'm beat. I get myself situated with a pillow and blanket and try to get comfortable in all my sweaty hefty-bag gear. I try to take a nap.

Respiratory arrives and administers Curtis' "Windex." When they leave, I try to go to sleep again. They come back, disconnect the Windex canister, and leave again. They forget to turn the lights off. I get up, turn them off, and grease Curtis' eyes again. I try to settle in for a nap again. I start to fall asleep.

Shirley shouts from the hallway that Curtis has visitors. I ignore her. She shouts, "Lisa, Curtis' family is here!" I shout back, "So what!" I adjust my pillow and close my eyes again. I don't care. We're taking a nap. Shirley says, "C'mon, Lisa, only two people at a time. It's their turn."

I get up from my chair, fuming. I turn off BeBe and CeCe and remove all my hefty gear. I grab my backpack from outside the door and storm off. I thought they couldn't police visitors. They sure can throw me out all the time. I barely glance at who all is there, but I do see Curtis' mother. There are at least four people in the hallway, all already in their hefty bag gear. Clearly, Shirley thinks the two-person rule only applies to me.

I am pissed off. I know they'll be here all day, if not longer. I once again decide that I am going home and I'm not coming back until Curtis calls for a ride home. I am tired and as ornery as I can be.

Maybe Dawn will let me stay home this time. Curtis is doing much better. It will take him a lot longer to get home if I'm not there taking care of him, but he'll get home eventually. I go home and take a nap. I talk to Dawn later and tell her I am done. Again. Seriously, this time, he's doing better, he'll be fine. I have no more energy for the trampling and confusion that comes with those Wrights underfoot. Really, not one more ounce. There are too many of them, they win.

I was wrong. Dawn will not allow it. I hear the story again about this mythical "somebody" who can help. She is incensed by this hospital and their lawless, insensitive policies. By now, she has repeated every infuriating story to anybody that will listen at her hospital. They are all as aghast as we are. I repeat the stories to Ginger, who spreads them all over the office. Everybody repeats these stories to all the people they know. By now, half the city knows what's happening to us at Memorial Hermann Hospital and fears for their lives or the lives of anyone they know who suffers the tragic fate of being placed in this fine facility.

Dawn gets me back on track and reminds me I can't leave Curtis. If taking care of him means I have to battle his family, then so be it. I can't leave him there. She talks some more about going over people's heads. Good for her, to have the energy for that, because I sure don't. It's like beating your head against a brick wall, knowing the result will be a smashed skull, but hoping you'll knock that wall down. It's self-torture as far as I am concerned.

I go back to Memorial Hermann. In the lower hallway, between the parking lot elevator and the burn unit elevator, I pass the blood bank and see Andy and Mrs. Andy giving blood. It warms my heart;

his relatives finally are doing something useful. I still wonder how many units of blood he's received. There is constantly a bag of blood hanging with his cocktails, even after all these weeks. He should have long since been discharged. He really isn't a burn patient now.

He sure gets a lot of blood. And he gives it all right back through his mouth. Somebody at the blood bank might know. No doubt they are billing the insurance company. Because of HIPAA, they can't tell me anything; try Medical Records. Medical Records is closed. I never give up my quest to find out how much blood he's received. This is an easy question for somebody to answer. I just have to find the right somebody in this sea of humanity.

I keep watch over Curtis while tripping over his family. I'm in a bad mood, but Curtis is holding steady at forty. I spend more time wandering all over the place than I do in his room. One time when I get back to his room, the only person in there is his mother. She's been in my chair all weekend. She says hello when I come in, and I ignore her. She asks how I am. I tell her I am tired and she is in my chair. She says she didn't see anyone's name on it. I go back to ignoring her.

Curtis' splints are off his hands. I work out his hands, fingers, and arms. I put lotion on, then put the gloves, wraps, and splints back on. I kiss him on the forehead. He's cold. *Finally*! I put a blanket **on** him. I am tickled. His blood pressure starts getting erratic, but I know it is just the equipment. I reposition his arterial line, and it starts reading correctly. I fix all his lines and hoses that have been shifted, bent, and tugged as he moves from side to side.

I suction his nose. I get a new suction piece, the kind I like better, and go to work on his bloody mouth. I know I should brush his teeth, but by now it is all but impossible. The bleeding is pretty much uncontrollable. I grease his eyeballs. I remove his boots and rub his feet. They are cold, too. I put lotion on them and put his socks and boots back on. I lotion all the dry spots on his arms. I check the abdominal drain bag. Pus is still coming out, but very little.

His chin and lower face are just mangled. There is no other way to describe it. It isn't getting any better, and it is clear to me it is going to scar, if it ever heals. This is really a shame. The burns on his face healed with no scarring at all, but now he is going to have scars from this...whatever it is. Pressure wounds from the garden hose and all its ties is the only thing I can think of, but they should have started healing by now.

I update the calendar. It has been a relatively uneventful weekend and I am tired, so I just X out Saturday and Sunday. I stand against the wall again, wishing I can have my chair. I call it a day and go home.

Dawn calls to tell me they've taken Curtis for a CAT scan. *Good deal. This is huge progress. He can leave the room.* That gut still nags at me, so I am happy to hear that they're checking it. She also says there's talk of taking him out of the rotisserie bed and putting him in a regular bed. That is also huge progress.

I have always worried that they'll take him off the sedatives when I'm not there. I can't imagine what it would be like to be him and start waking up. He's moving from side to side with his arms and legs splayed out; a machine is breathing for him; and hoses, probes, tubes, and bags of stuff are attached to every natural hole and some new ones. He'll probably wake up and think he is dead. That side-to-side motion might drive him crazy, as well. A normal bed will definitely be better. This is another happy day.

Dawn explained to me early on that the pulse-ox probe is a laser, so it needs to be moved every couple days or it will burn his skin. Shirley was in the room when Dawn was telling me this, and she said she'd never heard of such a thing. Dawn's replied, "You must be kidding. That's Nursing 101!" Shirley said she'd never heard of such a thing. Dawn said she'd print something out about it and bring it to her. My sister looked at me and rolled her eyes. She never printed anything out about it. With all the other drama, we really didn't care about proving anything to Shirley. It is just another of the many things my sister told me to keep an eye on.

Well, with all the Wright traffic over the weekend, I didn't move it. I've never had to move it anyway. I always take note of it, but it is on a new finger or toe every couple days. They always relocate it.

Curtis is still in his rotisserie bed when I arrive. He doesn't need anything; Dawn already took care of everything. His oxygen saturation is not right, but it's just the equipment getting a bad reading. This happens a lot. All these probes and monitors are probably getting accurate readings only seventy percent of the time. You can tell if it's the patient or the equipment after a bit.

I trace the line to his left pinkie toe. *It was there last Friday. They must have moved it somewhere else and moved it back by now.* I remove the probe. Dead center in his pinkie toe, exactly the same size as the laser, is a perfectly round, red dot. It looks like the Japanese flag on his toe. "Look, Dawn! I guess they figure he hasn't been burned enough! Geez!" We roll our eyes. Dawn gets a new probe from the cart and puts it on another toe. I can never get it on right. It really isn't that big a deal.

Shirley happens to walk in just then. Dawn points to Curtis' toe, "Look what the laser did." Shirley looks at his toe and brushes it with her finger. It is obvious it is a burn. She says, "Oh, no, that's not from the probe." Dawn says, "Yes, it is. We just took the probe off that toe and it hasn't been moved for several days. It burned his skin." Shirley says, "Oh, no. His toe always looked like that." Dawn and I just look at each other, flabbergasted. *Whatever.* Then Shirley says the only way to know for sure would be if his toe had been photographed when he was admitted, and we don't have photographs of the left pinkie toe. Shirley and her photography.

Later in the day, they arrive to remove the rotisserie bed. Thirteen days on the rotisserie. Farewell, and thank you for your help. We get kicked out for this significant event. It's time for Dawn to leave.

It is so good to see Curtis out of that monstrosity. He is finally still, so I can give him all the hugs he wants. They are weaning him off the Ativan and Fentanyl. He is starting to hear me now. I tell him all the same boring stories again, I give him all the boring, important instructions, over and over, all night long. They are dialing down the cocktails by the hour. I hate to leave him awake and alone all night. That sucks. He isn't responding to commands or anything, but he is closer and closer to the land of the living. I have no doubt that he can hear me. Whether he understands what I am saying, or even knows who I am, remains to be seen.

I head home. I can't wait to see him tomorrow. Just like in the early days, when he was only burned.

I reflect on Level 5 day. Man, it wasn't that long ago, but it feels like years. He has come so far so fast, just like I always knew he would. The gut nags me, but there is nothing going on now that is deadly. I am certain of that. He is on his own timeline now. I don't forecast any goals for him. He's been through so much, he can take all the time he needs. He's safe from harm. *Good job, Curtis. 'Atta boy.*

I am exuberant at work. Mandy stops at my desk. She can't wait to come to work in the morning and hear the latest news. I am mindful, ever since Secretaries Day, to keep it clean and brief. But she really seems interested. I tell her about the move to a regular bed, how well Curtis is breathing, and that they are moving the burn unit to a new part of the hospital tomorrow. It has been a week since Amy started her antibiotics, but she is still running a fever. I'm concerned; that's a long time for her to have a high fever. I'm driving Curtis' truck now, because my car is leaking antifreeze. One of my coworkers is coming over this weekend to fix it.

Dawn checks on Curtis after her class and tells me he is going to get vacuumed again. Well, this is a little out of the blue, but I had forecast at least one more. I am glad I predicted it because that means it isn't a cause for concern. We're right on schedule. *Vacuum away. Get the last of it out of there.*

I call Amy's pediatrician to tell them she is still running a fever and still has a sore throat. They say there's no need for them to see her, but I should call back if she still has a fever in two days.

One of my coworkers comes over after work to mow the lawn, since Ken officially passed the torch. Another one, Hooks, comes to babysit. As soon as he gets to the house, I race to the hospital to see how much Curtis has improved. I used to cry on the way home from the hospital. Now I cry on the way there, tears of joy.

I start reading Curtis' flow sheet while I'm putting on my hefty gear, like I do every day. I notice that his temperature has risen to over one hundred when some nurse I've never seen before comes out of nowhere and flips the paper over. She says I am not allowed to look at his flow sheet. HIPAA forbids it. *Something or somebody always has to set me off as soon as I walk in the door.* I tell her my husband has been here for almost eight weeks and I **always** read his flow sheet when I get here. Not today.

I look in to check his vent settings while I'm tying my mask. Curtis is gone. "Where is Curtis?" Another new nurse—Curtis' nurse for this shift—says he went for a Doppler. "What's a Doppler?" I don't like scary new tests. What happened? What have I missed? I'm told it's a test to check for blood clots. "Who ordered it?"

It is always important to know who orders tests. My faith is always in Dr. Plastic Surgeon. If he ordered it, then he is onto something. He doesn't do anything frivolous. If Dr. Gut ordered it, there's no cause for alarm. He's always checking the gut, and he will fix it pronto. If Dr. Lung ordered it, there is no need to worry at all—he's just throwing some business to his golf buddy, Dr. Blood Clot. But if Infectious Disease ordered it, then we have major trouble because Grandpa is right on the money. So, since nobody ever knows anything, I can glean a lot of important information just by knowing who ordered a test. This time, Dr. Plastic Surgeon ordered it. *Uh-oh. What happened? Why does he think Curtis has blood clots? I don't know a lot about blood clots except that they can travel to your heart or brain and kill you instantly, that's all.*

Dr. Doom and Gloom comes in. He says anybody can get blood clots at any time. I can get one sitting on the couch watching a movie. The Doppler is just a routine imagining test, a precaution for someone who's been immobile for as long as Curtis has. "Oh."

These people are determined to make every hair on my head turn white or fall out. I don't like surprises. But I can relax for now.

Curtis doesn't have blood clots. I go out for a smoke while I wait for him to return from his Doppler.

When I get back, Curtis is in his room. Nobody knows the results of the Doppler, but that's OK because I do. Curtis ESP'd me. Just in case I'm crazy, though, I always like to check with the medical people. They never know anything. I get to see his recent chest X-rays; they are still the same, full of clouds. His vent settings have increased. That is understandable because he has been out on a Doppler adventure. But he's been vacuumed today, so this is worrisome.

I kiss him on the forehead. *Oh, no, here we go again.* I know his temperature has to be over 101. I call the nurse. It's 101.3. Motrin please, not Tylenol. Off with the blanket. This is getting old. Two steps forward and three steps back. It's been two months now. Enough is enough. What now? In addition to yeast infections, this poor man must be hosting at least fifty percent of the world's population of bacteria. It is everywhere—in his gut, in his lungs, in his blood, in his IV entry points. They have him on broad-spectrum antibiotics. They change antibiotics all the time, but they are all powerful drugs. They are nuking him. For crying out loud, how can anything keep growing? I guess all those smart bacteria are learning.

I call to check on the kids. Hooks says, "Amy has a fever." I tell him, "Yeah, she's got strep throat. I gave her Motrin before I left. Give her Tylenol in another hour, I'll be home by nine." He says, "Her fever is 102."

*She is hotter than Curtis! Now I have something **else** to worry about.*

Curtis passes Amy about an hour later. He pulls into first place at 104. They are going to move his arterial line. I can't stay and see him awake; I told Hooks that I'd be home by nine. I can't take advantage of kind people who offer to babysit my kids.

I pull out of the parking lot at eight-thirty on the nose and call home. Hooks tells me that Amy still has a fever. "I'll be home soon. It's too early to give her anything else. She'll be fine." I am lackadaisical about it because she's had a persistent fever for a week. I called the pediatrician this morning, and they weren't worried, so y'know, I'm not alarmed. He says, "Her temperature is 105." *Amy lapped Curtis.* "I'm hurrying. I'm hurrying." I hang up and start to cry. *I am in Hell.* I call him back, "Put an ice bag on her head." He says, "She's been on the couch with an ice bag on her head for the past thirty minutes or so." I'm starting to panic. I can't get home fast enough. I ask him to put her in a cold bathtub. It is all I can think of. I apologize to him. I am so sorry. I had no idea she was this sick, and that's a heck of a thing to dump in the lap of a salesman from your office.

I call Dawn. She is concerned and tells me to call the pediatrician's office when I get home; they will have somebody on call. Then we both start thinking about acinetobacter. She says maybe I should take her directly to the emergency room. There's no telling what I disgusting bacteria I may have carried home, even though I always follow the isolation procedures to a T. Except when I smuggled in my camera. Oh, Lisa, you stupid, stupid woman. *Maybe I should just drive her back to Memorial Hermann so half my family can be together. What am I thinking? I wouldn't take anyone I love there, not for a million dollars. I suddenly have a flash of Amy hooked up to all the cocktails with a garden hose in her mouth. Curtis acquired all this bacteria just from being in a hospital. What am I thinking? I will shoot myself in the head before I take my baby anywhere near a hospital.*

I make the exchange to the last freeway that will take me home. Hooks is an older guy, y'know, just trying to help me out. I don't know that he is around young children too often.

Maybe he didn't take her temperature correctly. 105 is sky high. If Curtis ever got that high, it wasn't for long. He got close, but I don't ever think that high. That's brain-damage high. That's HOT. He must be wrong. Calm down, Lisa. I am a lot calmer by the time I get home. Amy is on the couch with ice on her forehead. I am tripping over myself with apologies to Hooks as I make my way to Amy. She is on fire. Hooks clears out pretty quickly. I find the thermometer and take her temperature. It's 104.6. Holy Moses it **was** 105! I think about the times she's gotten Motrin and Tylenol. I can't give her anything for at least an hour and it is Motrin's turn.

I call the pediatrician's office. A nurse calls me back. Another new nurse. I tell her about Amy's strep throat diagnosis six days ago. What antibiotic she's been on and how much. The persistent low-grade fevers, my earlier call to the pediatrician, her doses of Tylenol and Motrin tonight, and her spike to 105. She is pretty dismissive, "Oh, 105 is not that high. Call back if it gets to 106." My kids have had fevers before, and that's what they always say. If it's 103, call us back if it gets to 104. If it's 104 when you call, call us back if it gets to 105. I think 105 is pretty darn high. I've never known anyone to have a fever this high. This nurse is not instilling a lot of confidence, but then again, any confidence I ever had in medical people has long since been beaten out of me.

I step outside because I don't want Amy to hear me. I don't want to scare her. I give Dismissive Nurse a brief history of the currently isolated, bacteria-infected family member I am caring for. She asks if the kids have been up there. No, not since March twenty-first. I tell Dismissive about acinetobacter. This is important because it is a gram- negative resistant strain. She isn't one of those "Bless you, I will pray for you" strangers. She is still dismissive and unconcerned. "Call back if it gets to 106." OK.

What a night. I call Dawn back and tell her about Dismissive's advice. My sister sounds skeptical and she suggests again that I take Amy to the emergency room. Pfft! *Yeah, right, there's no way I'm taking my baby to a hospital.*

I am up most of the night with Amy; she has a bugger of a fever. It finally comes down to 103. I check in with the nurses' station throughout the night, as well. Amy and Curtis are in a fever race. Amy stays in the lead most of the night. They go up and down, competing for first place, over the next two days. It is enough to drive a person completely insane. But it is a good, clean update for Mandy at work. Everybody knows the word *fever*. It isn't scary or horrible or gross. The fever race keeps her entertained for the next two days. I am certain my hair is stark white.

Dawn is staying with Amy today. I do some research on the internet; I don't trust Dismissive. It doesn't take me long to diagnose Amy with scarlet fever. I don't remember the exact details now, almost two years later, but everything I read made me believe it was scarlet fever.

After all the coincidences, all the mishaps at the hospital, and especially after Curtis has proven me right so many times, I have stopped questioning myself. I am always right. You can't tell me anything now; I am dangerous. She has scarlet fever. When I call the pediatrician's office, I don't even waste my time with a nurse. I want the doctor to call me. I let the pediatrician know that Amy has developed scarlet fever, and I tell her all the symptoms. Call in the nukes; it's scarlet fever. Well, of course nobody is going to take my word for anything. I'm not the expert. They want to see her. Dawn takes her in.

They don't agree with my diagnosis, of course. They say it's just a bad case of strep throat. My sister stays home with her the rest of the week. We continue with the strep throat antibiotics, and Tylenol and Motrin. Amy maintains persistent high fevers through the end of the weekend. She had scarlet fever. You will never convince me otherwise.

Today is moving day at Memorial Hermann. At long last, the move to the new, state-of-the-art burn unit. The employees at Memorial Hermann have been so excited about it; they had a party and everything. I am just glad Curtis is stable enough to be rolled down the hallway. Dawn is going to meet me at the hospital after her classes. My brother is staying with Amy.

I get to Curtis' room; he is gone. All his stuff, personal and medical, is still here. I had picked out his new room ahead of time. I figure he's been here long enough that he should get first pick. For the last couple of weeks, I've been telling everyone what room I want him in. I go to the new unit and find that the room I picked out for Curtis is vacant. I'm not surprised. I find him at the other end of the hallway. He's in their new, state-of-the-art isolation room. This room is just as nice, so it's not an issue.

I see Dr. Plastic Surgeon and ask about the results from yesterday's Doppler. He says Curtis didn't have a Doppler yesterday. "Curtis was taken from his room yesterday, and his nurse said he was having a Doppler." Dr. Plastic Surgeon asks me who ordered it. "Dr. Doom and Gloom said you ordered it." He starts flurrying from one stack of papers to the next. He asks a nurse if Mr. Wright had a Doppler yesterday. She doesn't know. Dr. Plastic Surgeon asks me if I'm sure Curtis had a Doppler. *Sigh.*

Curtis' new room has an entry door, but you're not supposed to use it. There is another door that leads to an anteroom. This is where you wash up and put on all the hefty bags, and this room has another entry to his room. My sister explains it to me later, something about negative air pressure. When the door to the anteroom is opened, the room air is sucked up instead of being blown out. Something like that. Anyway, the normal entry door is never supposed to be opened. You're always supposed to use the other entrance to keep the bacteria away from all the other helpless burn victims.

I stand in the hallway, looking through the window in the door. The monitor for the blood pressure, heart rate, oxygen saturation, and all that is hanging on the wall, like a TV, in plain view. Behind that is an IV pole with all his cocktails and pumps. I can't see Curtis, but I can see the bottom of his bed and his legs, so logic tells me his head is behind the IV pole and all its cocktails. On the opposite side of the bed is his ventilator. I recognize the shape of the machine, but I can't see the screen with all the data on it. I wonder about an emergency. I think this machine should be on the IV side of his bed, closest to the door that is never supposed to be opened. I can't see how he is breathing. That's always one of the first things I look at.

I start to review his flow sheet and some medical lady starts talking to me. I walk her over to the door with the window and ask her what is wrong with this picture. She doesn't know. I express my concern about the location of the ventilator and the blocked view of the patient. "There, there, Mrs. Wright. We can see all that at the nurses' station." I dress in my hefty bags and go in. He needs to be suctioned. There is no cart and no equipment in the room. Nothing to suction him with. No supplies.I go out and ask his nurse where all his stuff is. It's still in his old room. She is trying to get it all moved as she finds time.

The room should have been ready for him before he ever moved. The nurses already have their hands full. Why are the nurses, who are already short-handed, responsible for moving patients, especially critical ICU patients? Boxes and paperwork are stacked haphazardly behind the nurses' station. *This place isn't ready for patients!*

I go back to his old room and grab the most important thing first, the supply cart. I wonder if I should wipe it down. No, they do that every day, and everything on it and in it is sterile. The new unit is upstairs, but you can walk down a long hallway that slopes upward, so you don't have to wait for the elevators or take the stairs. I push the supply cart to Curtis' new room. I suction him and get him all sorted out, then go back for more gear.

I carry all I can and walk back. Before I leave for my third trip, Curtis' nurse thanks me and offers me a rolling cart, similar to something room- service in a hotel would use. I roll the cart back to the old burn unit, load it up, and walk all the way back. I make two more trips like this. When I arrive at the old unit on my last trip, Dawn is here. It is pretty deserted, and I have almost everything from Curtis' room. We take down all the cards and pictures and the calendar. Dawn disinfects my chair and off we go, taking my chair and the rest of Curtis' stuff with us.

We are getting Curtis all situated in his new home. His mouth is bleeding again. It is constantly bleeding. This time, though, it has run down his face and gotten his pillowcase all bloody. It soaked through to the pillow. There are no washcloths or linens in the room. I go out in search of a linen supply closet. I walk back down the same hallway I've been using. No linens. Go down another hallway I haven't seen before. I find the torture room, so I figure there must be linens nearby. There is a linen closet, but the shelves are empty.

Throughout Curtis' time in this barbaric pit of Hell, I've had numerous occasions to go to the kitchen, or go to the linen closet, or go look for supplies in empty rooms. I am all over the place for one reason or another. I hear other patients in other rooms. Their screams, their equipment alarms, their ventilators quacking, you name it. I know which rooms are occupied, and then suddenly one day they are empty. I know it is because they died. I tell myself they went home, and I try not to think about it, but I know all around me people are dying. It is a depressing place to spend an afternoon. This is afternoon number fifty-seven.

Heading back to Curtis' room, I walk past a room that is all lit up. Half the wall is glass, like an observation room. A patient, wrapped in familiar white netting from head to toe, is in there. A new admit. A new burned person. A couple of white coats are looking at his back. I glance away as quickly as I can. I see a nurse who's headed into New Admit's room and ask her where linens are. She says Housekeeping hasn't come yet. I go back to Curtis' room and let Dawn know I am heading back to the old unit—again—to clean out the linen closet.

I find my room-service cart, go back, and grab as much as I can load onto the cart. I'm sure Curtis isn't the only patient who needs something, so I take several of everything: gowns, sheets, blankets, pillowcases, pillows, towels, washcloths, pads. I am tired of lugging stuff back and forth, and I know this is going to be my last trip. *They need to put me on the payroll. They owe me two months back pay. Bastards.* I pass the supply closet... *Uh oh! I'll bet they don't have any supplies, either.* I am already carrying more than the little cart can hold, but I don't want to spend my evening volunteering for the hospital, I want to take care of Curtis and spend time with him. I grab some of my favorite suctioners and 4×4 bandages. We use a lot of those.

At long last, I get all hefty bagged up again and bring Curtis a fresh pillow. Suction his mouth, lotion him up, all the usual things. He went code brown, so we have to get the nurse to help us move him and clean him up. He'd had a poo bag way back when. Well, they took it out after a couple days because he stopped having anything to put in it, and they stopped hearing any bowel sounds. Apparently, his bowels woke up today.

We have to wait about forty-five minutes. That aggravates me. He has diarrhea and shouldn't be left to lay in it. He is bloated up badly, and his muscles have atrophied. We can't move him by ourselves. They have been steadily weaning him from the sedatives, and he is becoming more alert. I keep up my repetitive conversation about all that is going on with him, that he has moved to a new room, and why he is hooked up to this and that. "Relax and try to take deep breaths, Curtis. They're trying to wake you up. Everything will be OK. Take slow, deep breaths, no matter what." He is more sedated than he was yesterday. His nurse says she had to kick it up because of the move.

Dawn and I leave together at about nine o'clock. We are walking out, chattering about all the things that have irked us tonight. Near the nurses' station, she grabs my arm. "Let's wait. I don't want to walk out behind that." In front of us is a guy pushing a body bag on a gurney, so we stop at the nurses' station. A nurse asks if she can help us. My sister points and says, "We don't want to follow that out." She says, "Oh, come this way," and leads us back down the hallway toward the torture room. A secret exit. We pass New Admit's room. The lights are off, and he is gone. He is in the body bag. Man, I hate being here, just hate it. I can't help but wonder if he is in the body bag because they didn't have any supplies on hand.

Amelia is Curtis' nurse today. She is a trauma float nurse who's taken care of him maybe three times before. We haven't seen her in a while. She is very pleased at how much better Curtis is doing. I notice that the abdominal drain bag now looks like it is full of Mountain Dew. This is new, so I ask Amelia what it means. "Oh nothing, that's just what's draining out of him." Well, all these weeks it has just been a slow trickle of thick goop; this is definitely something new. She says it isn't. A fresh new day of frustration is starting for Lisa. Again. I've seen this bag every single day for almost five weeks. This is a big, new development.

Shortly after I arrive, Curtis goes code brown. I press the call button and stand by the window. A voice on the speaker box says, "Yes, Mr.Wright?" I point to my rear and say, "Code brown." She laughs and says, "OK, we'll be along in a moment."

After twenty minutes or so, Curtis starts to squirm. Well, he doesn't actually squirm, because he can't move, but I can tell that the burning diarrhea on his butt is bothering him. I call the nurses' station again and remind them we have a code brown. They say they are busy and will be here soon.

Dr. Doom and Gloom and Dr. Soap Opera are now gone. They're residents, and their month is up. I have to train a whole new group. The very thought of him lying in diarrhea is intolerable to me. He will get diaper rash on top of everything else, for crying out loud. There is no way I can move him. I keep pestering every ten minutes for him to be cleaned up. Finally, his nurse comes in with two helpers and they kick me out.

I smoke and wonder about the Mountain Dew in the bag. Nobody on this floor is going to know anything. They are all new. I'll have to wait for Dr. Gut or Dr. Plastic Surgeon, both of whom are long gone for the day. I'll just have to wait until I'm lucky enough to trip over one of them.

Later in the evening, I point to the calendar pages on the wall and show Curtis how long he's been here. He is alert and hears me, but he can't turn his head to see the wall. One by one, I take the cards and pictures off the walls and read them to him. It is so exciting to have him awake. I let him know that my mother was here for a week; my cousin Jackie was here for a week; Jackie is coming back in a few days to stay another week, and this time she's bringing her husband with her.

I talk to him all evening. All positive. I never tell him his family sucks. I never tell him he almost died countless times. I am really proud of him, and I let him know it. I ask him if he wants his mother to come and visit. Does he want to see any of his family? He seems angry about it, so I let it go. Now that he is awake, I ask him every day. He is never enthusiastic about it.

After a while, he needs to cough. His chest buckles and his vent quacks. No crisis or anything, he just has to get some clouds out. I know this means he has to be suctioned. It is gross and disgusting, but he needs it, and I am used to it by now. He's been suctioned at least once an hour for the past three weeks. It's a part of his daily life now, but as far as I know, it hasn't happened to him while he is awake. I explain how they help him cough. I always check the canisters on the wall to see what new color is coming out of him today. The canister looks bloody, but this could be from his mouth, so I'm curious to see what today's color is. His IV has been blip-blipping, but this is not alarming. He has so many cocktails, something is always blip-blipping. There's a constant racket in that room. I know his nurse will be along eventually to cough him when she de-blips the IV pump. It's routine, normal. There is always something to tend to with him. He keeps me and his overworked nurses constantly busy. There have been some "Batman flying emergencies," for sure, but for the most part, it is just routine issues like this one. If he goes too long without being coughed, his oxygen will desaturate and he will start to suffocate, but that takes a really long time or a really big "loogie." This is just routine, time to suction him.

Well, once again, I don't go looking for something to complain about, but these people love putting me in a bad mood. Amelia comes in with her hefty bag on, but it isn't tied. She has one glove on, no mask, and no hat. She comes in quickly, hits a button on his pump, and leaves again before the door even closes.

Excuse me? I tell Curtis I'll be right back. I throw away my hefty gear and go to the nurses' station. *Remember, never be nasty to his caregiver.*

Batman, the charge nurse, is behind the counter. I tell him Curtis' nurse just went into his room with no mask and no hat. That is all I got out of my mouth when I hear behind me, "I just went in to reset his IV!" She says it in a snotty, sarcastic tone and keeps on walking. Now I'm mad. I say to Batman, loudly, "Curtis is an ICU patient in critical condition, and he has issues from head to toe. His nurse should **never** enter his room just to reset a pump. She should be gowned up, gloved up, masked up, and have her hair covered so she's ready to take care of the patient!"

I'm ready for the all-too-familiar, "There, there, Mrs. Wright," but Batman says, "You're absolutely right, Mrs. Wright, and I will speak to her."

All this time, all I've ever asked is that acknowledge and correct issues, and Batman does exactly that. Why can't they do this every time? I like Batman. I calm down like somebody hit a switch. I tell him Curtis needs to be suctioned, and ask him if he can please take care of that. He says he will.

Dawn arrives for a brief visit, and I give her the update. As we are leaving, we mention what a difference it makes for someone to say, "You're right, I'll speak to her." It's about time! We turn back and thank Batman. *What a difference!*

When I come back from walking my sister to the bus, I'm dreading having to interact with his nurse. Now she will hate me, and I think she is a bitch, and she's taking care of Curtis. This is not good. I'm not mad at her, except for her sarcastic tone. The problem is the hospital and their staffing policy. Things like this would not happen if he had a regular nurse. Their policy is, "To Hell with the patient's needs." She comes into the room not far behind me. I tell her I'm not mad at her, I am angry at the hospital. She is really nice. She says she understands and she is sorry. We're friends again.

I get kicked out for shift change, so I grab a BLT and head outside. Curtis is alert now and no doubt has plenty that he wants to say. I can't wait to hear it! He still has to wear those splints on his arms, but instead of bandages, he now has gloves and compression garments. His arms and legs are wrapped in Tubigrip bandages to help minimize scarring. Tubigrip is like a thick stocking. You cut off the length you need and stretch it over something that looks like a coffee can with both ends removed. Curtis'arm goes into the "coffee can" and you pull the Tubigrip off the can and onto his arm as you're pulling the can away, so his arm is covered in this thick, elastic garment.

His arms and hands aren't quite as heavy as they were, but it's not like he can hold a pen or anything. I thought about an Etch A

Sketch, but those are hard for me to manipulate, so no doubt he'd have a lot of trouble. I'll go to Toys"R"Us and look for something that might enable him to communicate.

When I get back from shift change, Curtis is code brown again. I make my announcement and wait. After twenty minutes, I call again. Yeah, they're coming. I cannot stand for him to be left in diarrhea, not for one minute. I note the time in case I am over-reacting. They always act like I am overreacting. Nope, it is now eight-ten; I came back at seven- thirty. That's forty minutes lying in diarrhea—thirty-nine minutes too long. We change our babies' diapers more quickly than that.

I try to clean him myself, and ask Curtis to bear with me. I lower the head of his bed so he is lying flat. I pick up his right leg and put it on my shoulder. I can see there is no way I can get it all off him by myself. It goes way up under his back. His ventilator starts quacking. He is trying to cough. I put his leg down and raise the head of his bed. Now he has a bloody mouth. I change my gloves and suction the blood out of his mouth. He has yet another bag of blood hanging with all the cocktails. It is coming out of his mouth like it is coming out of that bag.

After Curtis settles down, I change my gloves and lower his head again. I get his leg on my shoulder a little more quickly this time, and I already have a new pad ready. I fold the corner of the soiled pad on top of itself, so at least that area of mess isn't directly on his skin. Quack! Quack! I change my gloves, raise his head, and suction the blood out of his mouth again. He is choking on it. I call the nurses' station again. Instead of being funny about code brown, I ask if somebody can please help me clean him up. "We're on our way!"

Ten more minutes pass. Now it's eight-thirty. He's been lying in diarrhea for an hour. It's inhumane.

I get a damp washcloth ready and put a new pad between his legs where I can grab it quickly. Suction his mouth again, change my gloves, lower his head. I race to the foot of the bed, put his left leg on my shoulder, and tuck the other corner of the pad over itself. Quack! Quack! Lower his leg, change my gloves, raise his head, and suction blood out of his mouth. I get him settled and push the call button again. No answer.

At eight-forty-five, a nurse finally comes in. By now his blood pressure is up, his heart rate is up, and his oxygen saturation is down. It is clearly bothering him to be lying in diarrhea. It has been at least an hour and fifteen minutes, but could have been as much as two hours and fifteen minutes. I got kicked out at six-thirty and couldn't come back until seven-thirty.

I ask the nurse to order diaper rash ointment. She asks Mr. Wright if he'd like her to increase his sedative. Curtis gives her a dirty look that means "no." I say, "No, don't sedate him. Please help me clean him up!" She tells Mr. Wright she is going to increase his sedative so he can relax, and she is going to get somebody to help her clean him up. I am standing right here to help. Two of us probably can't move him by ourselves, since Dawn and I can't, so we'll probably need a third person. But I am smoking mad by now.

No, we do not want more sedatives. He has worked so hard to get off the cocktails and come back to life, and she wants to knock him out rather than clean him.

She blips a button on the cocktails and leaves. She doesn't sedate him too much. He is still alert, although his blood pressure comes down. *Mental note: Tell Karen not to pay for a dose of Fentanyl tonight because the patient didn't want or need it.*

Ten more minutes pass. I suction his mouth again. Blood, blood, blood. His face, mainly the chin area, is a mess of open sores with grease on them. It surely is going to scar. I change my gloves again and get a new warm washcloth ready because by now the other one is cold. I raise his right leg, start wiping his cheek, and try to get as far up under him as I can. I am going to need another washcloth. It is stinky and nasty, but I am desperate to get it off his skin.

Quack! Quack! Quack! "Calm down, Curtis, let me get this off you." Quack! Quack! "I'm hurrying Curtis." The washcloth is dirty. I put the clean pad under him as best I can. Quack! Quack! Quack! Lower his leg, change gloves, and run around to raise his head. Suction his mouth. I check my watch, now it is nine-twenty.

If they don't have this off him by nine-thirty, I am going postal. That will be two hours since I got back up here. I have half a mind to scoop up the poo and throw it in their faces. No, **smear** it in their faces as they have left it smeared all over Curtis.

I am furious! I change my gloves and get another new pad and warm washcloth ready. Let him settle down. It's now nine-thirty-one. He isn't going to settle down. He is choking on blood and lying in burning diarrhea. He is miserable and I don't blame him. I lower his head and race to the foot of the bed and lift his left leg.

Quack! Quack! Quack! Quack! Honk! Honk! Honk! I try talking to him as I wipe. He is choking on blood again. Lower his leg. Race to change my gloves and raise his head. Suction his mouth. Smoke is coming out of my ears, but Curtis doesn't know it.

Earlier, his vent would stop quacking when I raised his head to suction blood out of his mouth. Now it just keeps quacking. His breathing is getting irregular.

I am standing there sucking blood with a quacking vent when a new resident, Dr. Curly Hair, strolls by and peers in the window. She meanders away as casually as she'd come by, like a school principal checking in on a class. She saw me standing there with a hose in his mouth and heard his vent quacking. Why did she even bother to look? This tears it for me. I finish sucking the copious amounts of blood from his mouth. There is quite a bit in the canister. It will not stop.

I walk over to the "never-open-this-door" door and open it. Dr. Curly Hair is at the nurses' station. I hiss at her, "I want you to call the on- call administrator!" She strolls over smiling, asking if she can help me. Quack! Quack! Quack! I hiss at her again, "I want you to call the OA. Right now!" I am so angry that I'm shaking. Quack! Quack! Quack!

She asks if there is something she can help me with. "Yes, you can tell me what you saw when you looked in this window." I am shaking and trying not to scream, so I am hissing. Quack! Quack! Quack! She glances into Curtis' room and then back at me, wondering what my point is. She doesn't have an answer. I answer it for her and I am no longer hissing, I am screaming.

"You saw a f---ing IV pole, that's what you saw!" She steps back as if I had slapped her, and she finally catches on that I am beside myself with fury. "Why did you even bother taking a peek? I've been in here for two f---ing hours trying to get diarrhea off him when I have a break from sucking blood from his mouth! His mouth is bleeding so much he's choking on it! Am I the only person who's heard his vent going off for the past two hours? It takes you two f---ing hours to look in, and all you saw was an IV pole! Why'd you even bother to look? Go look at the canister on the wall! His mouth has been bleeding non-stop for weeks and nobody gives a rat's ass! I asked the nurse when I came back from shift change to help me clean him up and I've been asking for the past two f---ing hours! Why do you people do this to him? I want the CEO of this hospital to lie helpless in burning diarrhea for two hours, and I want to pinch his cheek and tell him he's getting the best f---ing care!"

There is a flurry of bodies in Curtis' room. They already have him on his side and are cleaning him up before I drop my last

F-bomb. His nurse starts apologizing. They just brought another patient back from surgery, blah, blah, blah. I tell her that I'm not mad at her, that it's not her fault she has a critical ICU patient on top of all the other patients she has to take care of. "It's the f---ing hospital!" I am worried that my behavior will upset Curtis, but he is calmer than he's been in two hours. He looks at me as if to say, "You go girl!"

Hmm... If all I have to do is drop a few F-bombs to get his butt wiped, than so be it. I don't know why they have to make everything so hard. I will be back tomorrow with a B-52 F-bomber.

I ask the nurse again to order some diaper rash ointment. I don't even need to look; I know he'll need it. Before I leave, I tell Curtis to try not to poo unless I am here. This is unlikely, I know, but what else can I do? He's done everything else I asked him to, so maybe it will work. I hate leaving him here at night. I can't think about what is happening—or not happening—to him when I'm not there. If I do, I will be a basket case. I've already witnessed miracles, for sure. That he has survived inept and neglectful care is an even bigger miracle. It is a miracle these dipshits haven't killed him. *Hang in there, Curtis. We need to get you off the garden hose.*

Now that he is alert, leaving him in diarrhea is an even bigger problem. It's one thing to be helpless in bed when you're warm and comfortable. It's quite another to be helpless in bed when you're lying in burning diarrhea. I don't want him wondering if this is how he is going to spend the rest of his life. He needs to stay committed to getting well. I never want him to fall into despair and think, "I can't take this anymore." And I can easily see that thought coming after spending hours lying in diarrhea. This is so easily preventable, and it is not going to happen to him again if I can help it.

Every person in the hierarchy of this hospital should be left lying in burning diarrhea for hours on end. They wouldn't do that to their husbands, wives, children, or anyone they care about. But Mr. Wright, their celebrity patient who has almost died countless times, is a different matter. He can lie in shit and his wife can eat shit. They just don't care. It is inexcusable and inhumane. If this ever happens again, I am going to tell the world.

But for the time being, I report to Dawn. She is as beaten down as I am, but she gives me her "Somebody in that hospital can fix this" speech. It's a lot weaker than it used to be. She says she is going up the ladder. I tell her to have at it. They've worn me out, and I don't believe anybody in this place can fix anything.

At four o'clock, after a productive day at work, I leave to see Curtis. When I get to the burn unit, the doors won't open. They are locked. There is a phone on the wall, so I pick it up and ask the person who answers to open the doors. I wait for the doors to open. *How dare they lock me out? They better give me a key. I am flying in on my B-52 F-bomber.*

Dr. Beverly Hills is here. He is an attending doctor on the burn unit, so he isn't somebody that leaves every month. I ask about the Mountain Dew in the drain bag. He explains that this is a good sign; the "plug" has drained, and the pocket of air that is left behind is now filling with fluid. Something like that, but it is a good thing. They have changed Curtis' central line and he's had more chest X-rays. I worry that he is going to get cancer from all these X-rays.

I ask Dr. Beverly Hills what can be done to prevent Curtis from lying in diarrhea for hours on end. He says Curtis doesn't lie in diarrhea for hours on end. "Yes, he does. It's happened the past two nights when I've been here, and no telling what happens when I'm not here." He seems surprised and says he'll speak to the nurse.

He tells me Dr. Lung examined Curtis' face this morning and determined Curtis has herpes. That's very common in ICU patients and some ointment has been ordered. I reply, "Those oozing, open wounds are pretty hard to miss, they jump out at you. It's hardly something you need to look for. His face has been like that for weeks!" He says, "The doctors don't usually go into the room when they're doing rounds."

What!? Pardon me!? I must have a hearing problem. I think I heard him say, "The doctors don't usually go into the room when they are doing rounds." I am appalled. The doctors don't actually enter the room to examine the patient? They read the chart, full of lies and omissions, and look through the window. Well, they can see a nice IV pole when they look in the window. I guess none of the dozens of nurses we've told about his face bothered to note in his chart, "Wife concerned about disappearing, bleeding face." This also explains his eyes. The doctors never bothered to look at the patient, and none of those nurses bothered to write, "Wife concerned about melting eyeballs." His tummy is changing every day. I never made any secret about my concerns about ongoing issues in the gut. I assume his doctors are noticing its changing appearance and rigidity. Sometimes it's big and swollen; sometimes, flat and hard. If they didn't notice his face or his eyes, then they aren't looking at his belly, for sure.

I ask Dr. Beverly Hills go in and look him over from head to toe, and I tell him to take a good look at his butt. I haven't seen it, but I have no doubt it is raging with diaper rash. Dr. Beverly Hills assures me he will come in later and go over Curtis with a fine-tooth comb. Dr. Beverly Hills didn't do this examination while I was here, so I don't know if he ever did, but he's a good guy and I believe he did.

You can go to the doctor with a mosquito bite and they look you over. But if you get really sick and you're in the ICU of one of America's finest hospitals, forget about a doctor putting his eyeballs on you. This is disturbing.

I go back to Curtis' room and his nurse tells me they've discontinued all his antibiotics. He is down to just a Fentanyl patch for the pain. This is huge! He's been on antibiotics for two months straight—massive doses of powerful antibiotics—and now he isn't getting any. Not a drop. Here come those leaps and bounds I've been talking about. I am beaming.

I brought in up a lap-sized board. One side is a magnetic board with alphabet-shaped magnets, and the other side is a dry-erase board. I brought some markers for whenever he'll be able to use them. For now, maybe he can manipulate the magnetic letters. I can tell that Curtis has things to say. We both just have to be patient. He tries the letters, but it doesn't work. He can't lift his hands yet.

These first couple days are frustrating for Curtis, Dawn, and me. We try so hard to understand what he is trying to tell us with his eyes and the very limited gestures he can make with his hands or arms. He can't use his voice. Surprisingly, within two days, both my sister and I can understand him pretty well and pretty quickly. His room has a fabulous, panoramic view. We can tell now when he wants the blinds open or closed, when he wants more blankets or pillows, what channel he wants on TV, all that stuff. I am surprised at how well we can communicate with him.

I ask Lydia, his nurse today, to order a wall clock for his room. I show her where I want it hung, in a place where he can see it and you can also see it from the hallway. I tell Curtis, until the clock arrives, that I'll be here every day before the evening news. I can't imagine what it's like not knowing where you are, what day it is, even what time it is. He must be going insane. I think a clock is important to help him get oriented and so he'll know when I'll be here, I know it is the highlight of his day.

Curtis is getting frustrated that he can't talk. I explain to him it is just going to take time. I explain the "little bit of fluid" in his lungs and the need for the hose, and tell him that he is getting better each day. I show him the numbers on the vent and tell him how well he is doing. He is still getting sixty percent of his oxygen from the ventilator, but the pressures are coming down and he is no longer on bi-level settings. I show him the sixty percent on the screen and tell him when it comes down to twenty percent he'll be off the hose. See how close you are? I've been watching every day, Curtis. When it's down to twenty percent, you'll be free of the hose and you'll be able to talk. I have no idea whether that's true, but twenty or thirty percent is no different from room air, so I know enough to know that I can't be too far off. I want him to have something he can sink his teeth into—a visual tool that shows him he's getting closer to his goal of coming home.

At shift change, I wander aimlessly away from the burn unit. When I return, Curtis is "code brown," so I call the nurses station. I do it again fifteen minutes later, and fifteen minutes after that, and fifteen minutes after that. That's four calls. Finally, after another fifteen minutes go by, I open the anteroom door and see Dr. Beverly Hills at the nurses' station. "It's been at least an hour and he's been lying in diarrhea. Believe me now?" He says he'll get the nurse. I guess he believes me now. Ten minutes later, they come to clean him up. This is a pattern; it isn't an isolated event. Every evening, either right before or right after shift change, he has diarrhea and is left in it for at least an hour, usually longer. I have no doubt this goes on when I'm not here, although I refuse to think about it. It happens every single time I am here, in spite of all the times I've complained to, all the people I have begged to please not to do that to him, all the F-bombs. Nothing changes.

To get to the new, state-of-the-art burn unit, you have to pass through another ward, which means all manner of traffic is coming and going past all those patients' rooms. I feel sorry for them. They have no privacy at all.

I arrive at the gates of Hell promptly at eleven and am greeted once again by locked doors. There are no chairs, no waiting room, nothing. You just have to stand here and wait. I pick up the phone. It rings and rings until, finally, someone gets around to letting me in. I hate these locked doors almost as much as I hate them leaving Curtis "code brown."*Mental note: Add these doors to my list of issues, in case anyone ever asks what he or she can do for me.*

When I get to his room, Curtis is sitting in a chair! Wow! This is unexpected progress. I am all over him telling him how proud I am, looking for improvement on the vent—none today—and chattering away. Chatter, chatter, happy chatter. "Wowee! This is amazing, Curtis. You are out of that bed! Wow!" Now, it isn't really a chair, it's more of a gurney. They slide him onto it, then raise the head and prop up the feet, so he is in a sitting position. It is the only way to get him out of the bed. But still...wow, hooray! I babble on about his remarkable view and, "Isn't it nice to move around and be in a different spot after all this time? You're practically home; the worst is officially over! You did it, baby!" I make a huge deal of it all day, but get no reaction from Curtis.

The Life Flight helicopter's landing pad is just above us and to our right, on the roof. I've heard a helicopter periodically the past couple of days, but this is the first time I've seen it. All day, this helicopter comes and goes. At first, I think they are doing test flights or something, but I soon realize that they are responding to calls and bringing back patients—hour after hour, day after day, night after night. I can't believe there are so many people being so critically injured as to keep that chopper so busy around the clock. These things just don't happen to people. Curtis was hurt really badly, but he didn't arrive by helicopter. It's hard to imagine somebody being any worse off than he was.

Every time that helicopter takes off or lands, it is a reminder of how lucky we are today, and it is a depressing reminder of where we were not that long ago. I always think of the person in that helicopter and what their entire family is about to go through. Every single time that thing flies by, I feel an instant jolt of gratitude that Curtis isn't worse and he is almost home. At the same time, I am awash in profound sadness and heartbreak for the misery that patient and their family are about to face. Curtis has a great view, but that chopper is a constant, evil reminder of pain and suffering. No matter how positive I try to be, I know that we are in Hell.

Hell isn't somewhere you get to instantly. It's not like you're on a bus and the driver tells you, "Next stop, Hell." Hell creeps quietly into every corner of your life. It infects you with its relentless misery. It's only when you're overwhelmed by it that you realize, "I'm in Hell." By then, there's no getting out. It has taken over. This is your new reality, and you better find some way to get through it. My way of getting through it is setting goals. The big finish, of course, is Curtis coming home, but we have a long way to go, so there are numerous short-term goals: get the Imipenem kicked in by 11:59 PM Monday night, get the temperature down to ninety-nine within four hours, get the ventilator down to twenty within a week. Whatever it is, I always set a goal for Curtis. He's reached darned near every one. I continually set short- and medium-term goals. The long-term goal never changes.

I chatter away, telling Curtis not to worry about his vent not changing, that sitting up is no doubt taxing and very hard work. "I am so proud of you!" I offer him the magnetic letters. He isn't interested in the letters or in anything I am saying. He is alert, watching cartoons on the TV. I offer to change the channel. No response. He looks so uncomfortable. He is so swollen, it me hurts to look at him. I remember how uncomfortable I felt when I was pregnant, when my toes and fingers were tight and painful from edema. Curtis looks four times his normal size. He is swollen everywhere, like somebody inflated him. His belly looks like Santa's. I offer pillows for his arms and feet, but get no response. I tell him I am going to bring his clippers and cut his hair for him because he's grown quite the 'fro. Nothing I say gets any reaction. Maybe he is just out of it. I'm not sure. I smell code brown. I ask him if he is code brown. Still no response. I lift his gown, and yep, he is code brown. But I also notice his testicles—they are swollen up to the size of a cantaloupe! *Ouch! Poor man.*

I call the nurses' station and display "code brown" through the window. We don't have to wait as long as usual, about thirty minutes. That's still twenty-nine minutes too long, but my blood is just starting to simmer. They have to put him back in bed anyway, as he's been the chair for an hour. They're all quite pleased with him for enduring the chair. Curtis is pleased that his nurses are so pleased with him. I guess I'm just chopped liver.

They don't throw me out this time; I stay and help get Curtis clean and back in bed. Curtis responds to his nurses. They get the eye gestures, the feeble arm motions. He doesn't give them blank angry stares. Curtis continues to ignore me until they throw me out for shift change. I go out to smoke cigarettes and think about this revolting new development.

If I didn't know better, I'd swear he is angry with me. Surely that can't be it. He's been through a lot. He might be dopey from drugs. Maybe he doesn't know who I am. No, no. I run through all these things and discount them. The only answer is that he is angry with me. But that just can't be. Maybe I accidentally stepped on his foot or something. I rack my brain and cannot figure out why or how he could possibly be angry with me. Stop being silly, Lisa. Ask him about it when he gets better. It must be something else. Maybe he is just spacing out. Maybe I overlooked something I was supposed to do for him. No, I am really thorough. Maybe it is really uncomfortable to sit in that chair and he has to concentrate to endure it. That must be it. He'll be in a better mood when he's recovered from being out of bed.

He's ignored me all day, for the most part. That's OK, as long as we're together and he's getting better. It is puzzling, for sure, but whatever floats his boat, y'know? I can never know what he went through, what all these drugs are doing to him. I can never expect him to be in a good mood, he has no reason to be. He doesn't know he almost died several times and I'm not going to tell him until he comes home. He can be as grumpy as he wants to be. A tiny, nagging thought lingers that he is ignoring me on purpose, and it hurts a little, but I can't be sure that is it at all and there's no sense worrying about it.

My only consolation is that Curtis is almost out of here. Karen has already told me to start thinking about a long-term acute care facility because he will need rehab. I don't like the sound of "long term acute care," but she assures me it is for rehab.

I know he no longer belongs in a burn unit. He still has open wounds on his abdomen, but it is too late for skin grafting. They will just take a lot longer to heal and close; they're not a reason for him to stay in a burn unit. Anywhere but the burn unit at Memorial Hermann is fine with me. I want him closer to home. Karen is putting together a list of possible facilities.

I get back from shift change and chatter away about this news. Maybe he'll cheer up, knowing he's getting closer to home. I never get much of a reaction from him. Every time I see a nurse, I remind her that I want a clock in the room and show her where I want it. I know it's useless on the weekend, but I always try. I tell Curtis I am still working on getting a clock for his room. My plan is to work every day until at least four o'clock, then spend the evenings with him. I ask Curtis if he wants his family to come and visit him. I ask him this all the time, now that he is awake. All I get is a blank stare.

Calvin stops by. Curtis seems very happy to see him. Curtis has a code brown, and we have to wait an interminable and unacceptable amount of time for somebody to come and clean him up. But since Curtis seems happy visiting with Calvin, I don't get too bent out of shape. Finally, someone arrives, and we are excused for the cleaning.

While we're waiting for them to finish, I talk to Calvin about the family. I tell him that Curtis has been cognizant for a few days now and that I keep asking him if he wants his family to visit him. I never get a reaction, but after seeing how happy he was to see Calvin, I wonder if he'd like to see them. Maybe Curtis is sick of Dawn and me. Heck, I don't know, but he was happy to see Calvin and I want him to be happy. I ask Calvin if he can call the family and ask them to come. I also ask him to tell them to please let me know their travel plans, but I realize I'm beating my head against a brick wall with that request. Calvin didn't stay long, he never does.

Curtis and I spend a relatively quiet evening together. We've been watching TV, and I am lounging in my recliner. Quack! I look at his vent, but it is over as quickly as it happened. He's been quiet and still, so I know it isn't a cough. Everything is fine; it must have been just a hiccup or something. Something is constantly beeping, blipping, quacking, ringing, buzzing. I ignore almost all of it except the ventilator. I always glance at it and at him when it quacks. It usually means he needs to be suctioned, but not this time. So we go back to watching TV.

A few minutes later, Quack! Quack! I get up this time and look at Curtis. He is fine. It is so odd for his vent to quack when he hasn't moved a bit. I check his vitals; all is well. I watch him breathe several times and watch the vent. All is normal; all is fine. The graph shows the disruptions to his breathing when the machine quacked. Both times, he really didn't take a breath at all. I trace all the hoses, wires, and tubes to the vent. Everything appears connected.

Quack! Quack! This time, I am looking right at the screen when it happens. Large red letters flash, **WITHOUT VENTILATION 0:00:00:30**, and I notice the main hose shudder a little. It is over as soon as it happens, but I've never seen the screen display **WITHOUT VENTILATION** and start timing tenths of a second before. This gives me a jolt of terror, I push the call button. "Yes, Mr. Wright?" "There's something wrong with the vent." She says, "I'll page Respiratory."

I stay by his bedside and talk to him. I am outwardly calm, but I've had a spurt of adrenaline. There is nothing wrong with him; there is something wrong with his vent. I already know this much, and I don't want to see another Batman flying emergency due to defective equipment. I'm awake now.

Quack! Quack! Quack! Quack! **WITHOUT VENTILATION 0:00:15:10**. Fifteen seconds is a long time. The vent quacks and flashes the **WITHOUT VENTILATION** screen intermittently, and the hose shudders and then rights itself. I inspect the main hose a little more closely. It goes from Curtis' neck to the machine, but it has some slack in it so it makes the letter U on the side of his bed. The belly of the U is full of water, and it appears that air can't get through. This is our problem. There is a canister at the base of the machine; it appears that the U-shaped hose drains into this canister. This, too, is full of water. I surmise this canister is to capture the condensation and, since it is full, the water is backing up into his hose. This indicates to me that it's been a very long time since they've emptied the canister. This has never happened before, although he's been on the vent for over a month.

I check his oxygen saturation. It's down to ninety percent, that is no cause for alarm. I call the nurses' station again and tell her he can't breathe because the hose is full of water. She says she paged Respiratory.

Shouldn't ICU nurses have enough training to drain a hose? Most kindergartners can do it. There must be something highly delicate and technical about draining this hose if only the most specialized medical personnel can attempt it.

I stay at Curtis' bedside, calmly telling him for the millionth time that my cousin Jackie is coming for a second visit, all the way from Michigan. She will be here in three days. Last time she was here, she took the kids to Wal-Mart and had their pictures taken. I never had a chance to pick them up, so she is going to pick them up when she comes back. Blah, blah, blah...

Quack! Quack! Quack! **WITHOUT VENTILATION 0:00:25:50.** The hose shudders and rights itself, but then it goes right back to quacking and timing. It shudders and rights itself again, and goes right back to timing and quacking. I get Curtis to focus on me and take slow, deep breaths. This happens three times in a row. I study the hose again and wonder if I can disconnect it. It has a wire running through it. What if I can't get it hooked back up? What if that wire is something important? I'd better not go disconnecting his life support machine. Some people might construe that as murder. I wonder if I can drain the canister.

Quack! Quack! Quack! Quack! **WITHOUT VENTILATION.** The thing is screaming at me. **WITHOUT VENTILATION!** I pick up the hose and straighten it so every drop that the overflow canister can hold will leave the hose. This gives Curtis a reprieve so he can catch his breath. His oxygen saturation dips below ninety percent. I push the call button, "Somebody really needs to get in here and drain this hose. He can't breathe." She replies, "We're working on it." Well, she obviously hadn't paged Respiratory stat. I could have ridden up and down the elevator four times by now. What if Respiratory is trapped outside the locked door?

Quack! Quack! Quack! Quack! There is no stopping it this time. Quack! Quack! Quack! **WITHOUT VENTILATION.** The hose keeps shuddering. I hold Curtis' hand and tell him to look at me and take slow deep breaths with me. "You can breathe, Curtis." He has that familiar wild-eyed, frantic look on his face. He can't breathe. I know it, and a state-of-the-art machine is telling us so. It is letting everybody in the world know, as it is designed to do. Batman doesn't come.

It's been over a minute. That's a long time to go without breathing. This thing is honking and quacking like it is desperate for somebody to come running. *Yeah, you and me both, buddy.* I keep holding Curtis'hand and calmly, slowly telling him to look at me, to breathe with me. Well, he isn't taking his eyes off me and he is gripping my hand. I know he is desperate for air. He is suffocating right in front of me. My adrenaline level is sky high. I'm so scared, but I have to stay calm for Curtis. I want to grab the phone and call 911. Here he is, in a world-class facility, surrounded by the best equipment money can buy—yet nobody is coming, nobody is helping him. I want to call 911, but I don't dare let go of Curtis' hand.

One minute, fifteen seconds—he is starting to turn blue. His oxygen saturation drops to the low eighties. I don't want to see seventy percent. I drop his hand and run to the door, still calmly and slowly telling him to take slow, deep breaths. I open the "never-open-this-door" door, look right at Dr. Beverly Hills at the nurses' station, and desperately cry out, "He **can't breathe**!"

Curtis' nurse is passing the nurses' station, on her way to the room next door with her arms full of supplies. Dr. Beverly Hills stands up and looks at her. She never stops moving but says, snottily, "I paged respiratory. Whaddya want me to do?" She disappears into the other patient's room. Dr. Beverly Hills doesn't move. I go back to Curtis. I am not going to let him die while I am bickering with these hateful people. I hold his hand and try to keep him focused. He is panicked, wild-eyed, and turning blue. He's suffocating, and there's not a damned thing I can do. It's difficult to describe the range of emotions I'm feeling—helpless to do anything to save him, terrified that he's going to die any second, furious that nobody is coming to help.

After more than two minutes, Respiratory finally strolls in. He is putting on his hefty bags in the anteroom and I try to rush him into the room, "Forget about all that. He can't breathe; the hose is full of water!" Respiratory strolls in with me nipping at his heels, "Drain that hose. Quick, quick!"

Respiratory is some Jamaican guy—apparently, the "Don't Worry, Be Happy" song was written about him. No Batman here. He takes his sweet time getting the bag onto Curtis' neck. Finally, he starts pushing in desperately needed air. He drains the hose while he bags Curtis. He gets Curtis all hooked back up, and we watch him for a few minutes. Watch his color come back. Watch his oxygen saturation come back up. *Whew!* Jamaica suctions Curtis for good measure. He stays and watches him for about ten minutes, then finally flashes me a smile, "He is good, Mon." I remind him to drain the overflow canister, as well. He does that and leaves.

I can get a Big Mac at McDonald's faster than I can get oxygen in this hospital.

Visiting hours are over, and I have to leave. I'm still shaking as I drive home. I know it is a very real possibility that Curtis will die while I'm not there. It tortures me to leave him. Everybody is too busy or too indifferent to take care of him. If I think about it for one second, I can picture him lying there all alone, desperate for air. So I try not to have those thoughts. If he dies, that will be the cause.

If that happens, I'll call the police immediately and have his room marked as a crime scene and every piece of equipment, including the monitors at the nurses' station, confiscated as evidence. I'm sure all that sophisticated equipment records everything somewhere. They'll have to explain it to the entire world. There is absolutely no excuse for what happened tonight.

I get to the burn unit at eleven and wait outside the hateful locked doors. I pick up the wall phone and hear, "Curtis is getting his bath. We'll call you when we're done." I ask, "Do you have my cell phone number?" They hang up! Just where are they going to call me? There are some chairs out by the elevators and there is a phone on a table, but it isn't hooked up. I study the doors, trying to locate the locking mechanism.

I go to the chairs by the elevators. Somebody left a Sunday paper. I've been thinking about getting Curtis a recliner before he comes home, but I don't have time to look for one. I flip through all the ads. A couch catches my eye. It's on sale for five hundred dollars. I keep looking for recliners and eyeball the comfy couch. I add the circular to the never-ending stash of papers in my backpack.

I try the locked doors again. Nobody answers the phone. I stand there for fifteen minutes or so, hoping somebody will come in or out. Somebody finally does, so I sneak in. They tell me, "Curtis is still being bathed. Come back later."

Had I known I'd have an extra hour or so to kill, I could have done a bazillion things at home. But instead, I'm having another cigarette. I don't feel like calling anybody, and I have no updates to give. I am bone tired, after another sleepless night with the suffocation terror.

I am finally allowed in at twelve-thirty. Curtis is cold. I go out to the linen closet to get him another blanket. Of course, this means the whole decontamination routine again, but I am used to it by now. I grab an extra pillow for myself and get more 4 × 4 bandages from the supply closet. We can never have too many of those. The hellish days of suctioning blood from his mouth are over, finally, so I don't need to grab the suctioning tool. The herpes ointment is clearing up his face quickly. I still don't know why the inside of his mouth bled so ferociously for so long. I can only surmise that it's somehow related to the herpes, as it stopped as soon as they started using the herpes ointment. But it's something else to be grateful for. I get back to the room and give Curtis another blanket. I remove his boot splints, put socks on him, and rub his feet, chattering all the while. I call attention to all the progress he's made, "Vent is down to fifty. You're on your way, Curtis! Blah, blah, blah..."

Curtis is tired from his bath, and I am pooped. I get him comfortable, check for code brown, drain the Foley hose, and look everything over. I close the blinds and make my nest in my recliner. I get all comfy. As I'm drifting off, I hear the helicopter take off and feel a wave of relief at how lucky we are and, simultaneously, sympathy for the family whose lives are about to be torn apart. I hear the helicopter come back. A constant reminder. I am falling asleep when a voice on the intercom announces that Mr. Wright has visitors.

I get about ten winks before the voice comes back and announces the arrival of guests. I open my eyes and give the speaker on the wall a dirty look, as if it can see me, "I don't care. We're sleeping." I notice people in the anteroom, getting their hefty bags on. It is Curtis' brother Richard and his girlfriend Imelda. I haven't seen Imelda since Curtis' birthday weekend when we all had such a nice time. Richard keeps coming out here with his wife. I like Imelda, but I figure she hates me by now, just like the rest of them. They come in and I tell Curtis his brother is here. I can tell he is happy to see Richard, but he is uncomfortable having Imelda here, for whatever reason. Imelda senses it, as well. She says she'll wait in the nonexistent waiting room. I sure don't want to stay here with his brother. In spite of everything, I can see how happy Curtis is to see him, so once again I'll be gracious and leave

When I come back, the visitors are gone and Curtis is code brown again. I start my code brown announcements and start timing. He finally gets cleaned up at nine o-clock. Ninety minutes. I still try to move him and get it off him as well as I can, but he is still too heavy for me to move. I can get a leg up on my shoulder and clean what I can reach, but it isn't enough. This is how we spend the evening: trying to get code brown off him and calling every fifteen or twenty minutes for somebody to help me.

I am really bitter about the diarrhea. I don't know how many times I can say it. It is inhumane and inexcusable. I never shut up about it. I am pissed off about it. They leave him in it constantly. I beg, bitch, and plead with anyone on the staff that will listen, "Please don't do that to him." It continues to happen regularly.

I plan to work until four o-clock. Curtis is out of danger. As much I want to be there watching over him, folks all across the state need to pay for their roofs, and I need to keep my job.

Dawn has spoken to several people in administration, and there is talk of having a meeting. I'm not interested in a meeting. I know that nobody cares, and yelling at them doesn't make me feel any better. Every minute of the day is precious to me. I want to spend as many minutes as I can with Curtis, since he is awake and alert. My sister and I agreed that she will handle this meeting. These are important issues, but I know Dawn can handle it and she'll speak perfectly well on our behalf. She is still convinced that somebody in the hospital can help and she's determined to find that person.

Dawn calls me to let me know that I have to be present. They refuse to have a meeting with only Dawn. HIPAA forbids it. I call Twila and explain that I need to spend my weekdays at work and my evenings and weekends with Curtis and that we have appointed Dawn to speak for us. She says that I have to be present at the meeting to comply with HIPAA. I ask her if we can meet on the weekend. No, it has to be during a weekday. *Of course.* She knows what a long road Curtis and I have been down. If this were a mediocre facility, they would bend over backward to accommodate us. But this is a world-class facility. I must be confused about the definition of world class. This attitude is typical of our whole experience and it is exactly why I don't want to bother with a meeting. It is just a meaningless gesture on their part.

The meeting is eventually arranged for next Thursday, May eighth. The attendees will be me and my sister; Twila and her boss; the director of patient relations; useless Mitzi, manager of the burn unit; Mitzi's boss, the director of the Burn Unit; and the Vice President of staffing. I don't see why Mitzi and the VP of staffing are needed. We need to be meeting with the CEO so he can hear about the despicable treatment we've received in his hospital directly from the source. **That** will make me feel better. Now I'm stressed about missing work to go to a pointless meeting.

I get to Curtis' room before the evening shift change. He seems mad at me, probably because I haven't been here all day. I remind him again that I have to work so he'll have a house to come home to. I praise all his progress. I issue a code brown. I tell him about Jackie coming tomorrow. Curtis really wants to talk, so we try the magnet board again. He is able to move a few letters, but I have no idea what he is trying to say. I remind the nurses that he is code brown. I keep working on what Curtis is trying to tell me. He gives up. Something about a chain or a tire, something bizarre. I keep reminding the speaker on the wall that we have a code brown until I am evicted for shift change. I come back an hour later from shift change and he is still code brown!

I go to update the calendar. It's gone! A clock is hanging in its place. That's not where I told them to put it. We are now on the month of May. March and April were taped to the wall next to it. All the days were covered in X's and my strange notes—it is obviously a diary of this man's journey. It is gone. I look all over. There aren't that many places to look. All the walls are covered in pictures and drawings from the children and cards from well-wishers. The calendar is gone. I ransack all the cabinets and drawers in the anteroom.

No calendar. Each page is huge—17 × 22 inches. It's hard to miss, but it's gone.

I go to the nurses' station, find the charge nurse, and demand that she call maintenance. She needs to find out who hung the clock and where Curtis' calendar is. Right now. And he's still code brown! She calls the room a short time later and says she can't find out anything about the calendar because it happened during day shift. She is very sorry, but it will have to wait until tomorrow.

My husband has missed a big chunk of his life, and those pages are to help him get it back! I go back out and ask her where they take the trash when it leaves the room. She shows me to a room full of garbage bags waiting to be picked up. I go get some gloves and get to work. I start with the red biohazard bags. I rip open the first bag and start wading through other people's code brown, blood, burned skin and tissue, and who knows what all else. I tear through these trash bags, on the verge of hysteria. Please, please, let them be here. Why do I have to do this? What kind of asshole would take them off the wall and throw them away? I am desperate to find them and angry that they might be in here.

I find them in the fourth biohazard bag. May twenty-eighth has code brown smeared on it. The pages are wadded up, crumpled, and ripped. I take my gloves off and leave all the ripped-open biohazard bags just like they are. I go to the nurses' station and lay the pages on the counter. I show them to the charge nurse and ask her, "Who would do this? What kind of an asshole would do this? Everybody knows I am keeping this journal for him; it is taped to the wall!" I am crying. Damn these tears, and damn this place straight to Hell. She is nodding and saying she is sorry, she knows I've been keeping this for Curtis. I want to know who did this, I want to ask them personally why. She gets on the phone. I never get an answer tonight. A couple days later, Twila assures me the maintenance department has been properly scolded.

My cousin Jackie arrives; her husband is coming tomorrow. She wants to visit Curtis this time, so we decide she'll come to the hospital with me on Saturday. The first thing I notice when I get to Curtis' room this evening is his new poo bag. It's better than leaving him to lie in diarrhea.

Curtis seems angry again. He always seems angry with me. I don't understand it. After the strong spiritual connection we've had, how can he be mad at me? If I didn't know better, I'd swear he's ignoring me on purpose. He doesn't respond to any of my chattering. I lift my gown and turn my back to him so he can look at my nice butt. Not even a smile. He is ignoring me. He doesn't want me fussing over him or doing anything for him. I stand at the foot of his bed and lift my hat so he can see what's left of my hair. Nothing. He doesn't want anything to do with me. Well, fine then. We watch TV. He can be as grumpy as he wants to; I'm not going to take it personally.

Six-twenty. Ten minutes until shift change. His vent quacks; he needs to cough. I call the nurse. Suctioning his garden hose is never something I mess with. Dawn doesn't even do that. Well, I'll be damned! His nurse comes in and Curtis looks at her like she's Florence Nightingale. You can see the cartoon hearts popping out of his eyes in her direction. Whatever! He is so happy to see his beloved nurse. "Oh, yes, sweet angel, please suction my garden hose. Oh, bless you, you wonderful woman. I love you so much." It's disgusting. You poor, clueless man.

I leave for shift change and go out to smoke. I am miffed. He **is** ignoring me; he **is** mad at me. He doesn't want me touching him or messing with any of his equipment. Only his dear, precious, angel nurses. What an asshole! At this moment, when I have the thought that he is an asshole, I **know** he will come home. How do you like that? I call Ginger and tell her this story; it is actually kind of funny. She says, "He just has no clue, does he?" I reply, "No, apparently not. I guess he didn't hear me telling him to pee after all!"

I haven't seen him sitting up in a chair since Sunday. They do that in the mornings when I am at work. I try to get them to put Curtis in the chair after shift change, but they won't do it on the night shift. Curtis doesn't want any care from me, so I have light duty tonight. He is equipped with a poo containment system, so that issue is resolved.

Twila's boss taps on the window. I look at her, but I don't get up. I ignore her. The phone rings. She says she wants to talk to me. I don't like giving away my precious time with Curtis, but he doesn't seem to want me here, anyway. She escorts me to the room where New Admit was before he died. I start lamenting about all the new nurses, what a catastrophe it was when he was so sick. About the code brown. About Mitzi lying. About the family. About them letting his mother in at the crack of dawn, but telling me I can't come until eleven even though he was begging for me. About the calendar. About Dr. Lung never talking to me. About the staff ignoring the isolation procedures. About everything that has made our experience so hellish. I'm having to repeat all these distressing reports for another new person. What's the use? She takes a lot of notes. And she scolds me for my foul language. She tells me it "puts up barriers."

Please. My language didn't get foul with anybody until he'd been here almost two months, and then wow! Drop a few F-bombs, and he gets cleaned up. "If dropping some F-bombs is what it takes to get that diarrhea off him, then I'll come here every day with a B-52 F-bomber. That or Marvin Zindler and his camera crew." She says she'd rather have the camera crew. Yeah, I bet they would. They have the political spin machine down to a science. I wish they'd put as much effort into patient care as they put into covering their asses. This meeting is over. So is this day. It's time for me to leave.

Day 64: Wednesday, May 7, 2003

When I arrive, Curtis' sportin' new bag is gone and he is code brown. I start my code brown announcements again. I see another resident and go to ask him about it. He says Dr. Plastic Surgeon is not happy about somebody putting in a poo bag because it is another invitation for infection. It is forbidden. They will have to clean him up. I tell him they don't clean him up; they leave him code brown for hours. He doesn't believe me. He goes to tell the nurses' to clean him up. I tell him I haven't seen Curtis' booty, but I bet he has raging diaper rash. I make him go look at his booty. He goes and looks, but it is greased up in white diaper rash cream. Yeah, because he has raging diaper rash from being left in diarrhea for hours on end. I don't want him to get any more infections, but that single day without code browns was a nice reprieve. Now I'm back to the endless battle of trying to get somebody to help me clean him.

There is a new sign on the door to Curtis' room. It says "Call 555- 5555 if you observe any violations to infection control procedures. Please report the date, time, and nature of the violation." There are also flyers posted on red paper with warnings about "Arnie Acinetobacer,"Arnie is a character in the shape of a whole dill pickle with arms and legs and a face

I discover over a year later that Dr. Plastic Surgeon is on the committee that determines infection control procedures for this hospital. It makes perfect sense. I always knew he cared. I wish he were Chairman of the Code Brown Committee. I wonder if they realize that their procedures for controlling the spread of bacteria are not followed by over half of the caregivers that enter Curtis' room.

It's meeting day. I hate to be in the building and not be with Curtis. We all assemble in the office of the VP of staffing. She starts the meeting by letting us know she has only twenty minutes; somebody else is waiting for her. Well, this is starting off on the wrong foot. I have a job to keep, and I have a very sick husband in their burn unit. My time is unquantifiably more valuable than hers, and I am here to give this meeting all the time it needs. She sends the message that this is nothing more than a gesture.

I decide to let them choke on HIPAA, and I let my sister do all the talking. Dawn gets right into the issue of consistent caregivers. She recaps all the things that were overlooked while he was so sick. All the dozens of different people we reported his eyes, face, and everything else to. All the infection control violations. There are so many, there is no infection control. The Unit Director says that Curtis is no longer a burn patient and she can't devote burn nurses to his care. My sister reminds her we never asked for only burn nurses. Ever. Plenty of trauma float nurses took care of Curtis. We even put together our own rotation of nurses. There are fourteen shifts in a week. We easily came up with fourteen nurses, which is more than enough to cover Curtis' shifts and provide consistency. Half the people in this room, including this woman, have already heard this many times over. We never demanded burn nurses. We have told them all of this before, but their only response is "he's not a burn patient anymore." When he was so sick and it was such a problem, he was still very much a burn patient and he didn't get burn nurses.

My sister also points out that Curtis is not an indigent case. They are billing more than enough revenue to throw a couple nickels at the problem. Dawn tells them, "I am a shift supervisor at Haven of Loving Care Hospital. Scheduling nurses is part of what I do, and I understand the issues you encounter in scheduling. I can tell you this, though: My sister calls me **daily** and tells me how much she hates your hospital. If I had a patient or a patient's family member who felt that way about Haven of Loving Care, I would bend over backwards to change that opinion. Don't you want to change her opinion of your hospital?" Nobody has an answer for that, but they are all taking notes feverishly.

I go back to the days of Mean Nurse and Mitzi later lying about our conversation. "Curtis was afraid of this woman. It doesn't matter if you think she's a good nurse, a patient was afraid of her. Do something about it! You didn't even take it seriously! Curtis never complained about another person, just this one, so there has to be something to it." VP checks her watch.

I tell them how hostile their locked doors are. They are running a burn unit. Human beings are burned, maimed, and scarred for life—if they live. Where is the compassion and humanity in this facility? Unit Director says they have to lock the door because certain patients need privacy.

Excuse me? I remind her about the constant stream of Wrights parading in and out of his room night and day and how they were wearing him out and he couldn't get any rest. About talking to dozens of administrators and being told that the hospital can't police visitors, I can't police visitors, and Curtis can't police visitors. Anybody and everybody can visit him whenever they want. But now, suddenly, "We have to lock the door because some patients need privacy." Kiss my ass. Some special patients need privacy, but you won't help the sickest man in your ICU get a **nap**!

This fuels my fury and brings us right to the issue of the day: Code Brown. I look right at VP and summarize everything my husband has suffered since he's been here. I remind her how well he is doing now and how hard Dawn and I have worked to keep him in a positive frame of mind and encourage him to come home. I believe attitude and atmosphere have a lot to do with him getting well.

I ask her to picture herself trapped and helpless in a hospital bed. You don't know what time it is, you don't know what day it is, you don't know where you are, you have a machine breathing for you, and you're hooked up to equipment from every port in your body. You can't move. Your muscles don't work. You can't talk. It's hard enough to endure all this if you're all warm and comfy in bed. It's quite another experience to be trapped like this while lying in burning diarrhea. I am crying by now. *Damn these infernal tears*. I don't want Curtis to think, "I can't do this anymore." He's come too far to give up now over something so stupid. Rather than spend the money to get him and all the other patients adequate nursing, you put in a poo bag! I tell her I want the CEO of this hospital to lay in burning diarrhea for two hours and I want to come pinch his cheek and smile at him and tell him he's getting the world's best care! And VP says, "Actually, the CEO is a woman." At that, she has to leave. Her other guest is waiting for her.

They have all been taking notes vigorously. Dawn addresses yet another issue with the remaining figureheads. The only people who ever tell Curtis what is happening to him are my sister and me. All manner of white coats come into his room to do this or that, but they never say a word to him. They have all given him up for dead, and they treat him like a carcass in a bed. He can't talk, so they don't talk to him or explain anything to him. This has to stop. It did, after this meeting.

I speak up about my relentless pursuit to find out how many units of blood he's had. Why is this so hard to find out? I've been asking for weeks and weeks. This is an easy question for somebody to answer. I want to know how many units of blood he's had! That leads to telling them about Dr. Lung never calling me. It's been over seven weeks, I've asked **every single day** to talk to him, and he still hasn't called!

The meeting winds down, and Dawn and I head to see Curtis. Yesterday, Jackie picked up the photos of the children that she had Wal- Mart take during her last visit. I hang a 10 × 13 picture on the ceiling over Curtis' head. He pulled the feeding tube out of his nose yesterday. Rather than put it back in, they ordered him a liquid diet. I get there in time to help his nurse sit him up on the side of the bed. He has a food tray in front of him. The swelling has gone down considerably. Now he looks thin and frail. He's weak and shaky, and he looks light-headed from sitting up. It seems a little silly to have a tray full of food in front of him, and the smell of the cheese soup is almost enough to make me puke. I take a picture of him. Another big milestone. Sitting on the side of his bed!

I think he looks great. Dr. Pinch Hitter comes in to check on him and she almost faints. She is so excited; she can't believe he is sitting up with food in front of him. The last time she saw him was the Saturday before Easter when she vacuumed his lungs and tried to save him from Level 5. Save him she did. This is her work.

They've taken him for another CAT scan of his abdomen. This gut has been nagging at me for two months now. His belly never looks the same from one day to the next. The next time I see Dr. Plastic Surgeon, I am going to ask him to get a different gut special-ist to evaluate him. There is still something wrong with the belly.

Curtis is always having all manner of X-rays and CAT scans. I rarely find out the results, but I never stop trying. I can ask five different people and I'll get three conflicting answers. One will say it is fine, no problem. One will say they are deeply concerned about the hoosawhatsit. And the other three will shrug their shoulders and say they don't know. I have to surmise who is correct. It is maddening. When Dr. Beverly Hills is on, he shows me Curtis' chest X-rays for the day and lets me know what the lab is growing. I know I can trust Dr. Beverly Hills and Dr. Plastic Surgeon to have the skinny, but I don't see much of either one of them. Other doctors and specialists do tests that Dr. Plastic Surgeon never knows about. I have to get my own answers by studying Curtis—and his flow sheets, when I can sneak a peek. I can learn a lot just from knowing who ordered what.

Twila calls to tell me that Curtis has received forty-four units of blood to date. I have no idea how much the human body holds, but that sounds like enough to flush and fill a person many times over. No telling what other diseases and disorders will manifest themselves. He's had a lot of plasma, too, but I never tried to find out how much. You can't fight every battle. Curtis has more blood after today, but this is the only official count I ever received. Forty-four pints of blood.

My mother is back in town for Mother's Day weekend. My folks and my sister and brother come to the hospital to see Curtis and to take the kids to my dad's for the weekend. The children haven't seen Curtis in a long time, but they are not going to see him until he is off the garden hose.

Curtis still has to be suctioned on a regular basis. They still use the "put the smaller tube down into the hose" method, but now sometimes they disconnect the hose altogether and bag him to suck the clouds out—like you would plunge a toilet. This causes him to gag violently and cough something up. I can see how this would be a hard thing for a new person to watch, but I am used to it. I always watch carefully to see what comes up, how thick it is, what color it is. All the time he has been here, he's had all types of goo coming out of his nose, his mouth, his hose, his gut, his booty, you name it. I always check it to see how it is different from the last time. Anything new always means something. If he were a stranger and I were a casual observer, I would have been puking my guts out long before now. But he is somebody I love, and he is very sick. I have to pay attention to everything. I never think it is gross or disgusting; it is sad and heartbreaking.

This evening, the nurse is using the plunger on Curtis as my dad, mom, and sister come in. My folks hang back by the wall until it is over. I watch to see what comes up. A big blood clot of a "loogie." OK, now that had to be gross. I go to the canister to study it, and I ask the nurse why there is a cluster of blood. She says it is a blood clot. Well, this is new, what does it mean? She doesn't seem worried about it. Just something that had been in his lungs and now it is in a canister. It must mean we're getting close to the bottom of the muck and cleaning out his lungs. I take it to be a good sign. We see more blood clots during the next week.

The nurse finishes and leaves. My mom wants to show me some shoes she bought me. Curtis 'coughs.' Quack! goes the vent, and my mom almost jumps out of her skin. My mom and dad are standing on one side of Curtis' bed, and my sister and I are on the other. Curtis is not interested in anyone but my dad. Those cartoon hearts that never come in my direction are popping all over my dad. Curtis puts his hand up, and I tell my dad that Curtis wants to hold his hand. My dad grasps Curtis' hand, and Curtis brings his other hand over to hug my dad's hand between his both of his. My dad starts talking as he normally would, telling Curtis about a motorcycle trip he and my mother had taken. Curtis is in love. He is gazing at my father with so much ardor I can't believe any human being can be so enamored with another. It is comical. I wish I had a video camera. The rest of us are chopped liver; we don't even exist. My mom leaves to switch with my brother, who's is in the chair area by the elevators with the kids. I just can't glorify it by calling it a waiting room. Maybe Curtis wants guy time. My brother comes in, and he is ignored as well. Curtis only wants my dad. He will not let go of his hand, and he is gazing and smiling at him. It is silly. My dad is there for forty-five minutes, chatting and being loved and petted by Curtis.

When it comes time for them to leave, Curtis is not happy. He looks so sad watching my dad leave. All the rest of the evening he ignores me except that occasionally he gestures at the door and looks at it expectantly. He wants my dad to come back. Poor thing. I really have to wonder about brain damage at this point. He's been off the cocktails and alert and awake for well over a week now. It is a bizarre display. If it weren't worrisome, it would be hilarious. Maybe he is just starting to go insane from never leaving the room. Who knows? We have to get him off the hose and get him home.

I have settled on a long-term acute care facility that is practically right in our backyard. I toured and visited several facilities in the Med Center and all over town, but they are all depressing. I want Curtis to come home. Someone from the care facility is supposed to come and evaluate Curtis on Monday. I tried to arrange the evaluation for a time when I could be here, but I never got results. Oh, well, they're the experts. They should know whether or not they can admit him.

Jackie comes with me to visit Curtis today. We get all our gear on and are standing beside Curtis' bed saying hello, when the intercom voice announces the arrival of visitors for Mr. Wright. Well, Mr. Wright already has visitors. I ignore the voice coming out of the wall. Jackie, who can see the anteroom, says she'll leave because there are people coming in. I tell her, "No you won't. You've made two trips here, and this is the day you planned to visit him. You will not leave!"

I go to get his lotion from the cart. His arms are dry, and he doesn't have any compression garments on. Jackie takes a couple steps closer to Curtis' feet so I can lotion his arm. Right then, Curtis' sister comes into the room. Jackie and I are on the opposite side of his bed, furthest from the anteroom door. Sister can walk right up to Curtis on the side of the bed closest to the door. Instead, she comes around and muscles her way next to me to get close to her brother's head. "Oh, dear brother, it's Irma. I'm here baby!" *Give me a break.* I put the lotion away and tell Jackie, "OK, let's go. I'm not up for this dog and pony show." Some other ladies come parading into the room. They're wearing gowns, hats, and masks, so they all look alike. I don't know who they are, and I don't care. You think they put lotion on his dry skin? No. You think they call for code brown and make sure he gets cleaned up pronto? No. You think they put an extra blanket on him when he is cold? No. They just stand wringing their hands and ordering our Savior to do all these things for Curtis.

Jackie and I go home. They will be there all day; I have no doubt. I clean the pool, and that's about it. There is no housework or cooking to do; Jackie has it all done. There is no yard work to do; her husband has it all covered. I am restless. I don't belong here; I belong with Curtis. I wait until after shift change, then head back. The drama queens are gone. I barely get a look at Curtis before I am kicked out again. They have decided to give him his baths at night so as not to interfere with his rehab during the day. The only daytime rehab I know of is Curtis sitting in a chair when I'm not here. I ask if I can give him his baths since I am here at night anyway. The nurse says she'll check into that.

I go to Wal-Mart and stock up on sponges, liquid Dove, Gold Bond butt powder, toothbrushes, razors, shaving cream, all kinds of luxurious bathing equipment and devices. I pick up some car and motorcycle magazines. I even buy him a Sponge Bob toothbrush. We love Sponge Bob SquarePants. I bought so much stuff that some of it is **still** unopened, two years later. I went a little overboard.

Day 68: Sunday, May 11, 2003 — Mother's Day

I arrive at eleven carrying about six Wal-Mart bags full of toiletries. I also brought Curtis' clippers so I can cut his hair. I am tired of waiting for permission. I show him all the stuff I bought for him. He isn't very interested. He is never very interested in anything I have to say. He never smiles at me. He always seems irritated with me. But I carry on as if everything is fine. I could drive myself crazy trying to figure it out, but I just try to ignore it. If he wants to be grumpy, he has every right.

I fetch extra towels and get him all situated to cut his hair. Man, am I glad I did! His hair is nappy and it has nests of matted dandruff. That can't feel good. It takes most of the afternoon to cut his hair and wash his head. The spot that was once a baseball-sized lump is now a sore. He has a bedsore on the back of his skull. *Poor baby.* More invaders arrive, so I tell Curtis I am going home. He isn't happy about that. I tell him his family will be here all afternoon, it is Mother's Day, and I'll see him tomorrow between four and five o'clock.

I decide that when he moves to a new facility I'm not going to tell his family where he is. If he wants them to know, he can tell them. I told the case manager and everybody at Memorial Hermann that his new location is to remain confidential. I never want to see his family again.

Karen calls me at work, late in the afternoon, to tell me that a lady from the acute care facility called her from Memorial Hermann. While she was examining Curtis, someone in his family said he is going to a different facility, not hers. Karen also has a message from Curtis' sister, wanting to arrange his move with her. Karen tells me she let the acute care lady know that those people at the hospital were not decision makers, and as far as she knows, he is going to her facility. She did not return the sister's call. I call the acute care lady, clear the air, and let her know he is definitely going to her facility if they can take him. She says they can and they hope to move him this week. They are waiting for a private room to become available, maybe by the end of the week. I tell her not to discuss this with anyone else. She says she is sorry, she has given her card to the people in the room. *Where the heck is HIPAA when you need it?*

I really want Curtis to come home as soon as he is off the garden hose. Karen keeps saying rehab, rehab, rehab. Rehab, schme-hab. We have exercise equipment at home, and they can have somebody come to the house. I haven't seen any rehab equipment at the care facility, other than an empty outdoor pool. We have a pool. I want him off the hose and home.

My sister tells me she visited Curtis after class this afternoon and gave him a nice manicure. I am so glad she did; his nails had gotten quite long. I am afraid to cut them; I might introduce bacteria or make him bleed uncontrollably. She spent over an hour on that project. She soaked his fingers, cleaned and trimmed his nails, massaged his hands, and put lotion on them. She says he loved it.

Jackie and Brad are leaving tomorrow, so I go to the furniture store and pay for the five-hundred-dollar sofa. I'm not going to pay fifty dollars for delivery, what a waste! I will pick it up from the warehouse on Saturday.

Jackie is eager to get home. Her father, my great-uncle, needs heart surgery. He is seventy-seven years old, and he has only one lung. It sounds pretty bad. Within two days, Uncle Moke is on a ventilator. Jackie calls me the day after his surgery and says nobody at the hospital will tell her or her mother anything about Moke's surgery. HIPAA forbids it. *I am surrounded by insanity. Now it has infected my family, thousands of miles away.*

I take an empty suitcase with me to the hospital tonight. We don't know when Curtis is going to move—it could be tomorrow or it could be a couple of weeks—so I start to pack all nonessentials to bring home. At shift change, I grab a BLT. After shift change, he is code brown and then I get to spend the evening begging for him to be cleaned. I still can't move him by myself, so I'm not allowed to do his baths.

Curtis gets a dinner tray now, right at six o'clock. He doesn't eat very much, and I have to write down what little he does eat. I decide I'll start getting myself something from the cafeteria and bring it to his room so we can eat dinner together. I am always starving when I get here in the evenings. If I eat at all, it is during the shift change. Most days, I don't eat anything.

Now that Curtis is awake, he can attempt to cough by himself. He's getting better and better at it. Sometimes when he coughs, the garden hose comes flying off his neck and sails across the bed. He is still getting a lot of support from the ventilator; he can't breathe without it. That hose goes flying, and I fly after it in a panic and try to hook it back up. I'm usually all thumbs, and I swear I can feel my hair turning white.

It happened to Dawn once while she was on the phone with me. I could hear his vent quacking through the phone, but that thing quacks any time he moves. I didn't think much about it. My sister was looking right at him but paying attention to our phone conversation. She hung up on me suddenly. When she called back, she said he got that "wild-eyed, frantic look" that I've told her about, and she realized his hose was in his lap. She raced over in a panic and plugged him back in. It's happening more frequently. If it happens while I'm not there... That's another of the many things that will worry me to death if I let it. I refuse to think about what is happening—or not happening—when I'm not there.

I stop at the cafeteria to get dinner for Curtis and me before I go up. I really want a big, greasy burger, but Curtis is on a liquid diet and that would be rude. I get a salad for myself and soup for Curtis. Fifteen bucks! This is going to be expensive if I do it every day. I head upstairs to have dinner with my husband for the first time in months. I have to wait outside the locked doors for a while. It seems like they always want to make sure I'm in a bad mood before I see Curtis.

Curtis has a fever. It's a low-grade fever, but a fever nonetheless. Oh, no, not this again. He has no appetite. I don't now, either. So much for the fifteen-dollar dinner.

Dr. Beverly Hills gives me an update. Curtis has cardiomegaly. "Cardio-what?" He says his heart is enlarged. His heart, like any other muscle, gets bigger when it is worked out. His heart has taken a beating, and he now has cardiomegaly. When his health returns and his blood pressure and heart rate return to normal levels, there is no reason not to expect his heart to return to its normal size. Oh, OK. By the way his liver is congested; it's starting to have trouble filtering everything. That, too, should return to normal as his health improves. Oh, yeah, and his kidneys took a dip again. *Great! Here we go again.* His health has improved considerably in the past week or so. Why are organs starting to shut down now?

I go to work briefly this morning, then leave to take Jackie and Brad to the airport in a mad rush. Shortly after I get back to work, my phone rings. It's Dr. Lung!

"Dr. Lung? **The** Dr. Lung?" I clutch my chest and tell him to get the paddles. He thinks that's funny. Curtis has been on the garden hose for over seven weeks—fifty-one days—and this is the first time I've spoken to Dr. Lung. That's not funny.

I hang on his every word. I may never hear from him again. I repeat everything he says back to him, as I understand it, to be certain that I'm not misunderstanding him. That's another popular response at Memorial Hermann, "You must have misunderstood." He says he is aggressively trying to wean Curtis from the vent. I like the sound of that. I ask him if this is a gradual process, or suddenly one day you can just unplug it, just like that. He says interestingly enough, he is writing a paper on that very subject. It's an unknown. Popular medical practice is to wean gradually, but he is weaning aggressively. If Curtis doesn't need the vent but is still on it, he wouldn't become dependent on it. So it is OK to wean him gradually, but Dr. Lung is weaning aggressively. The term "aggressively" is right up my alley.

I tell him that Curtis will be moving soon, and ask him to please make sure he personally shares his aggressive weaning therapy with the new admitting doctor. He says of course, absolutely, he will speak to the new admitting doctor before Curtis is moved. Dr. Lung says Curtis is febrile—feverish—again and he is certain the central line is the culprit. He says they keep moving the central line, and he keeps getting infections. They can move it back down to his groin, but that is just another warm, moist place that bacteria love. He says he removed the central line and installed a PICC line—a peripherally inserted central catheter. He explains that a PICC line is a more durable, long-term IV port. It is inserted into the arm and snakes through the main artery to the heart. It can stay in for many months without risk of infection.

I repeat all this to make sure I understand. I ask him three times if the regular central line is already out, right now as we speak. "Oh, yes, I took it out this morning. He's got a PICC line. I put it in myself." Regular IV lines, most commonly inserted in the wrist, are not meant for long-term use. The powerful drugs Curtis is getting would eat right through his veins. The PICC line is the answer and he put it in himself this morning. *A great day! Dr. Lung called me and he rescued Curtis from more infections.*

About an hour later, another new doctor calls me. He says he needs consent to perform a TEE test. I ask what that is. He says TEE stands for transesophageal echocardiogram, a test for the heart. My blood turns cold. "What test for his heart?" He explains they go down his throat with a scope and look at his heart, to look for disease or infection. He starts explaining the possible complications. My head is spinning. Dr. Lung didn't say anything about this. "They told me yesterday he has a big heart, but what else are they looking for?"

He says he doesn't know. I ask who ordered the test. He says he can't read the signature. He is very nice. He says he'll let the doctors know that I didn't give consent and I can speak to his doctors later. "No, no, no. My husband's been there for over two months. It might be days before I get to talk to any of his doctors. I don't even know which doctor to speak to. They're not going to talk to me about this, or they would have already. If he needs it, then do it. I give my consent. If there's something wrong with his heart, we need to find out now." I am crying. I'm scared. "I don't want him to die because I didn't let you look at his heart." *Now it's his heart. What next? What the f--- next!?* "His doctors told me his heart is enlarged but that it should get back to normal when he gets better. I just don't know what else they're looking for. Can you call me back at this number when you're done and tell me what you find?" He says yes, yes, he will.

I wait a couple of hours. I call Dawn. He is getting better, he is on his way, and now we've got heart trouble. Then I remember the congested liver. Can't livers grow back? I know his heart really took a beating for a while there, but not for several weeks. What else? What now? My sister is upset, too. She says cardiomegaly isn't a big cause for alarm, but they are obviously taking a good look at his heart. If Dr. Lung ordered it, then I have nothing to worry about, just throwing business to his golf buddy, Dr. Gargantuan Heart. But he didn't mention it. Acid poured into my stomach for the next ninety minutes. Nice Heart Doctor said it would only take thirty minutes or so. I call back to the nurses' station and ask what happened with the TEE. Curtis' nurse comes to the phone and says that Nice Heart Doctor left without performing the TEE.

Oh, Geez! I'm sorry I freaked out. Curtis, please don't have a heart attack and die. I told him to go ahead and do it. I just don't know what to do anymore. I am distressed the rest of the afternoon. You think everything's fine and on course and then bam! it's one thing after another. Burns, skin grafts, gallstones, sphincterotomy, gallbladder, cholelithiasis, surgery to scoop out gangrene, infected pancreatic pseudocyst, bacterial and yeast infections from head to toe, abdominal drain, foreign pelvic fluid collections, sepsis, unstable blood pressure, elevated heart rate, respiratory acidosis, bronchoscopies, collapsed lungs, raging pneumonia, acinetobacter, blazing fevers, mechanical ventilation, kidney failure, oozing wounds from facial herpes, melted eyeballs, rotting athlete's foot, burning diaper rash, total muscle atrophy— which leads us to gargantuan heart and trouble on liver street. No wonder everybody thinks Curtis is going to die.

What else is left? His brain; that's it. I don't think there's much wrong with his brain up to now. Some senility, for sure; but overall, he is still Curtis. Time will tell. I am probably senile by now. Time will tell that, too.

I can't go to the hospital until after shift change because Hooks is babysitting and I have to wait for him to get to the house. He's the same babysitter who had scarlet fever duty. He brings his wife with him this time.

I get to Curtis' room and look for this fabulous PICC line. I don't see one. It looks like the same central line in his chest that was there yesterday. Hmm.... When the nurse comes in, I ask her if this is the PICC line. She says no, he doesn't have a PICC line. His fever is higher. I tell her Dr. Lung told me repeatedly that this central line was removed this morning because it is infected and that he installed a PICC line. She shrugs her shoulders.

I call Twila. I explain to her that Curtis has infections again and that Dr. Lung told me this morning that he took the central line out and installed a PICC line. The central line is still in use, Curtis is running a high fever, and there is no PICC line. Dr. Lung made a big deal out of this and somebody needs to get hold of him and let him know the central line is still in. Twila tells me to check with the resident on duty. The resident confirms that Curtis' central line has not been removed and she says there are no orders to remove it.

I call Twila again. This is important. Somebody needs to contact Dr. Lung! Twila says she doesn't have any better luck getting hold of him than I do, but she will try. I call Dawn. My sister says that she calls her boss at home for smaller problems than this and that it is inexcusable that they cannot get hold of their physicians after five o'clock. She is disgusted. There is nothing I can do except watch Curtis get more ill all evening while bacteria multiply and infect him. I think Dr. Lung is a fool. He told me he personally removed the central line. Nobody did anything; they didn't even relocate it. What a joke.

At seven-forty-five, Curtis' cousin calls. Up to now, he and I have only exchanged brief voicemails, so I answer the phone. He is in town driving Mary J Blige on her tour bus and they're on their way to Las Vegas. The bus is parked near the stadium, and he wants me to pick him up. I tell Curtis I am going to get his cousin. I chat with him briefly on the way to the hospital. By the time we get back to the hospital, the entrances are all locked and we have to go through a long security line. We finally get to Curtis' room and I find that he is code brown. I have a big strong man to help me, so we turn him and I finally clean Curtis myself. There's a big, ugly bedsore on his lower back.

I call Hooks. It is now nine o'clock, and I am supposed to be home by nine-thirty. I tell him I might be very late and I will send the neighbor over. I call my neighbor and ask if she can go stay with the kids for a while. I may not get home until eleven-thirty or so. She doesn't mind.

Cousin stays and visits with Curtis, and Curtis is very happy to see him. We leave at ten o'clock when visiting hours are over. I drive him back to the bus and he follows me to the house. We show off the bus to my neighbor and she takes pictures of me lying in Mary J Blige's bed. Cousin and I go back into the house and start chatting about all the family gossip he's heard. He says if he had a daughter-in-law who wouldn't let him see his son, he would be kissing her ass. He says he didn't believe a word of it and they are all a bunch of fools. After about thirty minutes of me telling him the real story, he starts laughing and says I should have told them all to go to Hell a long time ago. He leaves, and I finally get to bed about one o'clock in the morning.

I'm beat. And I am mighty angry about the central line. They should all be embarrassed, but they never are. They spin everything around, "You must have misunderstood. That's not what I said." I know what I heard. The one and only time I talked to that great healer, I hung on every word and I understood perfectly. *Same old shit, different day.*

I get to the burn unit at eleven, fully prepared to put my foot in someone's rear about the PICC line. While I am outside the locked doors, waiting for someone to open them, my cell phone rings. Shirley is calling me for consent to do a procedure. The reception is bad inside the building. "Unlock the doors and let me in. I'm right around the corner." She can't understand me. We go back and forth for a while until, finally, somebody opens the doors. I hang up and head for Curtis' room. The SWAT team is milling around. A guy comes up to me and says he is here to put in a PICC line. I ask him why they waited until today. He says he just got the order today.

He shows me a rubber tube and explains that this is a PICC line, a long-term IV that goes into his arm and directly to his heart. It is preferred for patients who need long-term IV therapy because the risk of infection is almost nonexistent. *Why they didn't put one in over a month ago?* He goes on to explain the risks to me, all of which are listed on a piece of paper, and he is goes down the list with me. Lots of horrible things can go wrong, all of them resulting in instant death.

I am starting to have second thoughts about the PICC line. I ask him whether they take Curtis to an operating room for this major procedure, since this PICC line is quite a big deal. He says no, they do it right at the bedside in his room. "Do you anesthetize him?" No, no, that's not necessary. He explains again how they insert this rubber hose into his artery and right to his heart. Possible complications... instant death.

Maybe it is best not to go tampering with the heart right now. What is wrong with an IV in the wrist? Well, that is not good for long-term use, and the drugs he is on will destroy his veins. Oh. I am so scared of this PICC line. Terrified. I sign the consent. I wonder if I'm signing Curtis' death certificate. I ask him to turn the monitor in my direction a little, so I can see his vital signs. I sit in a chair in the hallway and watch through the window. SWAT guy gets dressed in all his hefty gear and drapes Curtis in sterile cloths. My legs are bouncing; I can't sit still. My eyes are glued to the monitor, watching Curtis' heart rate and blood pressure. I am holding my breath and bouncing my legs, and I am quite certain I am going to vomit.

I am a nervous wreck. Curtis is watching TV.

SWAT guy gets down to business, and Curtis' heart rate increases by one beat per minute. I instantly have regrets. Call it off, leave his heart alone. My eyes dart to Curtis in a panic—Curtis is fine, watching TV, cool as a cucumber. I breathe and watch the monitor again. This goes on for ten minutes. Every time I see a change, no matter how slight, in his heart rate or blood pressure change, I panic and my eyes dart to Curtis. He is relaxing, watching cartoons, not even flinching. *This is making me nuts! I can't watch his heart explode.*

I pass Dr. Beverly Hills in the hallway and say something sarcastic about them finally putting in the PICC line. He says they all got a "come to Jesus talking to" this morning during rounds. Everybody is in big, big trouble for the mishap yesterday. I am shocked. I expected the usual "you must have misunderstood" speech. He says one of the residents misinformed Dr. Lung, and they are all in hot water. They probably got in trouble because Dr. Lung was embarrassed. No wonder Dr. Lung avoids contact with the family members of comatose, intubated patients. I go out to smoke and agonize over the heart-exploding rubber hose. When I get back, they are finished.

SWAT team guy gives me an owner's manual for the PICC line. He writes in the type of equipment Curtis has. He gives me a sign to post on the wall about how often to flush the line, how to flush it, and what to flush it with. And—very, very important—do not allow anyone to draw blood from his left arm.

"You have to know all this and make sure the instructions are followed." There is quite a lot to this PICC line. He says he always instructs the families so they know what to watch for. I am getting overwhelmed with PICC line instructions. I need a degree to keep up with all of this. He says, "Very, very, very important—alcohol wipes. They must always wipe the cap before and after each use." He says, "My mother had a PICC line once. I had to constantly watch and remind the nurses... You know, how hard is it to take a wipe? But no...."

I cut him off. I put my hand up and say, "OK, you have to stop talking now. My husband has been here for over two months and every single day we see things that are overlooked or not being taken care of. I'm scared to death to leave him here. I can't keep up with anything else. I can't take on PICC line responsibility. I can't take any more. Stop talking to me." He says he is very sorry to hear I've had problems in this facility and he isn't trying to scare me. Just make sure they wipe, and keep that sign up wherever he goes.

He asks, "You don't remember me, do you?" No. He says he helped move my husband a couple of times when he was in the ten-ton bathtub bed. "I took him for a CAT scan and took him to GI." He says he spoke to me in the room on the old unit. I vaguely remember a SWAT person in the room a long way back, but I don't recall any conversation of any significance. My sister is here a lot. We always wear hats, gowns, and masks, and we both wear glasses. Doctors and nurses are always mistaking us for one another. They think we are twins, but in reality, we look nothing alike. I have a pretty good memory, so I figure he must have me confused with my sister, and I mention this.

He says no, it was me. I feel bad that I don't remember him; I pretty much remember every minute of every day. I secretly think he has it wrong and that it was my sister. But then he says he saw my sister the other day in Curtis' room, giving him a manicure. He says she was doing a good, careful job and he could tell that she really cares about Curtis and that he has seen me taking care of Curtis from time to time. "Mr. Wright is a very lucky man to have people who care about him so much. You'd be surprised. A lot of the patients here, you wouldn't even know they **had** a family. He's a very lucky man." And then he God blessed us.

Well, that makes me break down entirely. I am always so tense and on guard just walking into this place. Everything is such a battle. Nobody ever seems to notice that all I ever want to do is take care of Curtis. Here is somebody who, on only very brief visits, had noticed. I am touched. This is only the second time I've ever heard praise. I'm not used to it. But what really made me cry is the thought of all those poor, burned people who are left here alone. I can't believe that anyone could be heartless enough to leave a loved one in this place, forgotten. No wonder so many patients die.

Way back on the day that the ophthalmologist examined Curtis' eyes, Karen Vidor told me that when Curtis hit the emergency room, his chance of mortality was 99 percent. That was just from the burns. That was before he ever got sick.

Why didn't anybody tell me that? I would have cleared out the family a lot sooner and things would have been a lot different had I known that. Why don't they tell families these things? And where do they get these percentages, anyway? No two patients are alike; you can't compare them. If you're going to start quoting statistics, you have to compare the whole picture, not just the injury, the patient's age, and their medical history. You have to look at the course of their hospitalization. What kind of care they received. This observation from the SWAT guy proves that.

Curtis would have been dead by the end of March if it weren't for my sister and me. It's that simple. Everybody is capable of this. If you pay attention and keep working at it, you'd be surprised what you can do.

They have to X-ray the PICC line before they can use it. I am kicked out for this, too. I spend more time at that hospital being kicked out than anything else. Not long after the X-ray, I am kicked out for shift change. I go down to grab a bite. I read the PICC line owner's manual, and I finally realize that it's just an IV—a harmless rubber hose. I was spooked because SWAT explained it to me so carefully. He did it right. He and Dr. Pinch Hitter and Dr. Eye are the three who did it right. I'm just not used to it. That's why I was so scared.

After shift change, his nurse is in Curtis' room, fussing over him. I notice that she is hooking a cocktail to an IV in his wrist. "Is something wrong with the PICC line?" She says no, and continues with her project. "Why aren't you using the PICC line?" She says it's "dealer's choice." She can use either one; it doesn't matter.

If it doesn't matter, then why did they put in a PICC line? If it doesn't matter, then why did they tell me his veins would be destroyed if they use a regular IV? This place is Contradiction City. I tell her his central line was infected and Dr. Lung made a big to-do about getting a PICC line in, and that I've been told by more than one person that the drugs he is on will destroy the veins in his arm if that type of IV is used. I don't even know why he has it. She shrugs her shoulders in exasperation and says snidely, "Do you **want** me to use the PICC line, Lisa? It really doesn't matter!" I tell her, "No, I just **want** to get the correct information. That's all I **want**!"

I am getting mad, so I leave. That PICC line came with a technical manual and I still haven't learned it all. So, no, I do not want Miss Attitude using it and exploding his heart. That place is so frustrating. Now I have to worry about his veins dissolving overnight. I steer clear of Attitude the rest of the night. I don't want to get in an argument with her and have her take it out on Curtis.

When I arrive this evening, I learn that Curtis stood up today. They stood him up! Wow. I wonder how that felt. I'd like to see that. Can we stand him up again? I want a hug. No, not tonight. It has to be when the rehab people are here, and they will be here tomorrow. OK, I can wait until tomorrow. I am getting a hug tomorrow.

The acute care facility still doesn't have a private room for him, so he isn't going to move until next week. I am anxious to get him out of here. I've already cleared his room of all nonessentials, so it is less homey and more like a hospital room. His belly is swollen up like a Buddha belly,and it stays like that all weekend. They have clamped his pee hose and they unclamp it every two or four hours. They are retraining his bladder to hold its own liquid gold so he can get off **that** hose. So, my new chore for the weekend is to keep the bladder clamping on schedule. He is still on the vent, and still getting suctioned, and still coughing the hose out of his neck and across the room.

I get up early and drive sixty miles to the other side of town to pick up the sofa. My brother is staying at my house for the weekend. He helps me unload it from the truck, then I dash up to the hospital.

I arrive before rehab. I am so excited! I can't wait to see him standing. Rehab finally arrives. They put a big belt around his waist and they teach me the proper way to help him up. What an event. He is so proud of himself. I am so proud of him. I get my hug. He can't stand for long, but it is long enough. I am beaming. I knew this day was coming. He's getting closer to home every day. Soon we'll be counting the hours. I always knew it, always.

Curtis doesn't eat much. They have to cue him to eat. He just spaces out and doesn't seem to know what to do with the food in front of him. I spend all weekend reminding him to eat. I get stuff from the cafeteria and eat with him. Man, I am starving! I eat like a king all weekend. He never consumes very much, but he keeps me busy all weekend trying to get him to eat, writing down what he eats, clamping his bladder hose on schedule, reporting code brown, and waiting and timing for it to be addressed. Other than the continued problem of them leaving him code brown for interminable lengths of time, there are no negative events.

There is a very, very positive one, though. Curtis actually takes a few steps—with a big belt on and everybody holding him up—but it's a few steps, nonetheless. It is thrilling to see this man rise from the dead. I no longer think I'm insane. Curtis is telling the whole world that his wife is not crazy.

When I found Curtis' calendar in the trash, I took the pages for March and April home, so he no longer has a visual on how long he's been here. I taped May to the wall with a mile of tape. They take out his abdominal drain. That bag finally came out of his gut!

Rehab comes today and Curtis stands up again. I get a hug, and he takes a few steps. This is thrilling! More of Curtis' family arrives, so I go home in the early afternoon.

I'm getting so excited! Curtis is almost home! He might even be home for my birthday, June sixth. My mission is to get him home the second the hole in his neck is closed. Everybody keeps saying rehab. Well, they can rehab him at home. He doesn't need to be in a hospital 24/7 just for a couple of hours of daily rehab. I try to sell the case manager on the financial benefits of caring for Curtis at home. Nobody is buying it. Rehab, rehab, rehab. I write a long letter to Dr. Lung begging him to discharge Curtis home as soon as he can breathe on his own. He never responds. The finish line is so close I can almost touch it. I'm not giving up.

I check with the acute care facility. No bed today, but they can admit him to their facility on the west side of town for a couple of days and then move him to the southern location. No way. I'm not moving him twice. And what if a bed never opens in the southern facility? He will be stuck even further from home. No, thanks. We'll wait it out here in Hell.

My children will be leaving at the end of the month to spend the summer with their dad. My sister thinks they should come and see Curtis before they leave. I disagree.

When I get to Curtis' room this evening, there is a porta-potty in his room. Now that he can stand, he can be moved to a commode. The problem is that he can't move quickly enough. This is another new challenge: get him to his target in time. It never works. Poor thing, he just has no control of his muscles. I spend the evening getting his bladder training back on schedule and visiting with him.

The new GI came and gave a second opinion, but there is nothing new. Something is wrong with his gut, but whatever it is will just have to correct itself over time because nobody can figure out what it is. I have often lamented that one day his belly is soft and the next day it is hard. It keeps changing. I am finally told that his belly is only "layman hard," not "surgeon hard," and it's nothing to worry about. Well, hard is hard, and a hard belly is not normal.

Curtis is scheduled to move to the acute care facility today. My sister will dispatch from the hospital, and I'll receive at the new facility. I start calling the nurses' station at eleven. They are still doing Curtis' paperwork. That is fine, as Dawn won't be there until a little later, after class. She calls me when she arrives. She says she's found some boxes and is packing supplies, but the nurse is throwing stuff away. "What do you want to keep?"

I don't understand, I thought we had pretty much everything. She says no, everything in his room and in the anteroom is his. It has been billed to the room, the insurance company has paid for it, and it is against the law to reuse it for another patient. I tell her to pack it all. It will be a good inventory and hard evidence of all the useless junk they billed the insurance company for. I am constantly on the lookout for the insurance company being overbilled and reporting things to Karen that they should refuse to pay for. She always brushes me off and says they go over everything. I still keep it up. I know this is costing a fortune. Why should the insurance company pay three hundred dollars for a mattress cover that sat on the nurses' desk for two hours and then disappeared without being used for Curtis? How will their auditors know that it's a bogus billing? Why should they pay for parts that somebody ordered for a trach that is not the type of trach Curtis has? Stuff like that.

My sister is busy packing stuff and trying to keep the nurse from throwing anything away over the next hour or so. At about two o'clock, she calls with an update. The ambulance is on the way. All his stuff is packed, and she is going to start taking boxes to her car. Boy, I have made those treks plenty of times. I know she'll be worn out. I figure he'll be at the new facility around three-thirty or so. An hour passes and my sister calls again. The ambulance came, but they didn't have a portable ventilator, so we have to wait for another ambulance.

His room is cleaned out. Dawn's car is loaded. Just waiting. She calls me at four. The long-term acute care facility doesn't have a bed for him. A patient crashed, and we are stuck like chuck. I know my sister is beat. His room is completely cleaned out. She's kept a package of 4 × 4 bandages; that's about it.

I have to take the kids with me tonight, as I have no babysitter. My sister thinks they should visit Curtis, anyway. Amy and Ben hang by the wall for a few minutes and seem OK, but then Curtis has to cough. His vent quacks, and my daughter starts crying. This is too scary for them. I have to take them home and try to move again tomorrow. My sister is worn out, and we are both just as aggravated as we can be. In the parking garage, we transfer all Curtis' belongings from Dawn's car to mine.

When I was young, I thought all daddies flew airplanes. I have a long talk with my daughter tonight. I tell her not to be scared and not to think that this happens to everybody when they get older. I tell her Curtis is still a young man, and most people never know people who know somebody who knew somebody else who had a distant relative have something like this happen to them. This is a tragedy. It isn't normal. It is very rare. Curtis is going to come home soon and he'll be just fine.

Moving day, at long last. Again. My sister can't dispatch today; I am on my own. The acute care facility has a bed for him, and he is moving today. I call both facilities in the morning to check on his status. The new facility says the hospital has to ship him, so they don't know when he'll arrive. I triple-check that they have a room for him. I call the nurses' station every hour. I call at least twelve different people in administration and confirm that they ordered an ambulance with a portable ventilator. I find out which ambulance company is picking him up, and I call their dispatch office and confirm that they are sending an ambulance with a portable ventilator. I make sure they know what room and what hospital they are picking up from and where they are delivering him to. I check in with the burn unit again. The nurse tells me Curtis will not be moved without somebody letting me know. I start laughing. I check in every hour.

Finally at about three o'clock, the ambulance is on its way to pick him up. I head to the hospital. The ambulance arrives shortly. *They're here to get you, Curtis. We're outta here!* I almost can't believe it and I start holding my breath.

The paramedics have to do a lot of paperwork at the nurses' station. A lot. It sure takes a long time. Finally, they come into the room to start packing up Curtis for shipping. I tell the paramedics a little about Curtis' history. I am so proud of him. He is a miracle.

He has risen from the grave. I explain where Curtis' oxygen should be, what his normal blood pressure and heart rate are. I tell them that he needs to be suctioned sometimes, that they need to watch him because his lung collapses at the drop of a hat, and everything else I can think of that they should know. They are very friendly and they seem to appreciate all my information— dramatically different from the folks here at Memorial Hermann.

The paramedics get Curtis all hooked up to the portable ventilator and attached to who knows what else. They are very friendly and nice. I put a mask on Curtis' face. I take a picture of Curtis being prepared to exit. I am so excited! We're outta here! I drain his bladder right before they wheel him out of the room. I take another picture of Curtis rolling down the hallway, waving goodbye.

Just like that. Another miracle. I ask who's driving. I ask him if he is going with the sirens on. He says no. "Oh, c'mon. He's been here over two months, and he's getting closer to home. Give him a thrill; turn the sirens on!" I ask him to tell Curtis when he is passing the El Dorado Street exit. That is our exit and he will know how close to home he is because the new facility is only one exit further.

Goodbye and good riddance Memorial Hermann. Thanks for everything, anyway. I skip all the way to my car. My parking pass expired yesterday, so this works out well. I never look back.

Curtis is already in his room when I get there. A nurse starts firing a bunch of questions at me. All this information should already be in his chart, but I answer all her questions anyway. A lot of people are going in and out of his room with no protection at all. One lady introduces herself as his nurse for the night. It is after six o'clock, and it is right at shift change. *They don't kick people out for shift change. I love this place.*

I ask if Curtis is off isolation. She looks at me questioningly. I tell her he's been in an isolated room since April twelfth. Maybe they just forgot to take him off isolation all this time; that would figure. She asks, "Why he is isolated?" I tell her, "Well, acinetobacter in his lungs, primarily." I thought all this time we were waiting for a private room because he had to be isolated. She asks, "Assa-who-a-what?" I tell her, "Acinetobacter," expecting that she knows what it is. It is very common in burn patients and ventilated patients. They have a floor full of ventilated patients; surely, they know all about acinetobacter. She leaves to check on something, and I go into Curtis' room.

It is a lot smaller than the hospital room, so a lot of his homey gear will have to stay at home. It is also cold. I try to adjust the thermostat, but it doesn't work. The ventilator isn't nearly as sophisticated as the one at Memorial Hermann. It is very rudimentary. I note that he is getting one hundred percent oxygen. I ask Curtis if the ambulance driver told him when he was passing El Dorado? He smiles and nods yes. "Isn't it exciting, Curtis? You're practically in our back yard! Can you feel home?" He smiles and nods again. He is cold. It feels strange to be in his room wearing my street clothes and with nothing covering my hair.

I go out to find the linen closet. A nurse is wheeling a supply cart up to his door. It has gowns and masks. There's no place to wash your hands and no hair coverings. It is their weak attempt at isolation. The night- shift nurse comes up to me and tells me she is pregnant so she switched patients with another nurse. Well, that is an overreaction.

Do they not know the condition of a patient they are admitting? Curtis has an extensive history, and I assume it is well documented. What else don't they know? I thought they evaluated him and knew everything there was to know. Dr. Lung assured me he would instruct the new admitting doctor about the aggressive vent weaning. This is most important. I find a blanket and take it to Curtis. Boy, this room is frigid. Curtis has a code brown. They come in immediately and clean him. *I love it here.*

I let them know about his diaper rash. I have his ointment from Memorial Hermann with the basic supplies I brought. I tell them about how he got such a severe diaper rash. I also brought wax for wounds. They spot his angry bedsore immediately when they turn him. One nurse tells me that his paperwork from Memorial Hermann documented no bedsores. No surprises there. I point out the bedsore on the back of his skull.

I tell them they had a porta-potty by his bed at Memorial Hermann and we were working on getting him to it in time to hit the target, but haven't been successful yet. I ask if they are going to bathe him tonight. Yes, they are. I show them the Tubigrip, tell them it has to be on his arms and legs, and show them the coffee cans to put it on with. I tell them that he must wear compression gloves at all times. I point out the open third- degree burns on his abdomen and groin; I have the Xeroform gauze for that, too.

I post the PICC line sign. They ask about its serial number or something, whatever SWAT had written down, so I got the owner's manual out. Just basic stuff like that. No doom and gloom. I don't even get into all the horrible things that have happened to Curtis. I figure they already know, and who wants to talk about that anyway? That's all in the past. I am so proud of Curtis, and Hell is officially behind us. Before I leave, I ask them to check his temperature periodically; we still have to keep an eye on that. I am so happy he is almost home!

When I get home, I start sorting through all the boxes of stuff to decide what is going to stay at home and what he will need or want in his new room. He'll definitely want his Bible. I come across his extra set of compression gloves and put them on the coffee table to wash. He has wear gloves 24/7. We have two pairs. Every couple of days, I put the clean pair on Curtis' hands and wash the other pair in his bathroom sink.

Brownie, our Boxer, has been acting differently ever since Curtis has been gone. I know she can smell him on me, and smell his sickness. She follows me around acting depressed and sad, and she makes spoons with me in bed at night. When I put those gloves on the coffee table, Brownie leaves her perch by my side. She gingerly puts her nose to the gloves, then takes two dancing steps backwards, crying her heart out. I can practically see the tears coming down her face. She's whining, crying, and looking from the gloves to me, like I'm supposed to do something. "I'm trying, Brownie. I'm trying. Why do you think I've been in such a bad mood for over two months?" She has been despondent the entire time he's been gone, and tonight is beside herself with heartbreak. It's so sad. I feel as sorry for her as I do for Curtis.

I continue my sorting, taking note of the crap that was ordered unnecessarily so I can inform the insurance company. Most of this stuff will have to stay home. I take a few of the cards and photographs. There's no way they will all fit in his new room. The calendar, of course, is already hanging there.

Halfway through emptying one box, I come across a laminated piece of paper that I have never seen before. The items in this box have come from the supply cart. I am intimately familiar with the supply cart's contents, but I have never seen this paper before. It has several thumbtack holes in the top, like it has been posted somewhere and has been taken down and hung back up several times. I wonder where it was hidden. It is the brochure from the organ donor people with instructions on what to do when organs become available. They had called for the organ donor people to evaluate Curtis and see what they could harvest. They never said a word to me.

I had planned to donate his organs if it came to that, although he was so badly infected that I doubt they could have used them. In any event, serious talk of harvesting organs from a dead loved one is a highly sensitive and very personal matter. Nobody discussed it with me, and my sister is the only person who knew I planned to do it. It is violating and hurtful to pull this brochure out of a box and realize that some strangers had come and looked him over like he was a junkyard, to see what they could salvage. "Every time a death occurs or is imminent, notify LifeGivers*. Be armed with the following information... Cardiac death or brain death? Any active sepsis? Tissue or organ donations? Important facts... brain death criteria... call LifeGivers!" That was a close call, we are so lucky

Thank goodness, we never have to go back to that miserable place. Never. We've reached a huge milestone. Just like I knew we would. I finish sorting the hospital stuff, then take my suicidal dog and go to bed.

Day 79: Thursday, May 22, 2003

I get the kids up and leave a little early this morning. I can drop them at school fifteen minutes early, go visit Curtis, and still make it to work on time. The sun is shining, the birds are singing; he is right in our backyard. I pull into the parking lot. Instead of walking a thousand miles, riding endless elevators, and paying a king's ransom for parking, it's like parking in my driveway and going into the house—boom! it's right there—and it's free. I love this place! There are no locked doors. There really is a Heaven on Earth.

I smile and say, "Good morning!" to Curtis. He smiles back at me. I haven't told him good morning in over two months. Oh, happy day! I tell him I have to wash my hands and I'll be right in. A doctor is on the phone at the nurses' station. I am beaming. As I'm washing my hands, I hear the doctor say, "We get ventilated patients and do okay with them, but we're not set up for this." I hear some um-hums and ah- hahs, but I'm really not paying attention to him. I am thinking about how nice it is to see Curtis smile. And to have him so close to home. And to be able to see him before work. And how he might be home for my birthday. I am at the cart, gowning and masking and smiling idiotically at Curtis. He is smiling just as stupidly back. He has his hand up like he wants a hug. I hear the guy on the phone saying something about blood and saying some numbers.

I go into Curtis' cold room and make a mental note to get him another blanket before I leave. I can only stay about fifteen minutes.

I give him a hug and tell him how excited I am to be able to start my day by seeing him. I check his vent; he is still getting one hundred percent oxygen. *That's not right! Maybe they just overlooked it. Aggressive weaning, folks, aggressive.*

I am telling Curtis I can take the kids to school early and come see him every morning and that I brought him a few things but I have to be at work by eight, so I can't stay long. He makes a sad face. I tell him I can spend my lunch break with him and stay with him later at night because it is only five minutes from home, and I am going to see if I can spend the night. He smiles.

The doctor comes into the room, holding a mask to his face. He asks if I am Curtis' wife. I grin and say yes. I ask him why his vent is still at one hundred percent oxygen. He asks me to come out to the hallway so he can talk to me. I frown at Curtis and he frowns back. I have only fifteen minutes. There's always something.

Dr. Nervous says they are a small facility designed to take care of ventilated patients and try to wean them from their vents, and that they do OK with that. But my husband has a very complicated medical course. He had drawn blood this morning and Curtis' platelet count is only fifteen thousand. Do I know what is normal for him? No. No lab history was provided with his chart, so Dr. Nervous doesn't know, either. He says a normal person's count should be about a hundred and fifty thousand—ten times as high as Curtis' count. He says they don't have a blood bank, and even the hospital across the street doesn't have one. They are not equipped for trauma or critical patients, and Curtis could bleed to death by the time they order blood from a blood bank and have it delivered. My adrenaline is rushing and my rage is coming back. I look in at Curtis. He's watching TV. He is fine. He isn't bleeding to death. Something isn't adding up. I ask him if he talked to Dr. Lung before Curtis came here. He says no, no. He checked his paperwork and said the only doctor he's ever spoken to is Dr. Richard Head. *Dr. Lung, didn't talk to him like he said he would.*

I give him the number of the burn unit nurses' station and tell him to call and ask for Dr. Plastic Surgeon. It is early, so maybe Dr. Plastic Surgeon is there. He goes to the phone and I go back to Curtis. I'm not smiling like a dope any more. *No, no, no! This can't be happening. We've had more than our fair share already. Everything's fine.* Just for good measure, I lift up Curtis' blanket and look all over for signs that he is bleeding to death. He isn't bleeding to death; he is fine. His vitals are fine.

Dr. Nervous comes back and summons me to the hallway. He says according to Dr. Plastic Surgeon this is a new development; it is not normal for Curtis. He goes on again about having no blood and Curtis being in grave danger of bleeding to death. Terror strikes my heart. I look at Curtis again. *He's fine! What the Hell is going on?* Dr. Nervous doesn't say anything else. I ask, "Well, are you helicoptering him back to Memorial Hermann, or what?" He says no, an ambulance is on its way. "Yesterday it took all day for the ambulance to pick him up." He says, "Oh, no. The ambulance is coming right now."

I go back to Curtis, trying to be all happy and calm, and tell him everything is fine, but he has to go back to Memorial Hermann. They aren't quite equipped to meet his needs here. He is confused. So am I. I tell him I have to run to work; I'm going to be late. I'll come back here later. If he is already gone, either Dawn or I see him at Memorial Hermann. *It was nice while it lasted.*

I dash to the office to tell them what happened. I have to pack Curtis' things. I call Dawn on her cell phone and ask her if she can meet him at Memorial Hermann. She is as confused as I am. She is very, very angry, and she is scared Curtis will die before he arrives. I don't think that at all. I tell her he is fine. I don't have much time to talk, so I tell Dawn I'll call her back when he is loaded up here. She is pissed.

I tell Mr. Mann what happened and that I have to run back. They might forget to put him on a ventilator if I'm not there. I'm not joking. I also leave a message for Karen, the case manager.

I dash back to the acute care facility. The ambulance is already here. The paramedics note that he is on one hundred percent oxygen! I tell them he was down to forty percent yesterday, but they had to turn it up for the move and never turned it back down. "Just leave it. My sister will sort all that out at the Med Center."

They load him right up. I tell him to enjoy the ride and I'll see him this evening. At least he got to see the great outdoors for a quick second.

They came, they evaluated, they said they could take him. The insurance company shouldn't pay for this move. The long-term acute care facility that screwed up should eat the cost! I express this to Karen, like I always do.

I go back to work. My sister is in the burn unit raising Hell when Curtis arrives. She tells me she's sorry, but she yelled at his nurse and was crying in his room right in front of Curtis! She asked the nurse how, how could they have missed this? Curtis surely must have thought he was doomed after her display. The nurse called Dr. Plastic Surgeon, and Dawn calmed down after she talked to him. Dr. Plastic Surgeon says his platelet count is fine and his take on it, basically, is that they just don't want to take care of him. His history is too complicated, and they don't want responsibility for him.

My dear, sweet, gentle Curtis. He is a living, breathing, bona fide miracle, but they don't want him. They are afraid of him. We are back in Hell.

This is taking its toll. We have enough stress and turmoil without unnecessary drama, and all this is wholly unnecessary. Will there ever be just one person who can make any part of this, any small part, a little bit easier? Just a little? Anybody?

I go to the hospital in the evening, while Dawn babysits. It's a shock to be back at Memorial Hermann. Just a few short hours ago, I was elated that I'd never have to see this place again. *How did this happen?*

I get to Curtis' room and help him with his dinner when it arrives. I keep up with the bladder training. I am getting fed up. I want some semblance of a normal life. He is back in his old room with the fabulous view. They still have him on isolation. I find this a little moronic, given his adventures into the world of bacteria and germs in the past twenty- four hours.

All the facilities I toured mentioned food service in their brochures. They all said the same thing, that patients' families could order guest meal trays with advance notice and for an additional charge. I never got a Memorial Hermann brochure, but I'd venture to guess they're no different.

I don't know why I never thought of that. I can have dinner with Curtis every night. We can have dinner together. That is a normal thing to do, and it is the only chance I have to eat every day, anyway. As much as I hate to talk to Mitzi, I bite the bullet and ask her about ordering a guest tray. She says I can't, they don't do that here. *Yeah, right.*

I call Twila's boss and ask her if they serve guest trays. She says of course they do. I should talk to Mitzi, and she'll set it up. Aha! Now I have proof that Mitzi is just petty and mean! I tell Twila's boss that I just asked Mitzi, and she said they don't do that. Twila's boss doesn't know what to say to this. She says she'll make some calls. Well, I know from experience that these administrators are totally useless. They cannot accomplish even the simplest thing. They just pat shoulders. I decide to make my own calls. I hit "o" for the operator and ask for the patient meals department. I ask the girl who answers the phone whether they serve guest trays. She says of course they do. I ask her how to arrange it. She puts me on hold for her manager.

Martin*, the manager of patient meals, picks up the phone. I give him my name and tell him that my husband is a patient in room 834 in the burn unit and that I'm trying to arrange a guest tray, so I can have dinner with him. "When would you like that, ma'am?" I tell him, "Well, every night I'd like to have dinner with him." He asks if that is all. "Yes, that's it. How do I arrange payment?" He says there's no charge. It's included in the room charge, and my dinners will start coming tomorrow.

My guest tray arrives as promised and I have dinner with my husband. There **is** one person, just one person, who can do the simplest little thing to make this a little better. I am almost in tears. I call Martin and tell him how much it means to me to have dinner with my husband, that he has been here for over two months and it has been nothing but Hell. Thank you, thank you, thank you. It is such a small thing, but it means so much to me. Martin is on the ball. He hooked me up with lunch, too, on the weekends. I love him. He is world class. He probably arranges guests' trays all the time. It probably isn't a big deal to him. It meant the world to me. He came to meet Curtis and me a couple days later, and I had to restrain myself from giving him a bear hug.

I never heard back from administration. After a couple days, I call Twila's boss and tell her how easily I got a guest tray. And it is included in the room charge! I am trying to prove to her my point of how easy this is and how hateful Mitzi is. Her ears perk up when I tell her Martin said there is no charge. I shouldn't have said that. I am willing to pay for it and I don't want to get my hero, Martin, in trouble. I want to get Mitzi in trouble. I leave well enough alone after that. They just don't get it; they never will. Curtis is a miracle, risen from the dead. We should all be celebrating his victory, but all the people involved in his care just can"t stand each other.

Since we are back in Hell, I decide to do things right this time. I go to the mall and buy perfume for all of Curtis' favorite nurses and therapists. I have a theme going. Sonny got a scent called "Miracle," so she can remember her miracle patient. She's the first one I asked, "You've seen sicker patients than Curtis, right?" She's the one who pointed to the ceiling and said, "It's in God's hands now. We have seen miracles before." I don't remember who all got what, but I was buying the names, "Lifetime," and "Love," stuff like that. I gift-wrap everything and off I go.

For the next couple of days, whenever somebody comes in that Curtis has a gift for, I put it in his lap so he can offer his friend the gift. They're all very touched, and Curtis is very proud of himself. Sonny was so touched by her "Miracle" that she left the room in tears.

The bladder hose is gone! He has a bottle to use whenever he has to go. Progress, progress, progress. Well, he has a lot of misses with this bottle. By the end of the day, I am on point, ready to spring into action with the bottle. Changing linens is a big job. I don't want to ogle him while he is taking care of business, so I help him get the bottle in place and then let him take care of himself. It keeps going everywhere.

I finally watch him take care of business. Well, there's the problem. His equipment suffered third-degree burns. Third-degree burns eventually heal themselves, but they do so with a lot of scarring, especially when they're in a sensitive area where you can't use any type of compression garment. So a tube has been stuck up in there for two-and-a-half months and scars have been forming around it, and the combination has mutilated his hoo-hoo. He will need a wading pool to aim at. It sprays all over the place. *Sigh.*

I page Shirley, and she comes to inspect his hoo-hoo. She says she'll note to have a urology consult. Well, urology and neurology are about the only specialists that haven't treated Curtis yet. Everybody else has.

Urology says Curtis needs to be circumcised, but it's not urgent and it can wait until he is more stable. I tell Urology that he is circumcised. No, he's never been circumcised, and that's what he needs. Well, maybe it doesn't matter, but what if it does? I can't let these doctors keep acting on bad information. He is circumcised, but this guy keeps insisting he isn't. Yes, he is. "No, he isn't. You see this here?" We have quite a debate over Curtis' hoo-hoo. In the end, it didn't matter, but I invested a lot of effort to prove that he was. I even called his mother. She says he was.

Curtis still has a lot of swelling. He is on the vent sometimes and getting oxygen from a mask from the wall other times. He keeps inching closer to breathing on his own. He really wants to talk. He's been awake and alert for three weeks now. It has to be frustrating and maddening for him. I really feel for him and I admire his patience. This man is amazing. Today we get the news that, at long last, speech therapy is coming to evaluate him. Oh, OK, another new specialist. Well, poor Curtis, as soon as he hears this, he starts lighting up every time a white coat enters the room. He thinks it's the person who is going to make him talk. All we know is speech therapy is coming "this week."

Dr. Soap Opera, a resident from the hellish month of April, comes in to say hello. He's here as a visitor, not as a doctor. Well, Curtis doesn't understand that. He looks hopefully at Dr. Soap

Opera and points to his throat. He tries to make sounds. It is pathetic. All week, I keep explaining to him, no, not yet. This is not the person who can help you talk. Stop trying to talk; you're going to tear up your vocal chords. It is a hard week for both of us. He's been through a lot. He is a very patient and cooperative victim, but he is desperate to talk. I really feel for him.

Day 84: Tuesday, May 27, 2003

Only one dinner tray arrives. The ticket on the tray says "Guest 834." I call patient food and ask how many trays they sent for room 834. They sent two. The kitchen is locked. Mitzi won't let me in to check the cart; she says they only sent one tray.

Curtis has been on the vent all day except for two hours. Sonny is his nurse today. She is proud of him because he hit the call button for help when he needed air. That scares the Hell out of me because every time I get here, his call button is on the floor.

Dr. Plastic Surgeon comes by. They are hopeful Curtis will be off the vent and ready for rehab by the end of the week. There are more rehab facilities to consider. I ask Dr. Plastic Surgeon if Curtis can just come home and rehab at home. He says that in-patient rehab will be better for him and me, less anxiety. *Haha* I tell him and anybody else who will listen to me that I want Curtis to stay put and have rehab in this hospital. As long as that hole is in his throat, he needs to be with people who already know him and aren't afraid of him. He needs to get rehab in this hateful place until the hose from his throat is gone.

They have discontinued all of his antibiotics except one that starts with an "F." He is downgraded from critical to intensive. Another big milestone. Speech therapy evaluated Curtis and determined that he won't be able to talk as long he is on the Bivona cuff.

A Bivona is like a sponge, more form-fitting than other cuffs. It is more comfortable than the other kind, but it doesn't allow for the proper movement of air. He can't talk with a Bivona. Curtis is a very patient man, but he is not happy with this news.

Sonny is his nurse again today. How lucky. She says speech therapy is going to come tomorrow and evaluate him for speaking. I tell her they already came and they said that as long as he's on this cuff he can't talk. "Are they changing the equipment?" Oh, she doesn't know about that. She just knows a speech therapist is coming. "What for?" She doesn't know. Curtis hears all this and gets excited that he can finally start talking.

The unit director calls to check in. She doesn't know anything about the condition of Curtis' heart and hasn't seen any doctors. She ignores me when I ask her why I can't stay during shift change. I tell her that Curtis has been code brown for at least an hour because I am the only one who cleans him. But they kick me out. For shift change. She just says, "Oh, he'll be going to rehab soon. He needs rehab." I don't know why she called to check in. Just to say she did, I guess.

Another of Curtis' cousins shows up tonight to visit. Curtis writes to him on the dry-erase board that he will be able to talk tomorrow. I hate to keep dashing his hopes, so I don't say anything.

Day 86: Thursday, May 29, 2003

Curtis has another new nurse tonight. He says speech therapy came to evaluate him today, but he can't talk yet because he is on a Bivona cuff. I tell him I know, they already came and said that. Are they changing his cuff? No, they just came to evaluate him. I email the case manager and tell her not to pay for a second billing by speech therapy. Curtis is in a bad mood all evening because he thought he was going to be able to talk. *They should have sent a cardiologist, not a speech therapist.*

He is getting close to home. Now I constantly evaluate what he'll need at home. I am forever emailing the case manager about all the details that have to be arranged. I know the bathroom has to be modified before he comes home. This is a big one, I keep reminding her, but she always says the hospital will send people to do a home evaluation. I keep wondering when that is going to happen.

I am worried about that bathroom. It has a whirlpool tub that's three feet off the ground. There's no way he will be able to get into it and there's no way he can get up the stairs to the other bathroom. This issue needs to be addressed, but nobody will do anything about it. Every day, I bring it up.

Brownie's eye has been looking weird, and now she won't even open it. Dawn takes her to the vet. The vet says she has hairs growing inside her eyelids that are scratching her eyeballs. She will need surgery. Dawn takes Brownie back and forth to the vet and pays all the bills, and Brownie has her eyes operated on.

They change Curtis' cuff to a smaller one, a size six instead of an eight. They keep making the airway in his throat smaller and smaller, until eventually it will be gone. *Man, this is taking forever. I can still hear Nice Blond Lady Doctor saying three or four days. Sigh.*

I spend the evening getting my children packed for their summer vacation. Ben passed the third grade; another miracle.

I take the kids to the airport. They are gone for the summer. I arrive at the locked doors. After they are finally opened, I get my hefty gear on and start tending to Curtis. About fifteen minutes later, I am thrown out. More of Curtis' family has arrived and I am reminded "Only two people allowed in the room!" I go home for the day.

I get a call at work. It is Curtis. He says, "Good morning!" I am thrilled. He can talk! OK, the insurance company can pay this bill! They changed his cuff. He can talk. I can't wait to get there tonight. He is still getting oxygen from a mask on his neck, but he is off the hose almost around the clock. They still give him inhaled medications and do that ghastly suctioning constantly. But he can talk. I get there tonight and he is a big yapper. His voice is raspy and it's an effort to talk, but he has plenty to say.

He wants to know where his motorcycle is. He never had a motorcycle! He is mad at me because he thinks I got rid of his Harley. He goes on in great detail about his Harley. He parked it at Dave's house next to the trailer. We don't know anybody named Dave, and we don't know anybody with a trailer. This Harley is very real to him, he knows right where he left it, and he wants to know what I've done with it.

He tells me it is down the street from the bar I always go to with my big-haired friends. The same bar we have to pass to get home. He names a bunch of people I don't know. I don't have big-haired friends. I don't hang out at bars. We don't have to pass a bar on the way home. He can't believe I don't know any of these people. Or remember where we live. He reminds me of the time Steve and Rick got into a knife fight. We don't know anybody who gets into knife fights. We don't know any Steve or Rick. "Where's my Harley? I'm calling Dave. Give me my phone. What's Dave's number?" He is muttering at me about leaving him there while I hang out at the bar with my big-haired, hoochie friends.

Well, this is not a good night. I am not going to indulge his fantasies, but I'm not going to argue with him, either. It is worse than I thought; he is totally insane. He **was** mad at me all those times. Unbelievable. This means that I am insane. All that ESP never happened. This bond I thought we had is totally one-sided. He has no clue. He is pissed off at me for getting rid of his motorcycle and neglecting him to party with my big-haired friends.

This hurts. I always saw his accident and the long stay in the hospital as a blessing in disguise. I thought it would only bring us closer. We had a connection, a strong one. But it never happened; it is all in my head. I am partially insane. But he has gone completely around the bend.

I email the case manager again about having the house evaluated. There's so much to do. Nothing happened.

Curtis'cuff is down to a size four. He can stand up with help and take a few steps to the porta-potty, but we are still having target practice. He is still big and swollen. They are planning to move him to the rehab floor tomorrow. I'm always asking the nurses if we can wheel him around in the wheelchair with a portable oxygen tank. No.

He needs to get out of this room. He is still harping at me about the Harley. "What did you do with my motorcycle? Did you call Dave? Where are the papers to my Harley? What's that paper over there? Let me see that." On and on. That Harley is very real to him. He knows right where it is, he doesn't trust me, and he doesn't believe me.

I talk to him about real things and real people. I show him pictures of the house and Brownie and the children. They are plastered on the ceiling above his head. He keeps coming back to that Harley. He's always wanted one so badly. He must have spent some time in Heaven and they must have had one for him there. It is very real to him.

They are going to move him to the rehab floor tomorrow. The sooner the better; he is nutty as a fruitcake. It is very depressing to have him so angry with me. This isn't the happily ever after I'd envisioned at all. He is always glad to see me when I arrive, but he is nasty to me while I'm here. I just have to ignore it. You can't talk sense to somebody who doesn't have any. It isn't his fault. Time will make it all better. Still, I just can't believe all that ESP was only in my head. It was so real. *Yeah, Lisa, as real as the Harley Davidson Fat Boy.* We'll get our happily ever after when he gets home.

He is going to the rehab floor today. The fourth floor. I call through-out the morning to see when he is moving. I call my buddy Martin to let him know we may be moving to the fourth floor. He says he's all over it.

Later in the day, they say they won't have a room for him after all. Sorry. Maybe tomorrow.

I get to the hospital after work. After dinner, they tell me they have a room ready downstairs. Dawn is with me. She helps me pack up the last few things, we let Curtis have target practice, and we are off. She and the nurse maneuver the bed and portable oxygen. We stack a lot of supplies on his bed, and I push the supply cart, which is also loaded.

We get down to the rehab floor and find that he is assigned to the same room that my coworker Willy was in. Home, Sweet Home. A good sign. Dawn and I are on cloud nine. Goodbye locked doors. Goodbye and good riddance to the hags running the burn unit. Woo-hoo! We are outta there! This is a huge milestone. There is no way he is going back this time.

We get him sorted out in his room and I head back up for more stuff. His commode is the next important thing. It always has to be close by. I get back with the commode just in time; he needs target practice. His stomach hurts. This is new. I make a few more trips upstairs to get the rest of his stuff. We fill that little room right up. I start weeding through things, looking for more stuff to take home. He is still in isolation, so the gown-mask-hat cart is outside the door. We are all relaxed and jovial. I can spend the night with him this weekend. They don't have hostilities toward families on the rehab floor.

Curtis has to use the commode again. Dawn and I get him up and onto it. His tummy hurts, and he doesn't feel well. I kiss his forehead; it is too warm. This is all too familiar. It's like somebody just has to remind me they can take it all back in a New York minute. I rack my brain trying to think of anyone I wronged today. Nobody. I didn't do anything. Leave Curtis alone, for crying out loud.

I find a package of disposable thermometers and take his temperature. He is running a fever. Oh, no! What the Hell now? It is about nine o'clock. I call for his nurse and ask for Motrin. She takes his temperature and finds a doctor to ask if Curtis can have Motrin.

His breathing is getting labored and erratic. My sister asks for a pulse-ox. This is just a regular room. He isn't hooked up to anything except an oxygen hose. They don't have any monitors. This is a rehab room; it is not equipped for sick people.

My sister monitors his pulse with her fingers and her watch. His color is starting to change, and I am getting scared. My sister **demands** that the nurse bring her a pulse-ox right now. I dial his oxygen up to sixty percent. The nurse comes in with a little yellow thing; it looks like the multimeter that Curtis keeps in his toolbox.

My sister hooks it up and turns it on. It says his oxygen saturation is seventy percent. Holy cow! We can tell he is struggling, but that seems alarmingly low.

We call for the nurse and tell her to call Dr. Plastic Surgeon. She says that Dr. Plastic Surgeon is no longer his doctor; Dr. New Person is his doctor now. What? The only reason I kept him here is that I wanted Dr. Plastic Surgeon to still be able to watch him. She goes to get a resident.

Our happy mood is gone. Dawn and I are both tense. Curtis hasn't been this sick in weeks. *What the heck? We just got here!* And I'm really scared, now that Dr. Plastic Surgeon isn't taking care of Curtis anymore. We are in big trouble. This portable pulse-ox does not monitor steadily. You have to turn it on every time you want to get a reading. It seems like its batteries are low or something; this can't be right. Curtis is crashing right in front of us. It keeps saying his oxygen is in the seventies.

Dr. Resident strolls in. By now it's been at least an hour since Curtis had Motrin. He evaluates Curtis and turns his oxygen up to one hundred percent. He asks us a few questions, like, "Was he sick before he got here?" No, it's been weeks since he's been this sick! I tell him about the frequent visits to the commode and the aching tummy. This is just like the hellish night way back in March when I walked in his room and he went to pieces. He is falling apart right in front of our eyes, just like that. He is burning up and having a difficult time breathing. Dr. Resident orders an EKG.

It is at least another hour before the EKG guy shows up. My sister and I are struggling with the portable pulse-ox and she's taking his pulse manually. We never see another medical person until the EKG guy shows up. She listens to his lungs and whispers to me that they're "crackling," and that isn't normal. Well, they are so full of goop, who knows what that means. He is burning up and his breathing is jagged and labored.

After the EKG, I go to the nurses' station to see what's up. Dr. Resident is on the phone. He turns his back, but I hear him say, "Possible PE. Uh-huh. OK." He hangs up and turns around. I throw up my hands and ask, "Pulmonary embolism?" He says it might be. "Great! Here we go again!"

He says Curtis needs to be in ICU right away. By now it is about almost midnight. This cannot be happening. Dr. Resident says they are sending him right back to his old room upstairs. Nurse asks if she should give him more Motrin because his temperature is 102. Dr. Resident says no, there's no time for that. Call transport and move him stat! *Holy shit!*

I ask if I should start taking his stuff back upstairs. He says yes. I tell Curtis and Dawn that they're moving him back upstairs. Curtis is getting incoherent. *This sucks out loud. Right out loud.* I roll the supply cart to the elevators and go back up to those hated locked doors. Back to Hell. I wait for the doors to open and roll the cart back into the anteroom. *Sigh.* I'd have rather be doing just about anything else.

A nurse I've never seen before walks past me near the nurses' station. I smile and say hi to this New Lady, then say to a familiar nurse behind the desk, "Can you believe this? We can't escape!" She smiles and says she knows, she is sorry.

I go back down for more things. Dawn is still there struggling with Curtis. She asks me where the transport team is. I don't know. I take his suitcase and another box of stuff and head back up. We are very concerned. The rehab nurse never comes to the room. Nobody else comes to the room. Nobody is around. This is not good. Maybe I'll bring a burn unit nurse back down with me. I call for the doors to be unlocked and go through them.

New Lady stops me, "I'll take his things." I look at her questioningly. She says, "You are disrupting the whole floor and you can't just be moving his things in and out." Oh, that tears it! I'm not disrupting anything. She says as long as she is on duty, I am not going to move his things. They have transport people that will move his things.

"Whatever I don't carry will disappear! Lady, I've been here for almost three months and I know better! By the way, where the **Hell** is this transport team? The resident downstairs said he needed to be moved **stat**, and that was over an hour ago! My husband is down there burning up and struggling to breathe, and nobody's with him but my sister. What if he dies while I'm standing here arguing with you?" She rolls her eyes and assures me that the nurses and doctors know how to take care of him. "What doctors and nurses? Did you hear me say there's nobody there?"

She says visiting hours are long since over and I am not allowed on the burn unit. I can't just be carrying things around; he is an isolated patient. I tell her, "It's the same way he left here a few hours ago. It wasn't a problem then!" She kicked me out.

I leave his stuff with that hateful woman and go back downstairs. I am tired, I am exhausted, I am stressed out, and that woman had no right to treat me that way and completely ignore this very sick man downstairs. That's just the way they are on their world-class burn unit. Very typical.

Curtis' oxygen is hovering in the eighties and his pulse is racing. I tell my sister about the bitch upstairs. She goes out to the floor and finds the nurse. I can hear Dawn yelling. "Where is the transport team?" His nurse says she has to finish his paperwork. Dawn says, "You do your paperwork later! Did you hear the doctor tell you to move this patient **stat**? Did you hear him tell you there is no time to give him Motrin? That was two hours ago! I **demand** you move this man **immediately**, do you understand?" Oh, my sister is boiling mad. Nothing is ever easy here. It's not like the movies at all. It is Hell.

About fifteen minutes later, some guy shows up with a gurney. I tell him he can't move Curtis on that gurney, he has to stay in his bed with his air mattress. He says, "Ah, he's on oxygen?" He has to leave to find a portable oxygen tank. This guy wanders back eventually. This is their transport team. Some guy.

My sister hooks Curtis up to the portable oxygen tank and the "transport team" asks us if we can help move Curtis because he can't push the bed and the tank and the IV pole by himself. I answer with more than a hint of sarcasm, "Of course we will, but we aren't allowed on the burn unit anymore tonight."

We all head up to the burn unit. The "transport team" has a magical credit card that opens the hated doors. I want one of those. I deserve one.

We come around the corner and New Lady puts her hand up in front of me to stop me. She takes the IV pole and says she'll take him from here. I remind her that Curtis' commode is still downstairs. She tells Dawn and me that we have to leave; she'll call us. *Oh, yeah. "We'll call you." If I had a dollar for every time I heard that and every time I didn't get a call, I'd be a millionaire.*

During the drive home, I slide into some really depressing thoughts. *Curtis is never going to escape that place. He is going to slowly die there, and it is going to take a really, really long time. His body is going to fail him one small piece at a time. He is young and healthy and wants to come home so badly—that's why it is going to take so long. That hospital is never going to let him go. It could take six months to a year, but he is going to die there. I finally believe it.*

It is four in the morning by the time I get home. Since New Lady wouldn't let me take the rest of his stuff to his room, I had to bring it home. The only thing left in his room is his porta-potty, and I am willing to bet a million dollars it will never make it to his room upstairs. A million bucks. I take everything into the house and notice a red envelope in a box. I look into the box and find are more red envelopes. They are the copies of his charts that were sent with him to the long-term acute care facility.

I take a quick shower, then start reading those charts. At least forty percent of what is in these pages is illegible. I now realize why my sister is getting into the computer age of medicine, but I do not see why she needs a Master's degree to have charts neatly typed. These pages are trash. A lot of pages have strange equations and polynomials in the margins and scattered about the page. Some pages are full of illegible and unintelligible gibberish, followed by new handwriting that says, "Examined patient and I agree." There are some interesting highlights, though.

Over and over, on the pages I can read, the nurse ends her notes with, "Wife at bedside. All questions and concerns addressed." *What the...?* Now, that is a flat-out lie. This statement is written again and again in his chart. I check the eyeball days, the face days, and other days that Dawn and I had asked questions or expressed concerns that they couldn't answer. None of our concerns were ever noted in his chart. Not once.

The notes by all the administrators are clearly written, "Met with wife who is resistant to patient being visited by family because they worry about him." Rude Attitude's note is also easy to read, "Met w/ patient, who said he wants his parents to visit. Nice Blond Lady Doctor said he is of sound mind."

Of particular interest with this one is that Curtis said, "I want my parents to go home right now." That is enormously different from, "I never want to see my parents." Rude Attitude talked to him on Saturday afternoon. The nursing notes from Friday, Saturday, and Sunday, both shifts, note that "patient is confused, agitated, and delusional." Yet, they think he's of sound mind. If she had asked him, "Do you want your parents to go home right now?" He would have said, "Yes, please." If she had asked him, "Did your doctors tell you that you could go home?" He would have said, "Yes." We found out much later that Curtis' parents were standing right there in the room when Rude Attitude asked Curtis if he wanted to see them. Well, *that's* a great way to ensure an honest answer!

Dr. Pinch Hitter took careful notes the day she had to vacuum Curtis and she gave me all of his lab tests. Her handwriting is very neat. She details Curtis' dire circumstances; she notes that she explained the procedure and all the risks, and that the burn team and the wife agreed to proceed. At the bottom of this page, in parentheses, she wrote: "Wife seems unrealistic in her expectations for recovery." I enlarged that and hung it on my wall at work.

Here's an entertaining piece:

Final Report

Verified by Twila's cohort on April 29, 2003 Source: doctor's order

Reason: psychosocial issues

Patient/family current situation/problems. Patient's sister called me from [out of state]. She said that Lisa called her mother three times on Sunday and told her mother not to visit again because she felt that this would kill her husband. The patient's sister said at one point the patient's father got on the phone and spoke with her and then needed to take his nitroglycerin. Mr. Wright said Lisa used profanity when speaking on the phone with her. The patient's mother is desperate to know how her son is doing.

I will contact Patient Relations and give them this information

It's time to go to work, so I find some clothes on the floor to wear. I know I must look like Hell. Folks at work comment on it. "Rough night?" Yes, yes it was.

Curtis is going to die there; he is never going to get out. He wants to come home and he is capable, but that hospital is going to kill him. This is the life I have to live until they finally kill him. It

is so sad that he's gone through so much just to die anyway. What a waste! What a tragedy.

Of course, that nurse never calls to let me know how Curtis is doing and whether he had a pulmonary embolism. It doesn't matter anyway. It doesn't matter how much he pees today. It doesn't matter what his temperature is. It doesn't matter what his stupid oxygen is dialed to. It doesn't matter what color goo is coming out of him today. It all results in the same thing. I always saw little signs as arrows pointing him towards home, but I finally get the bigger picture. He is doomed. So it doesn't matter that nobody called.

I work all day, but keep thinking about that report. It is preposterous! Why would his sister make all this up and call and "tell on me" to the hospital. What is that? It eats at me all day. I call my sister and she tells me that HIPAA allows a person to correct information in their medical records.

I send a fax to Twila's Cohort: Re: Your "psychosocial issues" report dated April 29, 2003. This is what I faxed:

> I have called Curtis Wright's mother, Helpless Wright, once, and that was Friday, May 30, 2003 to make a specific inquiry regarding Curtis' medical history that only she would know, and is relevant. It was a very brief conversation. No profanity was used; the topic of visitation was not addressed. She made no inquiry about Curtis' condition. I have never spoken to Dad Wright, Curtis' father, on the telephone.

> I myself have been "desperate to know how Curtis is doing" during the month of April. I have kept in touch with Curtis' brothers and cousins regarding his condition since his admission to the hospital. **When Curtis was admitted to the hospital he specifically requested**

I do not discuss his condition with his mother. Curtis asked that his brother Andy be my point of contact with his family. I resent the tone and implications of this "psychosocial issues" report that is "verified" by you on Tuesday, April 29, 2003 as you have never brought these outrageous accusations to my attention, and I am appalled at the irresponsibility of placing such rubbish in a patient's chart.

Lisa Lindell

All the administrators have the same attitude toward me, except Annie from the graveyard shift. I wonder if she remembers me. I sent a copy of my response to Karen Vidor.

I face my daily fate of going to the hospital after work. I am so tired. I have been up for thirty-six hours or so. Mitzi is at the nurses' station and tells me all the residents have seen Curtis and they are waiting for Dr. Lung's opinion. As far as they are concerned, he is ready to go to rehab. They aren't going to monitor him anymore. What about the bloody stool? Dunno. Were the cultures negative? Dunno. Why does he still have a PICC line? Dunno. How did the EKG compare to the last one that was done May twenty-first? Dunno.

I don't care; I am tired. The burn unit doesn't want to take care of him anymore and nobody else does, either, once they have him. He is too much trouble for everybody. I guess I just feel the need to continually beat my head against a brick wall. I go into Curtis' room. He doesn't have a fever. Well, that is nice. Maybe he'll have a relatively comfortable day before his heart explodes or his liver clogs completely or who knows what's in store. There is no portable commode in the room. *I want my million dollars.* I make my nest in my chair and start to fall asleep instantly.

Half an hour later, the unit director's voice comes over the speaker, "Mrs. Wright?" I ignore her. She tries again. I tell her to leave me alone I am trying to sleep. The phone starts to ring. I pick up the phone and ask her if she heard me tell her I was trying to sleep. I remind her I was up all night and I had to work all day and I want to take a nap. . She says she just wants to talk to me for a few minutes, it is important. Well, nothing she has to say to me is important, nothing. But she isn't going to let me sleep, either. I am full of attitude; I readily admit it.

We go to her office. Her minion Mitzi is there, too. She says the doctors have no explanation for last night; there is nothing wrong with Curtis. Maybe he got too comfortable being in his room here for so long and it is just a psychological thing. Who knows; these things happen. She suggested to the doctors that they move Curtis to a private room on the unit, the normal transition a patient makes as they progress, but the doctors said no, they want him in ICU. *"Can I go back to sleep now?"*

She says they aren't going to monitor his vitals anymore. *I don't care what these people do or don't do.* She says it might do him some good to get out of that room. I tell her she is way behind the eight-ball. I have been saying that for weeks; I constantly ask his nurses and the rehab people if we can get a wheelchair and wheel him around the nurse's station or something because he is rock-solid insane. They always say no. She asks me who I've talked to. I rattle off the names off all the nurses and rehab people I have asked over the weeks. She says well, the burn nurses are too busy to do something like that, they're not rehab nurses. "Yeah, I know all too well how busy the nurses are up here. They're always too busy to take care of Curtis. All the time. I know. I see it every day and I don't need to talk about it. Are we done?"

She says she isn't going to ask his doctors—*I don't believe that for one second*—but does she have my permission to take him outside in a wheelchair? "Hell, yes! Let's go right now!" I stand up. She says well, she can't do it right now and she has a really busy day tomorrow, but she will make the time to do it before she leaves for the day, tomorrow at four o'clock. "I'll be here."

I could have been a little more gracious about it, but even if I wasn't having a bad attitude today, they should have done this for Curtis weeks ago. Weeks! I asked until I was blue in the face. She's framing it like we're sneaking behind the backs of doctors that don't examine him anyway. Like it's a favor. Feels more like a prison instead of a hospital.

I go back to my nap and sleep until it's time to go home.

I leave work at three and go to the hospital. A wheelchair and an oxygen tank are in the anteroom. He is really going outside. I ask Curtis if he wants to go outside. He just looks at me, confused. I tell him we are going to go for a walk outside and ask if he needs to use the bathroom.

Curtis still doesn't have a commode. I sit him on the side of the bed and put his shoes on. He seems nervous. Director shows up and we get Curtis situated in the wheelchair. He is still big and heavy and swollen.

Director hooks him up to the oxygen. I put a mask on Curtis and a hefty bag over him—he is still isolated. She pushes the wheelchair, and I walk next to Curtis. I start chattering and pointing everything out to him. "There's the room I had picked out for you. There's the nurses station. These are the locked doors I'm always complaining about." I shoot Director a dirty look with this last observation.

The main floor has a little museum and all the original tile work from the hospital. We tour this little area. Chatter, chatter, chatter. We go all over the ground floor. We pass the cafeteria, "Look, Curtis. This is where I always go to get my Pepsi when I'm kicked out of your room." I shoot another dirty look at the Director. We pass the emergency room and I tell Curtis this is where he first entered the hospital. This upsets him a great deal and we turn around. We walk down the same hallway that I come in from the parking garage.

"Your truck is parked right down that hallway, Curtis. Those are the elevators I used to take to your old room." We go outside.

Oh, he is all smiles. His reactions are very childlike. He obviously isn't right in the head, but I don't care. He has a happy day, and I hope he has a lot more like it before this hospital kills him. He can talk, but he doesn't do it a lot. It is an effort. We stay outside until Director has to leave. Curtis gets a lot of stares from other people in the hospital. It is obvious, now that he is out in society, that this dude is really messed up. He has become one of those people you can't help but stare at. Strangers say "God bless you" and "I'll pray for you." I don't see what they see; I think he looks great.

We got back to his room and get him back into bed. He is tired. We both take a nap.

When I get to work this morning, I'm greeted by presents on my desk and a cake for me. It is my thirty-fourth birthday. I had forgotten and it doesn't seem important, but it is nice of my coworkers. I'm going to take Curtis outside again today, with or without permission.

It occurs to me that I should have arranged a birthday party in Curtis' room. Something different to do for him, something to give him a scale of time. He would like to be at his wife's birthday party. Well, the Curtis I knew before would have. Too bad I didn't think of it sooner. The more I think about it, the more I think it would be a good idea. I call my sister, "Can you and Mike and Dad come to the hospital tonight? I'll get a cake and we can have a little birthday party in Curtis' room." She says, "Oh, well, I'll see what everybody's plans are." She doesn't seem very interested. I guess my family can only do so much; they've already done a lot for us.

Dawn calls back shortly, "Aww, Lisa. Dad says I should tell you. We've already planned on giving you a party tonight at the hospital, but not in Curtis' room. The Director gave us permission to take Curtis to the conference room outside the burn unit, and she arranged for his night shift nurse to have a full oxygen tank."

Aww. Aww. Now I am crying again. I should have known Dawn would do something like that. I don't deserve it; I don't do anything for anybody anymore. I didn't even go to Mother's Day dinner when my mom was here, thinking there will be time for all that after

Curtis comes home. That was back when I actually believed he was coming home. I work until three, then go the hospital.

A wheelchair and an oxygen tank are in the anteroom. There is a new commode in his room. *Mental note: Send an email to the case manager and tell her the insurance company shouldn't pay for a second commode. They should take it out of that nurse's paycheck.* I hooked Curtis up myself and took him out for a stroll, all by myself. We still get "God bless you" and "I'll pray for you" comments from passing strangers. We get back just in time for me to get kicked out for shift change.

Not long after shift change, my sister taps on the window, "C'mon, c'mon!" I ask Curtis if he wants to go to my birthday party. He looks confused. "I guess." I am nervous; maybe we should just eat cake in here. My sister says, "No, no, c'mon." I meet her in the anteroom. She looks at the oxygen tank and says it is only half full. I tell her about our adventure outside. She finds Curtis' nurse—another new one—and asks where the full oxygen tank is. New Nurse doesn't know anything about it. She doesn't know anything about Curtis leaving the unit for any party. My sister puts her foot down and tells her that she can call the Director at home and confirm it, but Curtis is leaving for a short while. We let Curtis have target practice, then we get him into the wheelchair and wheel him out. Twice in one day. I'm chattering all the while. "We're going to eat birthday cake."

My brother and dad are in the conference room. The table is decorated and covered with presents, a big cake, and about twenty bottles of coffee-flavored Frappuccino, my favorite. They have gone all out. I get to work on the presents quickly. I am nervous about having Curtis in here with no medical personnel. Well, Dawn is here, but he is far away from his garden hose. I open a ton of presents and we eat cake. Curtis got me some perfume—sneaky devil.

Even my dad is beaming. Last time Dad saw Curtis, he was getting blood clots sucked out of his lungs and holding my dad's hand in loving delirium. He's come a long way in a short time. But I know how suddenly that can change. We finish the cake and load everything up. My dad and brother go and pack everything into the car while my sister and I put Curtis back into bed.

It has been a good day, but I no longer have all that excitement. Now I know better than to expect another. I am ready for anything.

I have to wait a really long time for somebody to open the locked doors. The entire floor is a noisy mess of people. Curtis' room is no different. His oxygen hose is disconnected from the wall, and oxygen is just blowing into the room. His oxygen saturation is in the nineties. *Hey, he is doing pretty well on his own!* By the looks of things, he's been in this predicament for a while. His head is turned away from the door and it never moves, even after I start talking to him. I realize that the oxygen tube is hooked on the bed and he can't turn his head. I free him, and I see a deep welt across his cheek, where the hose had been stretched and stuck for a good long while. I hook him back up to his oxygen. It is dialed up to one hundred percent. I turn it down to forty percent. *What is going on?*

Curtis and his bed are a mess. His room is a mess. I get busy. He's been on his own for a while. My chair is gone.

About an hour later, some guy comes in with Curtis' lunch tray. He is Curtis' new nurse for the day. I ask him why the oxygen is on one hundred percent. He says, "Curtis is on one hundred percent, isn't he?" I tell him, "No, and the hose was on the floor when I got here, so he was getting zero percent oxygen. When's the last time you were in here?" Oh, not long at all. "Well, I've been here for an hour. Is there a guest tray for 834?" Uh, no, ma'am.

The nurse tends to Curtis and goes on to apologize. He says he's not supposed to talk about other patients, but they have a new admit. Some guy was being chased by the police; when they caught him, he poured gasoline on himself and lit a match. He has third-degree burns on eighty- five percent of his body. The whole floor is busy with him. It is all over the news.

I ask where my chair is. "Uh, another patient's family member needed a chair." I ask him if he wiped it down before he took it out of the room. He has to think about what the correct answer is and he says he did. I tell Curtis I am going to find a chair. I see my chair in another patient's room with somebody else in it. They are in the bad luck room, the room where New Admit expired. I never want that chair back. I find a chair in a vacant room. It isn't as good, but it is better than nothing. I find some disinfectant and wipe it down, then roll it to the anteroom.

I go to the kitchen. It is unlocked, I check the meal cart. There is my guest tray. "Guest 834." That's me. Thank you, Martin.

My washing machine finally quit working yesterday. It is probably something Curtis could fix easily, but he is never coming home. I get up early, go to the Sears Outlet, and buy a washing machine. The neighbor who wanted to visit Curtis comes over with three other neighbors, and my washing machine is inside the house and hooked up in less than five minutes. "Thanks a lot! I gotta go to the hospital." They ask how Curtis is doing. "He's hanging in there!" I can't tell them he is never coming home; they'll just feel sorry for me. "He's hanging in there" is my new answer.

I'm still planning and thinking about all the things that need to be done at the house. Just in case he comes home. I have no time to do anything at home, and I don't know where to start. Curtis is going to divorce me when he sees the state of his garage. I keep pestering the case manager about a home evaluation and the bathroom, but nothing ever happens. I don't know who else to ask.

Curtis is getting a bad case of cradle cap. I wash his head thoroughly. He is still at forty percent oxygen, but he's not on the garden hose, just an oxygen mask over his trach. Calvin comes to visit today. Calvin's father suffers from diabetes. He has developed infections and is in the hospital. Calvin tells me his father had to have his leg amputated.

I dropped my "don't bother the nurses by calling" rule a long time ago. By noon today, I've called the nurses station three times to request that they help Curtis out of bed and into a chair. He's been in bed seventeen hours, and probably hasn't even been turned. When I get to the hospital after work, Curtis is on one hundred percent oxygen and hasn't been out of bed all day. Not even to sit on the side of the bed.

They did another Doppler and they finally did that TEE test. The TEE shows his right ventricle is depressed. I don't freak out. He is going to slowly erode; I know that now. He didn't get any rehab today. I want to find out if I can take him home for a couple of hours and show him his house, but I don't know who to ask.

Curtis is supposed to move back to the rehab floor today. I'm not holding my breath. It takes about forty minutes to get him from lying in the bed, to sitting on the side of the bed, to standing. I always get a hug when he stands up. Curtis takes a few steps, holding onto the wheelchair. He walks himself out of the burn room. Then we push him in the wheelchair the rest of the way.

The resident on the rehab floor tells me that Curtis is on one antibiotic, Cefapime. I think it's a new one; he said it's for acinetobacter. He says that whoever told me Curtis would have acinetobacter for the rest of his life was wrong, that it is colonized. Well, he's partly right. "Colonized" means the acinetobacter is still there, but doesn't cause symptoms. Dr. Lung told me a while ago that Curtis will always test positive for acinetobacter.

Another new doctor shows up today, a Dr. House*. She says she's his new attending, but she doesn't know the answers to any of my questions. She tells me it's up to the therapists to evaluate the house and asks if that's been done. No, not yet. But I keep trying.

I talk to Mitzi's boss to see if she knows who I am supposed to talk to. She says Dr. Rehab is Curtis' attending and Dr. House is a resident, and tells me that I need to talk to some lady named Debbie*, the manager of the rehab department.

Dawn is at the hospital today. She says Curtis is dressed and ate a good lunch. She also says that his trach is clearly capped and he is fine. We hope they can take all the stuff out of his throat on Friday. I'm on the phone all day, scrambling to get everything organized so I can take him home.

Nobody seems to know how to get hold of Dr. Rehab*, who's supposedly Curtis' attending doctor. Dawn says she's seen no doctor since she's been here. She also said nobody could help him to the toilet last night, so he was code brown again. That's inhumane and I'm sick of it. And he still hasn't had a decent bath.

I'm still trying to reach Dr. Lung about the trach, but I keep getting his voicemail. If they take the neck gear out Friday, I'm taking Curtis home. I find out that I need a prescription for oxygen at home—can't just go to the oxygen store and buy some. He may need prescription drugs, as well, but apparently nobody knows. He can't possibly be the first person who's ever been discharged and needs continuing care at home. I don't understand this place.

I call Debbie, the rehab manager, but get her voicemail. Then I call Dawn for an update. She says they "deferred" his therapy this afternoon because she couldn't get anyone to help her get Curtis to the commode so he pooed and peed all over himself. They still don't have anything for him to sit on in the tub so he can get a decent shower. Of course, there's nothing set up at home for that, either.

Debbie calls back and says I need to talk to a Dr. Affawal* about discharging Curtis. Another new doctor! It's like there's a conspiracy to keep him in the hospital. Who is Dr. Affawal? Why won't anybody let Curtis come home?

I get to the hospital with some regular clothes for Curtis. Dawn is still there. Curtis pushes the wheelchair all the way to the nurses' station and back. We hook him up to oxygen and take him outside in the wheelchair. By now, we are allowed to take him on little excursions. We go outside and sit and talk. He still has mild swelling, but you can see how much weight he's lost. His arms and legs are wrapped in Ace bandages. He is always wrapped up in compression garments. More often than not, I am the one who wraps him because the rehab nurses don't think to do this. It is important to prevent scarring.

We hook him up and take him outside every chance we get and stay out until we start running out of oxygen. My sister notices that the plastic tubing from his oxygen hose is irritating the tops of his ears. She puts gauze between the hose and his ears. She is always doing stuff like this for Curtis.

He always gets a lot of stares on our outings. I am so proud of him. Stare away folks; look at the miracle! We still hear the occasional "God bless you" and "I'll pray for you."

Day 100: Thursday, June 12, 2003

There is starting to be a lot more confusion, as if we don't already have enough. Poor Curtis is just not right in the head. He is surrounded by new caregivers, and he can talk now. So he talks to them. He tells them all sorts of crazy things, but they don't know he is nuts. It sounds reasonable, so they believe him. Just harmless things. He tells them he can breathe by himself. That he is going home for the weekend. That he walked outside. That he can dress himself. Curtis describes the Harley in great detail to anybody who wants to hear about it. He tells them all sorts of things that are not real, like his wife sold his motorcycle while he was gone. He is nuts but he sounds normal to someone who doesn't know any better, so it creates a lot of confusion.

Curtis pushes the wheelchair a few steps until he tires out, then he sits in it. Each day he tries to walk a little further. Today he is walking in front of the wheelchair, while the physical therapist walks behind him, pushing the wheelchair. When Curtis tires out, he sits down in the wheelchair. The therapist had the oxygen tank in the seat of the wheelchair, and Curtis sliced his back on the hook protruding from the oxygen tank. It is always something, constantly.

He finally got a decent shower today. For the first time in months, he sat on a bench in a real bathtub and got clean. Orchestrating this event is no small task. His PICC line has to be wrapped and waterproofed. His trach has to be waterproofed. His bedsore has to be unwrapped and redressed. He still has open, third-degree burns on his abdomen. He has to be undressed and dressed. He has to be helped to the tub. He can wash some of himself now. After the bath, he gets lotion from head to toe and compression on his arms and legs. It takes easily half a day from start to finish. It passes the time.

It truly is miraculous watching him rise from the dead. The first time he sat on the edge of the bed, when Dr. Pinch Hitter almost fainted, he looked like himself advanced to age ninety-five. I have been watching him get younger every day. Today he looks only eighty-six. He has been free from the burn unit for two whole days now; he has them on the run. I'm not trying to be crazy or anything, because I know now that he will die here, but maybe one little goal—just one secret, little goal—won't hurt. If he makes it to looking only eighty by the end of the weekend maybe, just maybe, he can still make it home. I'll be here all weekend to help him. *We can hit eighty; we can do it. He is coming home! Shh!*

Day 101: Friday, June 13, 2003

Another new doctor appears today, a brain doctor. He gives Curtis a wacko test. Curtis called me at work, annoyed because he thought the questions were insulting. "They held up a picture of a pencil and asked me what it was." Curtis is disgusted by the whole thing. He goes on and on about it.

I find out later that he didn't pass the test. He doesn't know what year it is or where he is; he is very disoriented. All his screws are loose. I think he got the pencil right. The initial diagnosis is "ICU Psychosis," he's senile from being cooped up in a hospital room. I'm told this should resolve itself over time. They want to do an MRI of his brain to check for a stroke or seizure or any kind of brain damage. Ultimately this can't occur because Curtis has a bullet lodged in his calf (before my time).

I pack myself a bag, as I get to spend the entire weekend with Curtis. It's the first time in over three months! I hook him up to the portable oxygen and take him outside. They've decided he is "medically unstable" and can't go home on a two-hour pass. When I initially asked about it, I was told that if the insurance company approved it, then I could take him home on a two-hour pass. I jumped over a lot of hurdles and got approval from the insurance company just like they asked, but in the end, they said no. They could have saved me the trouble. He is always watching cartoons when I arrive, and this evening is no different. Maybe there is nothing else on, but he is riveted to those cartoons.

I wander all over outside with Curtis for hours. We get the usual stares and "God bless you" remarks from passing strangers. He really must look a fright, but not to me. He looks like Curtis at age eighty- five is all. I could put him in the truck and drive him home, and nobody would be the wiser. I am sorely tempted, but I haven't figured out how to get him into the car by myself, and Dawn refuses to be a party to my scheming. It is in the back of my mind to make a run for it.

While we're on our walk, I hear hissing. I feel around the tank's connections and feel oxygen leaking out. *Holy moley! We have a bum tank.* I try turning the screw to tighten it; that just makes it worse. *Aren't these things explosive?* I turn the screw the other way. It stops hissing for a moment. It is low on oxygen. It must have been leaking since we left upstairs. I keep looking at Curtis; his color is fine. I discover if I hold my finger against the pipe, it doesn't hiss. It is bent or something. I hold my finger there and race back upstairs as quickly as I can with only one hand on the wheelchair. When I get to the rehab floor, I just let it leak. I disconnect Curtis' hose from the bomb and leave it in the hallway. I race into the room and hook his hose to the wall.

Right in the midst of escaping the bomb, Twila's boss comes by to check in. She beams at Curtis and tells him how lucky he is to have me and my sister. I think Curtis is starting to get sick of people tell him how great I am. He thinks I just hang out at the bar and I secretly sold his Harley. He is really mad at me about that.

After the leaking oxygen tank adventure, I am cured of the thought of taking him for a drive. The next best thing to making a run for it is to find somebody to bring his suicidal dog to see him. Somebody could meet me outside with her. My sister says no way.

I spend the night with Curtis tonight. Finally, after more than three months, I get to stay with him all night. Something wakes us up constantly. The IV pump goes "bloop-bloop!" periodically. Respiratory comes in. A nurse comes in. Of course, they always have to turn the light on. I get no sleep at all. It is the longest night ever.

Curtis is glad I am here. They bring breakfast in the morning. Later in the morning, I am bored out of my skull. I give Curtis a bath, then he takes a nap. I go to our favorite restaurant to get us a "to go" lunch of smoked sirloin.

I haven't even been here twenty-four hours, but it feels like a week. No wonder he is insane! I come back with our lunch and he makes me empty the contents of my purse. He is still looking for those Harley papers. He inspects everything. He is so mad about that motorcycle.

Curtis doesn't talk much these days. The most he ever has to say is about the Harley I have taken from him. I have long since gotten used to his silence. It's surprising how well you can learn to communicate with somebody who can't talk. We are both used to him not talking. We're sitting quietly, eating our smoked sirloin and watching cartoons, when suddenly I hear a loud, shaky whisper, "Gosh darn, this is good!" It makes me jump because he's always so quiet. He is in ecstasy over that smoked sirloin. *Bless his heart!*

Day 103: Sunday, June 15, 2003

I spend the night again tonight. It's another sleepless night. Respiratory people come in to give him his breathing treatments. They never do the same thing twice. How hard is it to read doctors orders? I get no sleep at all this weekend. I am happy to spend it with Curtis, though. It's a quiet weekend; just the two of us. I've been waiting since March fifth for this. It's now summertime.

My dad and sister come by. Thank goodness! I am so bored. We go out for another walk and stay outside for hours. I want to take Curtis home so badly that you almost can't hold me back. I watch all the traffic passing on the street and wonder if those people realize how lucky they are.

When I finally leave today, I feel disoriented. I can remember different people coming and going, but I can't for the life of me remember which day or what time. No wonder Curtis is nuts. I've been there only two nights and I'm a little disoriented. I have to get him out of here. We almost made our goal this weekend. Curtis doesn't quite look eighty yet; I put him at eighty-two. Close enough. He's coming home.

All the equipment is removed from Curtis' neck today. By the end of the day, he is off oxygen. He is breathing on his own. I write on the calendar "Heaven and Earth move." I can see pigs flying.

It's now or never. He is spending this weekend at home. We can do this the easy way, or we can do it the hard way. Knowing this hospital, I will have to get an order issued by the President of the United States. Whatever I have to do, he is coming home. He is not spending another weekend in this hospital. I turn up the heat. I tell every nurse or doctor that enters the room. "He's coming home Friday. Who do I need to see about that?" I get a different answer every time I ask, but over the course of the week, I ask everyone. The PICC line has to come out. He needs modifications to the tub at home. I want to get him a recliner that lifts him up, but the insurance company says no. One of my coworkers has a grandma who has one for sale, so I buy it. I send Karen, the case manager, a barrage of emails about all the little issues. I hammer and hammer and hammer her about the bathroom. I have been hammering her for a month about it. Bathing him is going to be a huge problem. We have so many things to take care of and arrange.

Karen cautions me not to get in a hurry. She tells me sometimes patients take a dive, and she reminds me of the night in rehab when Curtis crashed. Well, there is a fire department right behind my house. If something goes wrong at home, I can call 911 and have paramedics in my bedroom faster than I can get help in this hospital. He needs a nurse at the house while I am at work. Karen knows I am not going to give her a moment's peace until Curtis comes home. I remind her of the financial benefits of caring for him at home. She starts working as hard as I do. It is a Herculean task. She has all the insurance paperwork to get through. There are deadlines and forty-eight-hour turnarounds and you name it. It is a tense week, a constant race. There's one issue after another, but we are banging them out—all day, every day, all week long. Everything except the bathroom.

I find out that Dr. Rehab is the one who has to discharge Curtis. She says they will have a family meeting with all his caregivers on Monday, and I have to attend that meeting before they can discharge him. I need to be counseled in how to care for him, you see. I'm determined that Curtis is not spending another weekend here; he is coming home Friday.

Dr. Rehab tells me I have to contact some other lady in some other department. Karen Vidor and Other Department Lady and I have a three-way phone conference. Well, that conversation doesn't go well. I want to talk to people that can get him discharged Friday, not people who tell me he can't come home Friday. He is coming home Friday. If you can't make that happen, I'm talking to the wrong person. Other Department Lady is hassling me about the counseling. I try to get counseled earlier so he can come home Friday. "Oh, that will be impossible." She finally says discharging him is up to Dr. Rehab, not her.

I zero in on Dr. Rehab and let her know that Curtis is coming home Friday and I don't want to hear any more reasons why that can't happen. It is going to happen. End of story. It just has to. *Please, please, please, will somebody help me get him out of here?*

Curtis has me digging through every bag, suitcase, cabinet, and drawer for his motorcycle papers. Looking for Dave's phone number. "Why aren't you here when I need you? I want my Harley back. Do you understand me?"

Curtis is nauseous. *Uh-oh! I had my window and I missed it. I'll never get him out of here.* Every week has been stressful, but this one has been even more so. I've been watching him like I hawk when I am at the hospital, and emailing, calling, and running around like mad trying to get the house ready for him when I'm not at the hospital. I've always told him that he is coming home as soon as that garden hose is gone. If I don't make it happen now, it might never happen. It's now or never.

People aren't treating me like I am crazy now. The administrators we have done so much battle with come to Curtis' room and tell him how lucky he is to have Dawn and me. I want them to ask Curtis, "Did you want your parents to go home?" All my enemies tell him how lucky he is to have me. Calvin tells him. Everybody tells him. He smiles and nods, but he is angry about that motorcycle. He is anxious to get home to call Dave and get it back.

The phone is busy today. Karen and I are both on the phone all day. Issues, issues, issues. It is all coming together. They are going to discharge Curtis with the PICC line and a thirty-day supply of IV antibiotics. All the supplies are scheduled to be delivered tomorrow. It is coming together, slowly but surely. The in-home caregiver is becoming troublesome. *Oh, c'mon!* I know Karen is working her tail off to get Curtis home on Friday. She's probably calling in every favor she can think of. Really, it is all on her. There is only so much I can do.

Dawn is at the hospital during the day, making sure they don't kill Curtis at the last minute. When I arrive in the evening, Curtis is hanging in there just fine. He's breathing on his own, holding steady at eighty.

What a show off! Oh can it be, is this really going to happen? I can't deal with the thought of him being in here one more weekend. I'd rather drive myself off a bridge. I am really holding my breath now. This is it. If it doesn't happen tomorrow, it is never going to happen.

As I leave, I tell Curtis that I'll be here tomorrow before eleven to take him home. I never tell him anything that isn't true, so I am committed. It's real now.

I don't sleep a wink.

I climb the walls at work all morning. Elmer lets me leave at ten-thirty. I am fully prepared to spend the entire day battling to get Curtis released. I can see the finish line.

Dr. Rehab comes to Curtis' room about ten minutes after I arrive. She has Curtis' discharge papers; I have to sign them. I take a load of stuff to the car. I come back and another lady is already there, waiting to push Curtis' wheelchair to the car. Just like that. We leave. It's this easy?

By the time we get to the lobby elevators, Curtis has to go potty. Well, when he has to go, he has to go **right now**. The GI issues that plagued him never got resolved I hold my breath, and we wait for the elevator. We are stuck; there are no bathrooms nearby. We get downstairs and wheel Curtis to the bathroom. As soon as he stands up, he misses the target. I am afraid that Hospital Lady will tell on us and they'll make me bring him back. I act like this is no reason to return him to his room. I throw his pants away, clean him up, and cover him with a blanket. We continue on our journey. We roll Curtis down the hallway. I can see the exit doors. I can see the truck parked outside waiting. I catch sight of security guards. *Act like you're not doing anything wrong, Lisa, and they won't even notice you.*

We pass the security guards and go through the doors. I secretly exhale and act casual as I point to our truck. We walk to the truck and Hospital Lady helps me get Curtis situated. Ha ha! *So long suckers*!

I am elated. Curtis is nervous. I call my dad as I pull out of the parking lot. I'm bouncing in my seat. "I'm leaving the hospital! I'm in the truck driving away, and you'll never guess who's sitting in the seat next to me!" He says, "You're kidding!" He can't believe it. We escaped. I smile and look at Curtis. He is grim and staring straight ahead.

He never forgave me for losing his Harley.

Made in the USA
Coppell, TX
01 May 2020